The Truman White House

THE TRUMAN WHITE HOUSE

The Administration of the Presidency
1945-1953

Edited for
The Harry S. Truman Library Institute
for National and International Affairs
by

Francis H. Heller

The Regents Press of Kansas
Lawrence

Photographs Courtesy of The Harry S. Truman Library

The Truman White House.
Bibliography: p.
Includes index.
1. United States—Politics and government—1945–1953—Addresses, essays, lectures.
2. Truman, Harry S., Pres. U.S., 1884–1972—Addresses, essays, lectures.
3. Presidents—United States—Staff—Addresses, essays, lectures.
I. Heller, Francis Howard.
E813.T75   353.03'13'09044   79-15713
ISBN 0-7006-0193-7

CONTENTS

ILLUSTRATIONS

PREFACE

In early May 1977, twenty-two persons who had served in President Truman's administration as members of his cabinet, members of the White House staff, or senior officials in Executive Office agencies gathered in Kansas City, at the invitation of the Harry S. Truman Library Institute for National and International Affairs, to discuss the operations of the presidential office from 1945 to 1953.

The Harry S. Truman Library Institute was formed to lend support to the Truman Library and to promote its interests. The Library itself is, of course, maintained and operated by the National Archives with federal funds. But these funds are not available for the promotion of research and the development of the Library as a major research center. It was President Truman's wish at all times that the library that bears his name and houses his papers should serve scholarly inquiry, and he encouraged the creation of the Institute as a means to channel private support to the advancement of the Library's use by scholars and students. Throughout his life he took an active part in the affairs of the Institute; routinely, he donated to the Institute whatever fees he received for lecturing and speaking engagements. Following his example, a number of his friends and associates have made generous gifts to the Institute, and over five thousand persons, from all walks of life and all parts of the country, contribute annually to the Institute through its Honorary Fellows Program.

Since the Library opened its doors for research in 1959, the Institute has given over 250 grants to scholars working in the Truman period. In addition, it undertook two special research projects of its own. Every other year the Institute recognizes an outstanding book on the Truman period by the award of the David D. Lloyd Book Prize. Its conferences, held on the average of every other year, have generally been designed to focus attention on the potential of the Truman period as a research field and of the Truman Library as the major resource center for such research.

During the course of the Institute's 1975 conference on the Korean

Preface

War, Professor Richard W. Leopold suggested the need for an administrative history of the Truman presidency.[1] The suggestion was promptly seconded by others, and shortly thereafter the board of directors of the Institute agreed that the administrative operation of the White House during the Truman years should be the subject of the Institute's next conference. Plans for the conference were entrusted to a committee consisting of Charles S. Murphy and myself, both vice-presidents of the Institute, and Dr. Benedict K. Zobrist, secretary of the Institute and director of the Harry S. Truman Library.

Invitations to attend the conference were extended to forty persons. Regrettably, ill health compelled a number of them to decline. Several others, including Clark Clifford, George Elsey, John Steelman, and James Webb, were unable to clear their calendars of previous commitments or demands of supervening importance. But twenty-two former Truman associates spent two stimulating days together, reliving what they all agreed were among the most satisfying years of their lives.

To provide a frame of reference for the discussions, the organizing committee had provided each of the participants with a copy of Stephen Hess's book, *Organizing the Presidency*.[2] In addition, a list of fifteen questions was circulated in advance, with an invitation to the participants to prepare a statement in response to these questions. To his credit, the late Justice Tom Clark was the only one to take us at our word and to respond to each question with a one- or two-sentence statement. From other participants we received a widely varying array of responses, some reflections set down in an earlier day, some written in anticipation of the opportunity to review with colleagues the years of their White House experience.

A number of these statements about the Truman White House appear here in four groups, followed in each instance by a section captioned "Discussion." It should be understood, however, that these were not discussions of the preceding statements. The plan of the conference was to focus in each of the four sessions on one particular group ("The Cabinet," "The White House Staff: Early Period," "The White House Staff: Later Period," and "The Executive Office Agencies"). The statements in each section were written by the principal discussants for the respective session; the statements, however, had not been circulated in advance. Discussions usually centered on much the same topics as the papers, but there was no deliberate intent to relate one to the other.

---

[1] Richard W. Leopold, "The Historian's Task," in *The Korean War: A 25-Year Perspective*, edited by Francis H. Heller (Lawrence: Regents Press of Kansas, 1977), p. 217.

[2] Washington, D.C.: Brookings Institution, 1976.

Preface

The discussions were lead by four distinguished students of the presidency and executive organization: Dean E. H. Hobbs of Auburn University, Professor Dorothy Buckton James of Virginia Polytechnic and State University, Professor Louis W. Koenig of New York University, and Professor C. A. Newland of the University of Southern California. The conduct of the discussions was left to each moderator's discretion. The organizing committee is deeply indebted to these four outstanding scholars for the skillful manner in which they discharged their tasks.

As program coordinator for the conference and editor of the resultant volume, I wish to record my gratitude to the staff of the Harry S. Truman Library and especially to John Curry who rendered yeoman assistance throughout. To the secretarial staff of the School of Law of the University of Kansas I owe thanks for the efficient typing of the manuscript. Charles S. Murphy deserves credit not only for his initiative in the organizing phases of the venture but for generous support throughout. Last but by no means least, my thanks to Ben Zobrist, a comrade-in-arms in many ways.

Francis H. Heller

June 1978
Lawrence, Kansas

PANELISTS

Charles F. Brannan, *assistant secretary of agriculture, 1944–48; secretary of agriculture, 1948–53;* practicing attorney, Denver, Colorado, 1953–present; general counsel, National Farmers Union, Denver, Colorado, 1953–present.

Tom C. Clark, assistant attorney general, Criminal Division, Department of Justice, 1943–45; *attorney general, 1945–49;* associate justice of the United States Supreme Court, 1949–67. (Mr. Justice Clark died June 13, 1977.)

Donald S. Dawson, *administrative assistant to the president* and *director, Liaison Office for Personnel Management, 1947–53;* major general, USAFR-Ret.; president, Reserve Officers Association, and U.S. vice-president, Inter-Allied Confederation of Reserve Officers, 1965–66; practicing attorney.

Robert L. Dennison, career naval officer; member Joint War Plans Committee of Joint Chiefs of Staff, 1944–45; assistant chief, Naval Operations, 1945–47; commander, U.S.S. *Missouri*, 1947–48; *naval aide to the president, 1948–53,* director, Strategic Plans Division, assistant chief of naval operations, 1954–56; member, Joint Strategic Plans Committee of Joint Chiefs of Staff, commander, First Fleet U.S. Pacific Fleet, 1956–58; deputy chief of naval operations (plans and policy), 1958; commander in chief, U.S. Naval Forces, Eastern Atlantic and Mediterranean, 1959–60, commander in chief, U.S. Atlantic Fleet, supreme Allied commander, Atlantic, 1960–63.

W. Averell Harriman, U.S. ambassador to the Soviet Union, 1943–46, to Great Britain, 1946; *secretary of commerce, 1946–48;* U.S. representative in Europe with rank of ambassador, Economic Cooperation Administration, 1948–50; *special assistant to the president, 1950–51; director of the Mutual Security Agency* and senior adviser to the president on foreign and military policy, *1951–53*; governor of New York, 1955–58; ambassador-at-large, 1961, 1965–68; assistant secretary of state for Far Eastern affairs, 1961–63; undersecretary of state for political affairs, 1963–65; personal representative of the president to conversations on Vietnam in Paris, 1968–69; chairman, Foreign Policy Task Force Advisory Council, Democratic National Committee, 1974–present.

Ken Hechler, administrative analyst, Bureau of the Budget, 1946–47; assistant professor of politics, Princeton University, 1947–49; *special assistant in the White House office, 1949–53;* research director, Stevenson-Kefauver campaign, 1956; administrative aide, U.S. Sen. John Carroll (Colo.), summer 1957; U.S. representative, 4th District of West Virginia, 1958–76; delegate-at-large from West Virginia to Democratic National Convention, 1964, 1968, 1972.

William J. Hopkins, executive clerk, White House office, 1943–49; *senior executive clerk, 1949–66;* executive assistant to the president, 1966–71.

Roger W. Jones, successively budget examiner, assistant to director, *deputy assistant director, assistant director for legislative reference, Bureau of the Budget, 1945–58;* deputy director, 1958–59; chairman, U.S. Civil Service Commission, 1959–61; deputy undersecretary of state for administration, 1961–62; special assistant to the director, Bureau of the Budget, 1962–68; assistant director, Office of Management and Budget, 1968–71, consultant, 1971–75; member, Commission on Political Activity of Government Personnel, 1967; member, Board of Higher Education, Washington, D.C., 1968–73.

Leon H. Keyserling, general counsel, National Housing Agency, 1942–46; *vice-chairman (1946–49)* and *chairman (1949–53), Council of Economic Advisers;* consulting economist and attorney with various individuals, organizations, and governments, 1952–present. Founder and, since 1954, president, Conference on Economic Progress.

James S. Lay, Jr., assistant to the special assistant to the secretary of state, 1945–46; secretary, National Intelligence Authority, 1946; division chief, Central Intelligence Group, 1947; *assistant executive secretary (1947–50), executive secretary (1950–61), National Security Council;* deputy assistant to the director, Central Intelligence Agency, 1961–64; executive secretary, U.S. Intelligence Board, 1962–71; consultant, President's Foreign Intelligence Advisory Board, 1971–76.

Panelists

Edwin A. Locke, Jr., personal representative of President Truman, 1945–47, in charge of the American War Production Mission in China; *special assistant to the president, 1946–47*, special representative of the secretary of state, with the rank of ambassador, to coordinate economic and technical assistance in the Near East, 1951–53; executive assistant to the president, Union Tank Car Company, Chicago, 1953–54, executive vice-president, 1954–55, president, director, 1955–63; president, chief executive officer, Modern Homes Construction Company, Valdosta, Ga., 1963–67; Coastal Products Corporation, Blountstown, Fla., 1964–67; president, chief executive officer, American Paper Institute, 1967–present.

Charles S. Murphy, Office of Legislative Counsel, U.S. Senate, 1934–46; *administrative assistant to the president, 1947–50; special counsel to the president, 1950–53*; practicing attorney, Washington, 1953–61; president, National Democratic Club, 1956–58; counsel to Democratic National Advisory Council, 1957–60; undersecretary of agriculture, 1960–65; chairman, Civil Aeronautics Board, 1965–68; counselor to the president, 1968; practicing attorney, 1969–present. *Conference Chairman.*

Philleo Nash, special assistant to the director, Office of War Information, 1942–46; *special assistant in the White House, 1946–52; administrative assistant to the president, 1952–53*; chairman, Wisconsin Democratic party, 1955–57; lieutenant governor of Wisconsin, 1959–61; U.S. commissioner of Indian affairs, 1961–66; American Specialist Program (India), Department of State, 1966; adjunct professor of anthropology, American University (Washington, D.C.), 1971–73, professor, 1973–present.

Richard E. Neustadt, staff member, Bureau of the Budget, 1946–50; *special assistant in the White House office, 1950–53*; professor of public administration, Cornell University, 1953–54; professor of government, Columbia University, 1954–65; consultant to Presidents Kennedy and Johnson, 1961-66; chairman, Platform Committee, Democratic National Convention, 1972; professor of government, Harvard University, 1965–present; associate dean, John Fitzgerald Kennedy School of Government, 1965–75.

Walter S. Salant, economist, Office of Price Administration, 1945; economic adviser to the economic stabilization director, 1945–46; economist, Price Decontrol Board, 1946; *staff economist, Council of Economic Advisers, 1946–52*; special consultant, NATO, 1952; consultant, Committee for National Trade Policy, 1953–54; visiting pro-

xv

fessor, Stanford University, 1954, 1969; consultant, secretary of the treasury, 1961–present; member, U.S. Economics Survey Mission to Indonesia, 1961; consultant, Rockefeller Foundation, 1960–61; consultant, AID, 1963–66; advisory committee, Balance of Payments Statistics Presentation, 1975–76; senior fellow, Brookings Institution, 1954–1976, emeritus, January 1977–present.

Beth Campbell Short, *correspondence secretary to the president, September 1952–January 1953*; publicity director, Democratic Senatorial Campaign Committee, 1953–57; press secretary to Sen. A. S. (Mike) Monroney (Okla.), 1956–66; special assistant for research development and training to assistant commissioner, Social Security Administration, 1966–present.

John W. Snyder, federal loan administrator, April 1945; director, Office of War Mobilization and Reconversion, July 1945; *secretary of the treasury, 1946–53*; adviser, U.S. Treasury, 1955–73; president, 1953–66, and director, Overland Corporation, Toledo, Ohio, 1953–present.

Elmer B. Staats, joined *Bureau of the Budget* in 1939, chief, War Agencies Section, 1945–47, *assistant director*, Legislative Reference, *1947–49, executive assistant director, 1949–50, deputy director* under President Truman, *1950–53*, and Presidents Eisenhower, Kennedy, and Johnson, 1959–66; research director, Marshall Field & Co., Chicago, 1953; executive officer, Operations Coordinating Board, National Security Council, 1954–58; U.S. comptroller general, 1966–present.

David H. Stowe, chief examiner, Bureau of the Budget, 1943–47; *special assistant to the assistant to the president, 1947–49; administrative assistant to the president, 1949–53*; labor arbitrator (primarily in the industrial and transportation areas), 1953–70; member, National Mediation Board, 1970–present.

Theodore Tannenwald, Jr., special consultant, secretary of war, 1943–45; consultant, secretary of defense, 1946–49; practicing attorney (except for periods of government service), 1947–65; *counsel to* Averell Harriman, *special assistant to the president, 1950–51*; special counsel, Moreland Commission for the Investigation of Workmen's Compensation, New York State, 1955–58; member, President's Task Force on Foreign Assistance and special assistant to the secretary of state, 1961; judge, United States Tax Court, 1965–present.

Roger W. Tubby, director of information, Foreign Economics Administration, 1944–45; assistant to administrator, 1945; director of infor-

INTRODUCTION

The cover of Stephen Hess's *Organizing the Presidency*[1] shows the eagle and shield of the presidential seal neatly broken up into eight segments that are distributed on a schematic organization chart. The unidentified designer thus sought to symbolize the issue to which Hess addressed himself: "Has the growth of government outstripped a highly personalized presidency that has to rely on the involvement of the Chief Executive and his staff surrogates?"[2] With a somewhat different emphasis the question is, How can the presidency be organized to serve not only the needs of the president but also the postulates of a free and open society?

The presidency has always been a subject of popular attention. There is no other office quite like it anywhere in the world; and because the United States is a world power, the manner in which the office is discharged has assumed critical importance not only for the people of this country, but for the world at large. The very uniqueness of the office, however, makes it difficult to generalize about its characteristics and requirements. It has been pointed out that academics writing about the presidency in the late 1950s and early 1960s (including the present writer)[3] based their views on the presidential styles of Roosevelt or Truman, while the generally critical interpretations of the 1970s were colored by "the acid of hatred for the Vietnam War."[4] It is indeed difficult to look back thirty or forty years and not be mindful of events of the

[1] Washington, D.C.: Brookings Institution, 1976.

[2] Ibid., p. 10.

[3] Francis H. Heller, *The Presidency: A Modern Perspective* (New York: Random House, 1960).

[4] William G. Andrews, "The Presidency, Congress and Constitutional Theory," in *Perspectives on the Presidency*, edited by Aaron Wildavsky (Boston: Little, Brown, 1975), p. 38. A shortened version of this essay is included in *The Presidency in Contemporary Context*, edited by Norman C. Thomas (New York: Dodd, Mead, 1975).

Introduction

more recent past. Comparisons and contrasts suggest themselves at every turn. Thus Stephen Hess, in his rather brief chapter on the Truman administration, asserts that the modern presidential organization "started to come into sharper focus under Truman,"[5] obviously a retrospective observation. The contributors to this volume were—understandably—more inclined to stress the distance between the Truman administration and more recent presidencies. But whatever their intentions, allusions to more recent practices occur more than once in their discussions.

Perhaps the most vexing aspect of the American presidency is its unavoidable blending of continuity and discontinuity. It is easy to say that the office is what each incumbent makes it. This is, of course, the underlying assumption of James David Barber's widely acclaimed study of *The Presidential Character*.[6] But no president can erase the record of his predecessors. Not only do modern budget procedures and long-term funding obligations circumscribe and inhibit his initiatives, but the public also develops certain expectations about presidential behavior which cannot easily be cast aside.[7]

Presidents normally arrive at the White House on a wave of popular approval, buoyed by the promise that the new administration will do things differently—and better—than its predecessor. A long campaign's oratory has projected a collage of initiatives and innovations, not the least of which is the greatly improved management of the presidential office itself. Thus, when the outgoing and the incoming teams meet to facilitate the transition—a practice started by President Truman in 1952 but surely by this time one of the "continuities" of office which the public takes for granted—there is an inevitable gap in perceptions. Those about to leave stress the merits of their ways of doing things; the new arrivals can hardly wait to show that there are better ways. This was true even in the first organized transition as the comments of the contributors to this volume indicate.[8]

Mr. Truman's personal interest in an orderly transition[9] is fully attested to by his associates. It is attributed, at least by some, to his awareness of the difficulties he had encountered when, almost totally

---

[5] *Organizing the Presidency*, p. 57.

[6] Englewood Cliffs, N.J.: Prentice Hall, 1972; 2d ed., 1977.

[7] An example, if perhaps only of a symbolic nature, is President Carter's decision at the beginning of his term to do away with the traditional playing of "Hail to the Chief." Less than eighteen months later the practice was resumed, ostensibly because the public expected it.

[8] See Laurin L. Henry, *Presidential Transitions* (Washington, D.C.: Brookings Institution, 1960), pp. 467–487, 508–511.

[9] Harry S. Truman, *Memoirs*, vol. 2, *Years of Trial and Hope* (Garden City, N.Y.: Doubleday, 1956), pp. 508–509, 511.

Introduction

ignored by his predecessor, he found himself suddenly faced with the awesome responsibilities of the presidency. But it is probably also true that President Truman desired an orderly transition because orderliness was an important part of his personal make-up.[10]

Orderly processes were clearly a keynote of his managerial style. His staff meetings—which feature prominently throughout the discussions reported in this volume—were not only an effective device for planning and communicating; their regularity imposed order on the working methods of the entire White House staff.

Yet the manner in which President Truman conducted the staff meetings served still another purpose: it reinforced the personal relations between "the boss" and his staff. As all participants report, the atmosphere at this daily session was open and informal. "Even the lowest man on the totem pole" was free to speak up—and evidently did.

The picture that emerges in these pages of life and work in Mr. Truman's White House is clearly one of informality, enthusiasm, and camaraderie. Contemporary newspaper reports tended to stress conflicts and mishaps. This difference in perspective may be a case of those on the inside versus those on the outside. Another explanation may be the inherent tension between the White House and the press corps which Richard Neustadt and Roger Tubby refer to in this volume. Still another may be the general inclination of journalists to assume that a normal state of affairs simply is not newsworthy.

On the other hand, it would be rather startling if the veterans of White House, cabinet, and Executive Office service who gathered to talk about their experiences some twenty-five or thirty years ago would have had other than favorable recollections. The warmth of their memories owes just as much to the excitement of sharing in the exclusivity of White House operations as it does to the relationship they enjoyed with Mr. Truman. Their discussions redound with reflections on the family-like atmosphere that pervaded the staff and the crucial role the president played in setting the tone.

Much has been written about President Truman's loyalty to those who worked for him.[11] This, too, was part of his style: he gave his trust and took it for granted that the support and loyalty would be returned. Anyone following the discussions in this volume will be forced to conclude that the bonds so forged withstood the test of time.

[10] Richard Tanner Johnson, *Managing the White House* (New York: Harper & Row, 1974), p. 52.

[11] Ibid., pp. 56–57; Francis H. Heller, "Truman," in *The History Makers*, edited by Lord Longford and Sir John Wheeler-Bennett (London: Sidgwick & Jackson, 1973), p. 330.

Introduction

Another element in President Truman's management of the presidential office was, from all the evidence in this volume and elsewhere,[12] that the president himself was a prodigious worker. His familiarity with, and concern for, budgetary procedures are particularly noted—and noteworthy. Averell Harriman's story of being embarrassed by Mr. Truman's detailed knowledge of a report of which he, Harriman, had only read a summary has been repeated in countless variations by others. Part of the effectiveness of the staff meeting hinged, of course, on the fact that the president, unfailingly, had done his homework.

There is, however, nothing to suggest that the pattern that evolved in the Truman White House was the result of design or premeditation. Mr. Truman himself was not given to the pursuit of abstractions and tended to distrust people with rigid ideological minds. He was at all times a politician by instinct and craftsmanship, and many of those he asked to work for him had similar inclinations.[13] They gave little thought to administrative theories and organizational charts. Task assignments in the White House were relatively fluid; there were no rigid job descriptions—witness the discussion in this volume over the question of whether or not the Truman White House had a chief of staff.

David Fellman has observed that "successful Presidents must have a sense of personal security and experience in politics; it is not a job for amateurs."[14] Harry Truman was, without doubt, a professional, and he chose professionals to work for him. As Neustadt points out in his essay (and he and others in discussion), the Truman White House staff included a high percentage of people who had earned their spurs in a variety of jobs throughout the federal government. They had administrative experience and political savvy. Like the president, they were oriented toward practice rather than theory.

A number of books on the Truman presidency have highlighted a conflict between conservatives and liberals within the president's entourage, sometimes describing it as a contest for the president's mind.[15] Truman himself said that it was his deliberate choice to surround himself

---

[12] Johnson, *Managing the White House*, pp. 50–51; Dean Acheson, *Present at the Creation: My Years in the State Department* (New York: W. W. Norton, 1969), p. 73.

[13] Robert J. Donovan, *Conflict and Crisis: The Presidency of Harry S. Truman, 1945–1948* (New York: W. W. Norton, 1977), pp. 26–27.

[14] Review of Richard Neustadt, "Presidential Power: The Politics of Leadership with Reflections on Johnson and Nixon," *Annals of the Academy of Political and Social Science* 428 (1976): 164.

[15] Cabell Phillips, *The Truman Presidency* (New York: Macmillan, 1966), p. 164.

Introduction

with associates of differing, even conflicting, views.[16] His associates, responding to a pointed question about this reported cleavage, readily grant that it existed; those usually identified with the liberal group (Charles Murphy, for instance) assert that the president's political instincts were always with them; the conservatives (e.g., John Snyder) see the president as fundamentally in accord with their views. No better support can be found for the president's explanation than these differing perspectives.

What can be learned from the way Truman operated the presidency? The overriding theme of the following essays and discussions is that the style of the White House is—inescapably—the president's style. The White House between 1945 and 1953 was orderly because Harry Truman was an orderly person. It was profoundly human because that was Mr. Truman's way. It was a successful operation because Mr. Truman was a professional and surrounded himself with staff members who, in their different ways, were also professionals. Historical perspective is often dangerously clouded by hindsight; it is easy to say today that this or that should have been done differently. To those who wrote and spoke for this volume, it is clear that the nation was well served by the way Harry Truman managed his affairs in the White House.

---

[16] Truman, *Memoirs*, vol. 1, *Year of Decisions* (Garden City, N.Y.: Doubleday, 1955), p. 546.

The Truman White House

I

THE CABINET

Four persons who had served in President Truman's cabinet discussed the operations of the Truman White House from the perspective of their experiences: (in alphabetical order) Charles F. Brannan, Tom C. Clark, W. Averell Harriman, and John W. Snyder.

Charles F. Brannan was assistant secretary of agriculture when Mr. Truman succeeded to the presidency in 1945. Brannan was appointed secretary of agriculture in 1948 and served in that position until the change of administrations in January 1953, when he returned to his hometown of Denver. He has been a practicing attorney since then and is general counsel to the National Farmers Union. He is a member of the board of directors of the Truman Library Institute.

Like Mr. Brannan, Tom C. Clark was elevated from a subcabinet position (assistant attorney general) when President Truman chose him in 1945 to head the Department of Justice. He served as attorney general until 1949 when he was named to the Supreme Court of the United States. Justice Clark retired from the Court in 1967 but remained active, both as a senior justice and as director of the Federal Judicial Center. Justice Clark died June 13, 1977.

W. Averell Harriman served in the Truman administration as ambassador to the Soviet Union (1943–46), ambassador to Great Britain (1946), secretary of commerce (1946–48), U.S. representative in Europe for the Economic Cooperation Administration (1948–50), special assistant to the president (1950–51), and director of the Mutual Security Administration and senior adviser to the president on foreign and military policy (1951–53). He was elected governor of New York in 1954 and served in a variety of high-level diplomatic assignments during the Kennedy and Johnson administrations. Governor Harriman is a member of the board of directors of the Truman Library Institute.

John W. Snyder holds the record for longest continuous service in the Truman cabinet, having served as secretary of the treasury from 1946 to 1953. Secretary Synder is a member of the board of directors of the Truman Library Institute and chairman of the board of the Truman Scholarship Program.

In their essays prepared for this volume, Messrs. Brannan, Harriman, and Snyder all stress the importance to the White House operations of President Truman's attitudes and work habits. All three agree that having selected those who should work for him, Mr. Truman placed full trust in them and delegated authority to the widest extent. Justice Clark whose untimely death accounts for the absence of an essay from his pen, confirms these impressions in the course of the discussion.

All four discussants deny the validity of Stephen Hess's assertion that the Truman staff began the trend toward White House staff dominance that became so ominously evident in more recent years. The recollections of the four cabinet officers are clearly to the contrary.

CHARLES F. BRANNAN

As secretary of agriculture my relations with President Truman and his staff in the White House were as pleasant as anyone could ask.

I never found the president unwilling to listen. His responses came promptly and clearly and were never evasive. It was a wholly efficient and productive method of operation from my point of view. I must assume that the president found the arrangement satisfactory or he would have changed it or his secretary of agriculture.

I conceived it to be my responsibility to minimize the number of matters which needed to be referred to the president for his personal attention; and I believe that during Mr. Truman's administration the Department of Agriculture demanded a minimum of his time and gave him few occasions for concern. I also believed it to be our duty to support the president's goals and objectives to the fullest extent possible although another government agency may have had the primary responsibility for them. I have always been convinced that effective administration and efficient service to the particular constituents your department served were the best possible politics, but my support in political terms did not stop there. I think President Truman had similar views.

A few examples may be the best way to corroborate and support these conclusions.

One of the statutory duties of the secretary of agriculture during the Truman administration (it is not so now) was to announce annually the secretary's estimate of the total domestic consumption of sugar for the coming year. This was a highly important decision to sugar producers, both domestic and foreign. If this estimate was relatively high as compared to the historic average consumption, import quotas for sugar produced abroad would be increased, and at the same time the domestic wholesale price of sugar would decline. If the estimate was below the historic average, the effect would be to raise the barrier against sugar imports and, thereby, to strengthen prices for domestic producers. Obviously, the secretary's estimate had wide-ranging political implications. Hence, the first time I was confronted with this duty, I thought it advisable to discuss my proposed announcement with the president, and so I secured an appointment. I took along a brief memorandum reflecting the applicable statistics for the president's review. I thought it also might be helpful to give the president some background on the history of sugar legislation. So, I opened our conference with a brief description of the Costigan-Jones Sugar Act. The president politely interrupted to advise me that he had been the floor leader for the bill that extended this legislation and understood it very well. That he also understood the political implications became immediately clear, for upon finishing the memorandum, he asked me if I had discussed the proposed consumption estimate with Senator [Allen] Ellender who was not only the ranking Democrat on the Agriculture Committee but also one of the chief spokesmen in Congress for both domestic cane- and beet-sugar producers. Fortunately, I had talked with Senator Ellender and could report that the senator agreed with my proposed estimate. The president thereupon indicated his concurrence. He then went on to instruct me that when it became necessary to make this annual estimate in subsequent years, if I were able to reach a satisfactory agreement with Senator Ellender, it would be unnecessary to review the matter with him or with anyone in the White House. During the succeeding five years, the annual domestic consumption estimate was reviewed first with Senator Ellender and his concurrence obtained, thereby eliminating the necessity for the president to concern himself further with this matter.

This demonstrates the president's inclination to delegate broad responsibility. The president apparently had concluded that his secretary of agriculture would do a conscientious and thorough analysis of all the available facts and reach a proper conclusion for the benefit of both domestic producers and foreign suppliers and that Senator Ellender's concurrence was sufficient assurance that political reactions to the decision would not be a source of trouble.

During the entire period of time that I served as secretary under Mr. Truman, I received only one instruction directly from him to employ someone. The persons and circumstances involved are so unusual that I think it merits repeating.

One afternoon, early in 1949, I answered the White House telephone on my desk to find President Truman on the other end. He informed me that he was sending Mr. Paul Stark, a prominent horticulturist, to see me and that he wished me to employ Stark as an adviser on my staff, effective the same day. It should not be considered unusual that the president himself should evidence interest in the employment of a particular person. But in this case he was directing me to hire the brother of the former governor of Missouri, Lloyd Stark, who had been Mr. Truman's opponent in a bitter contest for the United States Senate. Governor Stark's campaign tactics would not have earned the commendation of the Fair Campaign Practices Committee had it then been in existence. But however President Truman may have felt about his opponent in that campaign, it did not carry over to the governor's brother. Mr. Paul Stark was employed forthwith and became a useful member of the staff. No reference was ever made to the former governor.

Major appointments were always discussed with Don Dawson who handled these matters for the president. And from time to time cabinet officers received suggestions and recommendations from Mr. Dawson. But at no time was any "pressure" applied by the White House staff for the employment of anyone.

One example of Mr. Truman's willingness to delegate responsibility to his subordinates is demonstrated by an occasion following the outbreak of hostilities in Korea.

At the first cabinet meeting following the entry of the United States into the Korean conflict, the president instructed me to submit proposals for preventing the anticipated escalation in food prices, especially sugar, which, newspaper reports indicated, was already being hoarded by housewives and merchants. Two days later I returned to the White House with a brief memorandum pointing out the total ineffectiveness of existing price-control legislation which had been emasculated by the Capehart amendment. I argued that the only effective way to prevent a rapid advance in the price of sugar would be for the United States to buy up Cuba's entire stocks and its forthcoming production. The United States had a contractual right to do this. The president asked how much money it would take. I responded: about $2.5 billion. He then asked where the money would come from. I reminded him that the Commodity Credit Corporation had almost unlimited borrowing power. The president thought for a little while and asked me again if this was the only way I thought a drastic price rise could be avoided, and when I assured him that it was the only effective and quick way available to us, he merely said, "I guess that's what you will have to do." I left the president's office and by noon of the second day the United States owned or controlled practically all of the world's supply of sugar. As a result, the price of sugar did not rise during the Korean War.

It is very significant, however, that there is not one written word of authorization from the president to me for the expenditure of over $2 billion of U.S. funds in about a twenty-four hour period. (This story is told much more readably in *Mr. President,* which was published in 1952.)

The Cabinet

It was my experience that President Truman relied primarily upon department and agency heads for the proper performance of their administrative duties and communicated directly with them on matters of major significance.

My relationships and contacts with the White House staff were frequent and cordial. In my judgment, President Truman's staff was the most efficient crew that ever served any occupant of the White House. Yet I do not recall ever having imposed upon them to present a matter to the president for me or having received through the staff instructions from the president on a major matter of policy or operations.

W. AVERELL HARRIMAN

When President Roosevelt died on April 12, 1945, I was in the American Embassy in Moscow. I immediately made plans to return to Washington as early as possible in order to report to President Truman on post-Yalta developments and difficulties in our relations with the Soviet government. I called on Marshall Stalin, who appeared gravely disturbed about the worldwide effect of President Roosevelt's death. This visit gave me the opportunity to tell him that he would contribute to world stability if he were to send Molotov instead of Vishinsky to the United Nations Conference in San Francisco. Against Molotov's protests, Stalin agreed.

I arrived in Washington on April 20, 1945, after a record forty-eight-hour flight across the Balkans and Italy. Much to my surprise, I found that President Truman had already read the Yalta Agreements and all the post-Yalta telegrams. He was fully familiar with the details of our difficulties and with Stalin's failure to carry out his agreements. This was my first experience in understanding just how avid a reader President Truman was. Throughout his term as president, it was my experience that he read an extraordinary number of documents and reports. In fact, once when I was secretary of commerce I was embarrassed to find that I had only read the summary and conclusions of a report I wished to discuss with him, whereas he had read the entire report. I never made that mistake again!

I found President Truman's approach to his responsibilities extremely modest. He told me, after Roosevelt's death, that he had no experience in international matters, and he wanted to know what I could tell him about Roosevelt's policies. He said that Roosevelt, not he, had been elected president and therefore that he must follow Roosevelt's policies as far as practicable. I was at first a little worried about his deference; but during the next few weeks as new problems arose quickly, he showed the courage and ability to deal with them on his own. He was a little

9

overaggressive in his first talk with Molotov on Poland. He also acted too fast in stopping the Lend-Lease shipments after VE Day on the advice of [Lend-Lease Administrator Leo] Crowley. With the help of [Secretary of State Edward] Stettinius we were able to get the president to reverse that decision; but it left an unnecessary scar on our relations with the Soviet government although the Lend-Lease adjustment with the Soviets was, I felt, generous.

President Truman's first act was to ratify the call for the United Nations meeting in San Francisco, and he gave full support to Secretary Stettinius and the delegation Roosevelt had appointed. Truman was always disposed to support the members of his cabinet, but he insisted on prior consultations on important matters.

Truman was a man of very few words. I still vividly recall a talk I had with him during the winter of 1946, shortly after my return from Moscow. When [James F.] Byrnes offered me the position of ambassador to Great Britain, I explained that I could not take it as I had already been overseas for five years and planned to return to private life. He told me I would have to talk to the president about it. So, marshaling all my arguments, I called on the president. He greeted me with a brief direct statement, "We, with the British, are in difficulties with the Soviets over Iran. They are refusing to carry out their treaty obligations to withdraw their troops. This may lead to war. I need an ambassador in Britain who knows them well and I want you to go."

I could only reply, "How soon do you want me to go?"

He said, "As soon as you can."

I got up and started to leave and then thought of all my reasons for not going. So I asked him not to consider this a normal appointment but to allow me to return as soon as was reasonable after the crisis was over. He agreed, and that ended the conversation. (At about this time, the president transferred Harry Dexter White from the Treasury to the International Monetary Fund. Years later, this action led to charges of the president's being soft on communism. His blunt statement to me, however, shows how false this accusation was.)

As it turned out, the Soviet troops were withdrawn from Iran and the crisis subsided. The president did not forget his agreement with me. I hold the record of serving as U.S. ambassador in London for the shortest term, approximately six months.

In September 1946 when the president accepted Henry Wallace's resignation as secretary of commerce following the foreign policy dispute that arose over Wallace's New York speech, it crossed my mind that Truman might well ask me to return to Washington to take that job. He telephoned me a few days later and offered me the position, which I accepted immediately.

As secretary of commerce he gave me complete latitude in the selection of the members of my staff. He approved my recommendations without question for Undersecretary William Foster, Assistant Secretary David Bruce, and Counsel Adrian Fisher, even though Foster was a Republican. All three men have since played important roles in government in many other jobs.

The president was always available when I had a problem I felt I should discuss with him either personally or on the telephone. He and his White House staff gave me the fullest cooperation in dealing with Congress. Of course, many matters had interdepartmental ramifications, such as aid to Greece and Turkey and the Marshall Plan. He expected the members of his cabinet to confer together on matters of overlapping responsibility, and he would, on occasion, meet with those members jointly on matters of importance. He held cabinet meetings regularly—as I recall, every Friday morning. Each member of the cabinet was given the opportunity to raise any subject and to report on matters of interest to the president. Not many decisions were made at cabinet meetings, but they served to keep all the cabinet members informed about important questions being dealt with by other departments and about the president's policies on these issues. This arrangement was very helpful in developing a team spirit within the administration.

In April 1948 I was in Bogota with General [George C.] Marshall attending an inter-American conference. The president telephoned me and asked me to go to Europe to be what was called the roving ambassador in charge of European operations, with headquarters in Paris. I said that I would be returning to the states shortly and that I would like to discuss the matter with him personally. When I met with the president, I told him that I would prefer to stay in Washington and help in any way I could during the coming campaign. He answered that I could do more good in Paris; he said that Paul Hoffman was insisting on it and that it was important that I go. I, of course, accepted.

Mr. Truman had given his unqualified support to the Marshall Plan. He organized preparations for the congressional passage of legislation in a most skillful manner. He appointed three committees: one, chaired by Dr. [Edwin C.] Nourse of the Council of Economic Advisers, to assess our financial and economic capabilities; a second, chaired by Secretary of the Interior [Julius] Krug, to review whether the resources were available; and the third, I chaired as secretary of commerce—a committee of private citizens drawn from business, labor, agriculture, banking, economics, and politics to analyze the European needs and to propose a program of recovery. Senator [Arthur] Vandenberg told me that these reports, particularly that of the citizens' committee, assisted greatly in getting congressional approval of the Marshall Plan.

Secretary Marshall's prestige was extremely valuable. His testimony before congressional committees and his speeches around the country were most effective. Undersecretary of State [Robert] Lovett and his carefully selected staff spearheaded the presentation.

Senator Vandenberg, the Republican chairman of the Foreign Relations Committee, played a leading role in the enactment of the legislation. He introduced certain amendments to make passage of the bill possible and insisted on the appointment of a Republican businessman to head the operation. President Truman was indignant, regarding this as an interference with his constitutional responsibility to nominate his own administrators. He wanted Dean Acheson. President Truman, however, agreed to appoint Hoffman and, in fact, forced him to take the job by announcing his appointment from the White House despite Hoffman's objection that he did not think he could take the job. I have always considered this action to be in the best Truman tradition!

(At first Vandenberg thought Paul Hoffman was too liberal for his conservative colleagues. But after going through a long list of businessmen—some of whom I pointed out were opposed to the Marshall Plan—the senator finally accepted Hoffman, who, of course, proved to be unbelievably successful.)

President Truman gave Paul Hoffman the fullest support with Congress in his annual efforts to get appropriations and the freest rein in appointments at home and aboard—many of which I, of course, recommended.

In the spring of 1950 I told the president and Dean Acheson that I thought the program in Europe was so well established that I could come home and that a successor could carry on. It was agreed that I would come home at the end of July or early in August and become the president's special assistant on foreign policies. State and Defense at that time were at logger-heads because of the personal rift between Dean Acheson and Louis Johnson.

I was in London the Sunday that North Korea invaded South Korea, and I did not return to Paris until Monday afternoon. On Tuesday morning I had a telephone conversation with President Truman. In his memoirs he recalls calling me; my recollection is that I called him. In any event, he asked if I could come back as soon as possible because he was short-handed with the war emergency problems. I replied that I would leave at once, and I took the afternoon flight to Washington. I attended the subsequent meetings at Blair House, where the president was then living. The decisions the president made in those days were the finest example of his courageous and decisive character.

He agreed that I should have a small staff of half a dozen highly capable individuals. They attended the appropriate interdepartmental committee meetings on military, political, financial, and public relations matters. These men were authorized by me to attempt to get the interdepartmental committees to make the recommendations I knew the president wanted, so that there would be interdepartmental approval before a subject reached the president.

I recall one case in which the president turned down a recommendation of mine. I urged him to get a joint congressional resolution supporting his action in Korea. This would have had almost unanimous approval at the time. But he said that he would not do so because it would make it more difficult for future presidents to deal with emergencies. Much to my surprise, I learned later that Dean Acheson had recommended against the joint resolution. Later when Robert Taft and others began criticizing the president, I was convinced that the president had made a mistake. This decision, however, was characteristic of President Truman. He always kept in mind how his actions would affect future presidential authority.

Later, when I was director for mutual security, I reported to him that the committees of Congress were considering establishing a watchdog committee. I suggested that I could get along with such a committee and that it was sometimes easier to get their approval before an event than afterwards. The president refused. He objected because he considered this committee to be an invasion of the president's constitutional power and administrative responsibilities. He said that as long as he sat in the Oval Office his greatest responsibility was to protect the authority of the president against the inroads of Congress. He pointed out that if the Congress invaded presidential powers, there would be chaos. He was, Truman said, the only one who represented *all* the people, whereas senators and congressmen represented people of limited areas. I fully agreed with his conclusions, having recently spent two years in France when the French National Assembly controlled the executive branch, leading to a change in government every six to ten months.

In early August I went to Tokyo and Korea with Generals [Lauris] Norstad and [Matthew B.] Ridgway. The president thought it would be a good idea for me to see Douglas MacArthur. He told me that he wanted me to tell General MacArthur two things: First, to stay away from Chiang Kai-shek, as he didn't want the Nationalist Chinese to get us into a war with mainland China. (Shortly before this, General MacArthur had paid an unauthorized visit to Taipei and had had his picture taken kissing Madame Chiang's hand on his departure. This had caused quite a stir in the press.) Secondly, Truman wanted me to find out what General MacArthur's needs were and to assure him that the president would do everything in his power to provide for them.

I spent a day in Korea with General Ridgway and General Norstad. Our forces were then holding only the small Pusan bridgehead. We three independently came to the conclusion that Lieutenant General [Walton H.] Walker, in command of the U.N. forces in Korea, was not adequate to the task and that he should be replaced. This consensus was revealed on our return flight to Tokyo when we compared notes of our impressions.

In my two long talks with General MacArthur I made the first point—to steer clear of Chiang Kai-shek—plain, and General MacArthur said that as a soldier he would obey orders. But the manner in which he spoke gave me some doubts as to whether, in fact, he would. On the second point, MacArthur presented to General Ridgway, General Norstad, and myself the details of his plans for the Inchon landing. General Ridgway recalls that the brilliance of MacArthur's presentation fully allayed his prior concerns and completely won him over. I have a long memorandum of the talks which I gave to President Truman at the time, much of which he quotes in his memoirs.

I scheduled our return to Washington so as to permit me to call on the president at about seven in the morning. I knew this would be the best time to catch him alone. I reported on our visit, particularly the full outline of MacArthur's request for approval of the Inchon landing with the necessary support. I had made clear to the president the difficulties of the plan, including the very heavy tide which would make landing any reinforcements impossible until the next high tide.

Ridgway had prepared a memorandum for the Pentagon recommending approval of the operation; it was signed by Ridgway, Norstad, and myself. President Truman gave me the impression that he approved the operation. He instructed me to go to the Pentagon and see Secretary of Defense Johnson and General [Omar] Bradley, chairman of the Joint Chiefs of Staff. I was to have them give the operation immediate consideration and report to him as soon as possible.

I went home to shave, shower, and have breakfast and arrived at the Pentagon a little before ten o'clock. Secretary Johnson greeted me with the statement, "What have you done to the president? He has been calling me up asking what we have decided to do about your report." Of course, I explained the situation to him and also to General Bradley. Within twenty-four hours the Joint Chiefs recommended approval of the operation and, as I recall it, of all the support that General MacArthur requested. President Truman forthwith authorized the operation.

14

W. Averell Harriman

I recommended to the president that General Walker be relieved and replaced by General Ridgway or General [James] Van Fleet. He told me to take that up with General Bradley, which I did. I always thought the Chiefs of Staff were a bit reluctant to approach General MacArthur and raise the question of replacing General Walker.

The fantastic success of the Inchon landings was clouded by the later disaster following the Chinese intervention when our forces were driven back into South Korea. General Walker was killed in a jeep accident, and General Ridgway immediately took his place. Within two weeks he completely reversed the situation and was able to drive the enemy back to the 38th Parallel. President Truman then decided not to go north again but to hold the line approximately at the 38th Parallel. This decision was based on full discussions with General Bradley and others, including General Marshall, who was then secretary of defense, and Acheson. Had the president decided otherwise, our losses would be great and the political advantages doubtful. The first objective of the United Nations had been achieved, namely to stop the invasion of the North Koreans and force them out of South Korea. I believe it was a wise decision, and it was subsequently accepted by General [Dwight D.] Eisenhower when he became president.

In conclusion I will give a brief outline of the immediate events leading to the relief of General MacArthur. There had been several provocations, which I won't repeat, that culminated in MacArthur's sending a most disloyal telegram to the Republican House minority leader, Joseph Martin. I had been in New York and took an early plane back to Washington for the cabinet meeting on Friday. After the cabinet meeting, the president called Acheson, Marshall, Bradley, and myself to his office. He described his problems with MacArthur and then asked each of us whether we thought MacArthur should be relieved. Each gave the reasonable answer, indicating that he would review the question in the appropriate manner. When the president came to me, I recalled to him the doubts that I had expressed in my report in August. I said that I thought there was nothing for the president to do now but to relieve the general. We had further meetings on Saturday during which each of the four of us reported on his particular field. We unanimously recommended MacArthur's recall.

The president took no action until Monday. I have always felt that he talked with Chief Justice [Fred M.] Vinson, in whom he had much confidence, but there is no record of that talk. He may also have talked to Sam Rayburn, whose judgment he respected, but this is purely a guess. In any event, we met with the president again on Monday and he informed us that he had decided to recall MacArthur. He planned to have Secretary of the Army [Frank] Pace, then in Japan, inform General MacArthur that day and to release his decision to the press on Tuesday morning. Unfortunately, Pace was in Korea and General MacArthur heard the news on the radio before Pace could reach him.

This step was, of course, one of the most courageous any president has ever taken. General MacArthur was a popular hero and was received as such on his return. President Truman told me he had made a great mistake when he had not insisted on MacArthur's return to the United States for a visit shortly after the end of the war with Japan. He told me that he had invited MacArthur then and that MacArthur had declined. In retrospect, it seems clear that MacArthur intended to have a triumphant return, leading up to a possible nomination for the presidency. As it was, he got a triumphant reception and President Truman suffered a sharp loss of popularity.

To me, this was a great constitutional crisis: should a military proconsul impose his will on American foreign policy over the objection of the president?

President Truman had the extraordinary capability to make decisions after full consideration and then to stop worrying. After reaching a decision he used to say, "I have done the best I can." He never rehashed the problem; he relaxed, went home, went to bed and soundly to sleep.

JOHN W. SNYDER

In order to place my personal relationship with President Truman in the proper context, I must go back a great number of years; Harry S. Truman and I had known each other as close friends and associates for many years before he became president.

During the '20s and '30s, Harry S. Truman and I spent two weeks together nearly every year as colonels of field artillery at various military posts around the United States in connection with Reserve Officer training. We came to know each other extremely well, learned of each other's background and family relations, discussed past military experiences, learned each other's philosophies and aims, and generally became very well acquainted. Our associations during these visits, coupled with the times that we would see each other during the balance of the year, grew into a warm and trusting friendship.

After Senator Truman went to Washington, I was with him on many occasions because between 1936 and 1940, I was manager of the St. Louis district office of the Reconstruction Finance Corporation (RFC) and my duties frequently required me to go to Washington. On these occasions we spent many hours together discussing politics, military history, the economy, and banking. We made many weekend visits to nearby battlegrounds to reconstruct the strategy of individual engagements.

In 1940 I went to Washington to organize and operate the Defense Plant Corporation, which would finance plants to supply defense materials. Shortly after that, Senator Truman set up his committee to investigate defense problems, irregularities, and spending. These two developments meant that we compared notes and discussed proper procedures on many occasions.

When I went back to St. Louis to take up my active preparation to become president of the First National Bank, we had many discussions of the problems that would confront the country in its economic rehabilitation following the war, which was then drawing toward an end.

The Cabinet

During this period our families became acquainted and closely associated. Later our daughters would attend the same college, join the same sorority, and have mutual friends.

In the summer of 1944, at Senator Truman's invitation, I accompanied him, along with Mrs. Truman and Margaret, to the Democratic National Convention in Chicago and remained with them throughout the entire session—up to and including his nomination for the office of vice-president.

This recitation of associations makes it quite clear that when President Truman succeeded President Roosevelt, we were much more than just "war buddies" and "political friends." As a matter of fact, I did not serve with Captain Truman in World War I, nor was I ever actively engaged in politics, except when Mr. Truman himself was involved in later years.

When I went to the White House to see President Truman on the day following his installation, I had no inkling of the pending developments. I certainly had no thoughts of taking a government job; my heart was set on remaining with the First National Bank in St. Louis permanently.

I mention our personal history to indicate that there was a deep understanding and respect between us as to our individual qualifications.

I became Truman's first major appointment as head of the Federal Loan Administration, and from that time forward I was always invited to attend cabinet meetings.

President Truman's first cabinet meeting was actually held with the members of President Roosevelt's cabinet, shortly after he had been sworn in as president at 7 P.M. in the Cabinet Room at the White House, on April 12, 1945. Everyone else, including Mrs. Truman and Margaret, had left the room. The entire cabinet was present with the exception of Postmaster General [Frank C.] Walker, who was absent due to illness. The first official act the president took was to announce that the United Nations Conference in San Francisco would be held on April 25 as planned by President Roosevelt. President Truman spoke to the cabinet briefly, assuring them he would be pleased if all of them would remain in their posts, though it was obviously clear to everyone that there would be some changes made in due course. The meeting was short and after the members left the room only Secretary [of War Henry L.] Stimson remained. It was then, for the first time, that President Truman learned of the atomic bomb.

President Truman held his first official cabinet meeting on April 23, 1945, at 10 A.M. In his first regular meeting he adopted an agenda and a style that continued throughout his entire administration.

John W. Snyder

He opened the meeting by reading a brief statement of current events, asked for pertinent comments, took up urgent specific matters, and then requested each cabinet member, in order of seniority, to give a report on any matters in his department which might be of interest to the cabinet as a whole. After the 1948 election, he returned to President Roosevelt's custom of asking the vice-president to be in attendance at the cabinet meetings and to sit directly across from the president at the cabinet table.

President Truman believed in cabinet-level group consultations as well as in individual discussions with heads of each agency and with individual members of his cabinet.

He strongly believed in giving each administrator an opportunity to explain his views fully on any subject related to his responsibility or to express his personal views on matters in other departments of government. The president stressed, however, that the final decision on policy matters would be his own, after having heard all views.

President Truman used his cabinet as the central control of his administration very effectively.

When the President took office in April 1945, there were ten cabinet departments and 125 independent agencies and bureaus in existence; all heads looked to the president for guidance in policy and administration. With this many individuals seeking personal contacts, as well as scores of others desiring conferences on matters of various importance to the government, it was a delicate matter for the president to try to make himself invariably available. This was particularly true because at times he had strong differences of opinion with certain cabinet leaders and other agency and bureau officials.

By and large President Truman had very cooperative and responsive relations with his cabinet members. Inevitably, however, some problems with individual cabinet members did arise. For instance, because of his unprecedented experience in various governmental stations, Secretary Byrnes had come to feel that he was truly the assistant president in many matters, particularly in areas involving the State Department. President Truman had some problems with Secretary Byrnes from time to time; these reached a peak during and following Byrnes's first trip to Moscow. Some months later, President Truman had a serious disagreement with Secretary [Harold] Ickes in regard to the appointment of Ed Pauley as undersecretary of the navy. This argument ended in Ickes's resignation.

In my own relation with President Truman, I tried to be as considerate of the demands upon his time as possible and tried to confine my official consultations with him strictly to Treasury-related matters which required his determination of policy. I found the Treasury De-

The Cabinet

partment an enormous operation, employing over 110,000 nonmilitary individuals (as well as the Coast Guard), and I soon discovered that it required my full attention. I made it my objective to abstain from injecting my personal opinions into the affairs of other agencies, except upon specific matters when the president asked for my personal views.

The budget had formerly been included in the operations of the secretary of the treasury. During F.D.R.'s administration, he set it up as one of the agencies in the Executive Office of the President. Although President Truman did not change this, he asked me to work closely with the director of the budget, and I maintained a close liaison with the directors of the budget throughout my tenure at the Treasury. I sat in with the president and the budget director on much of the planning discussions and was always present with the two men when the budget was presented to the press.

The president personally set the pattern for close cooperation between the Treasury and the Bureau of the Budget. He brought the secretary of the treasury into the budget work with himself and the budget director. His own personal and active interest in the budget

Cabinet meeting, August 10, 1945. *Left to right:* Clinton P. Anderson (Agriculture), Lewis B. Schwellenbach (Labor), John B. Blandford, Jr. (National Housing Agency), Julius A. Krug (War Production Board), John W. Snyder (Office of War Mobilization and Reconversion), William H. Davis (Office of Economic Stabilization), Leo T. Crowley (Foreign Economic Administration), Henry A. Wallace (Commerce), Abe Fortas (undersecretary, Interior), Robert E. Hannegan (postmaster general), Henry L. Stimson (War), James F. Byrnes (State), President Truman, Fred M. Vinson (Treasury), Tom C. Clark (attorney general), James V. Forrestal (Navy).

made the organizational problem almost irrelevant as far as budget policy-making was concerned.

The Hoover Commission Task Force report on budgeting recognized that the location of the Bureau of the Budget was not as important as presidential interest in the budget. It declared: "Nothing can quite compensate in the field of budgeting for presidential appreciation and understanding of the problems and implications of fiscal planning. Without these qualities in the President, any budget unit, wherever placed and however directed, is seriously handicapped." With President Truman taking an active role in the budget process, the organizational problem, as it related specifically to budget preparation, was therefore of no significance during my term in the Treasury.

Although I frequently saw the president every week, I had an arrangement with his appointments secretary, Matt Connelly, to keep my name off the visitors' list except when appearing officially with the president and others.

A great many of my consultations were carried on through a direct line to the president. On urgent matters that required personal contact, I usually went to see the president through the office of his personal secretary, Rose Conway; at other times he would call me to meet him at the White House pool after he had left the office for the day. I would sit on the side of the pool and talk with him as he swam back and forth. Quite a number of our more serious confrontations took place at this spot.

Frequently I would drop over to his office on the second floor of the White House to get clearance on matters of urgency just before he went to dinner. I also found it of great value to fly with him on trips to Missouri. When he had to go to Independence or Kansas City, he would drop me off and pick me up in St. Louis. I also benefited from both short and extended trips with him on the *Williamsburg*.

President Truman did not, by our mutual agreement, use me to make political speeches or to carry out campaign assignments; we both felt that my position in the Treasury Department required a great degree of nonpartisanship. This does not mean, however, that I did not spend a great deal of time with him in planning political strategy and fund-raising.

If my delineation of our relationship suggests that we were always in agreement, I must hasten to straighten out such a misconception. President Truman and I had many occasions when we sharply disagreed on procedural matters or on the strategy to be employed in accomplishing a desired result. I believe that the very fact that we could debate deeply, and at times heatedly, was of great value to him in reaching certain decisions. In these disagreements, his position prevailed in some instances and mine in others. But the strength of our friendship and of my usefulness to him was measured by the fact that once a decision was made, he could rely on me to try to the fullest extent possible to see the undertaking through to a successful end.

DISCUSSION

Louis W. Koenig (chair): To begin, I would like to ask those present who were members of President Truman's cabinet to describe what they saw as President Truman's concept of the cabinet member. I have read some comment to the effect that during the Truman years there was something of a restoration of the departments, compared to the Roosevelt period. Governor Harriman, you, of course, had experience in both administrations. Would you care to comment on whether that is a valid description, and if so what the justification for it might be.

W. Averell Harriman: Well, I think it was a matter of the personalities involved. Some members of the Roosevelt cabinet played a very great role, others did not. President Roosevelt wanted Mr. [Cordell] Hull for his secretary of state because of his great prestige, but he chose to do business through the undersecretary, Sumner Welles, because he did not want to get into arguments over the things he wanted done. Mr. Hull complained to me on a number of occasions that things were done without his full approval.

I knew something of the role of the Department of Commerce during the Roosevelt era because I was chairman of the Business Advisory Council for three years. Mr. [Daniel C.] Roper, who was F.D.R.'s first secretary of commerce, was not a particularly aggressive individual, but then came Harry Hopkins and the department became quite assertive. Of course, we know that Hopkins was not the only Roosevelt cabinet member who made his presence known. Harold Ickes and Henry Morgenthau certainly played important roles. I won't go down the full roster, but I think we would all agree that Henry Wallace played an extremely important role.

Now, during the war period, there was a general reduction in the role of the cabinet—and this may be the basis for the statement referred to by Professor Koenig. I was in Britain for two and a half years during

the war. There the war cabinet directed the war effort. The members of
the chiefs of staff were advisers to the war cabinet, and they would never
think of reporting to the Parliament. But in this country, the president is
commander in chief of the armed forces, and the chiefs of staff reported
directly to Mr. Roosevelt; even the secretaries of war and of the navy
services were sometimes left out. So it was not surprising that some of
the other cabinet members were left out as well, especially when you
remember how many war agencies had been set up. Certainly, the members of the cabinet did not play the role during the war that they had
before. Men like Mr. Stimson and Mr. Knox and then Mr. Forrestal
were to some extent, set aside. So was the State Department, because so
many of the decisions made during the war were made by Mr. Roosevelt
himself, without full consultation with Mr. Hull or the State Department.

KOENIG: While you are speaking of the State Department, would
you discuss President Truman's relations with the secretary of state?

HARRIMAN: Mr. Truman had four secretaries of state. The first one
was Mr. Stettinius, who did remarkably well. He has not been given full
justice, because his tenure of office was rather brief and because he came
from business and was not well known in the diplomatic field. As soon
as he had finished the United Nations Conference in San Francisco, he
was supplanted, and Mr. Truman appointed Jimmy Byrnes. I always
thought that there were two reasons for that appointment: one was the
fact that the successor to the presidency was the secretary of state, and
Mr. Truman did not think it appropriate to leave Mr. Stettinius in that
position. Mr. Byrnes was the logical man as successor; and then he *had*
gone to Yalta—but I think Mr. Truman was under the impression that
Mr. Byrnes had had more experience in international affairs than was
really the case.

The relationship did not work entirely satisfactorily. I really believe
that Mr. Byrnes always thought that he should have been president, and
he assumed authority which President Truman did not give him.

There was the incident after the first meeting of the foreign minis-
ters in Moscow (where I was ambassador at the time). I'm sure you all
remember the rumors of what happened. Byrnes announced on his way
home that he was going to make a report to the nation on radio. When
Mr. Truman heard that, he sent word to Byrnes that he had better report
to the boss before he reported to the nation.

There has been a difference of opinion as to exactly what occurred
in that discussion on the Potomac, but if one is to believe the Truman
version, Mr. Truman told Mr. Byrnes in no uncertain terms that he was
president and the secretary of state got his orders from him. Mr. Byrnes

has a different version. Which version is true I do not know, but, knowing Mr. Truman, I would accept his as being the more accurate. Byrnes did stay on for a period of time until General Marshall came back from China and was appointed secretary of state.

That was a very happy relationship. President Truman had great respect for General Marshall. He respected him as a soldier; he respected him as a man of unquestionable character; and he respected his judgment.

Dean Acheson was very active in the early days. He had been undersecretary under Byrnes and under Marshall up to June 1947, when he left the government for about eighteen months. Mr. Truman called him back when General Marshall asked to be retired. The Truman-Acheson relationship was very close and very happy. Mr. Truman had great respect for Mr. Acheson's judgment, and Mr. Acheson had great respect for the president. And that closeness lasted until the end of Mr. Truman's tenure and well beyond.

It was a very different relationship than had existed between Mr. Hull and Roosevelt. Nothing was done in the international field that was not discussed fully with the secretaries of state during the Truman administration.

When I became secretary of commerce in October of 1946, a year and a half after Mr. Truman had become president, he had had plenty of time and opportunity to deal with personnel questions—but he allowed me to make all of my appointments without any question. I made three principal appointments; one was Bill Foster, who is a Republican, as my deputy. I thought it would be good for Republican businessmen to feel that they had someone in the department they could talk to who was not affiliated with the New Deal. Then I selected David Bruce as assistant secretary for foreign and domestic commerce and Adrian Fisher as my legal adviser. Mr. Truman never questioned me about them. I said I would like to appoint them and he said, "Fine." He never asked what their positions had been in regard to supporting him. He gave me a completely free hand.

KOENIG: As far as the choice of your principal associates went, Secretary Snyder, did you have a similar freedom? And then a second question. There was during your administration a very important reorganization of the Bureau of Internal Revenue; what was the president's relationship, and also that of the White House in general, to the reorganization?

JOHN W. SNYDER: I quite agree with Governor Harriman about the freedom of choice. I do not recall that Mr. Truman ever declined to back me on an appointment that I made. I did not come into the Truman administration willingly. I had planned to be with the First National Bank of St. Louis—I was about to become its president. When Mr. Roosevelt died, Mr. Truman sent for me; and when I came in the room the morning after Mr. Roosevelt's death, he said, "How soon can you get down here with me?"

I said, "Mr. President, I can do you more good out there with the bank than I can here."

But he said, "I want you here with me."

About that time Jimmy Byrnes came in and Mr. Truman told him: "Jimmy, John's backing out of our plan."

Byrnes said, "Don't pay any attention to him. Remember who you are: order him to do it."

It was, of course, a great privilege to have had the opportunity to serve the entire period of Mr. Truman's administration with him in the cabinet. I was his first major appointment, to the Federal Loan Administration job which was open at the time. I quickly moved on to the OWMR [Office of War Mobilization and Reconversion] where there was a myriad of difficult decisions to make—transferring from a wartime economy to a peacetime economy—and I will say that the president stood foursquare on important decisions that had to be made. Governor Harriman remarked about how many agencies had been set up to run the war and that the cabinet members had lost some of their functions. Well, our job at OWMR was to put those functions back where they belonged and to discontinue a great number of the agencies that had been set up largely for the war. Judge Sam Rosenman and I were appointed as a committee by the president to push this program along.

We tried to do it politely, inviting agency heads in and telling them that they had finished a fine job and that now we were going to close it up. Before we could get back to our desks, however, there would be a call from a congressman or a senator saying that we couldn't do that. So we went over to see the president and said, "We need your authority."

He said, "You have it. Don't worry me with the details, go ahead." So we began to close up the wartime agencies as their work ran out. The point is that President Truman would back you if you had an important matter that had to be done, and he had confidence in your capacity to carry it out.

As to the Bureau of Internal Revenue, that was something that was rather evident from the day I first went into the Treasury. We had had a war, we had had a great manpower demand for the armed services, and we had had a great demand for capable accountants in the huge plants that were built. As a result the Treasury, and most of the government, had suffered a slacking off in its operations.

I started from the second month to try to organize a plan to bring the internal revenue service up to par because the income from taxes had grown enormously, and we needed more people to process the tax returns. O. Max Gardner was undersecretary at the time, and I gave him the job of starting to see what could be done with the Bureau of Internal Revenue. Before he left to go to the Court of St. James's, he gave me a memo that said, in substance, that we had to reorganize completely.

Lee Wiggins then came in as undersecretary and I gave him the same assignment. Wiggins had been head of the American Bankers Association and was a banker of stature. He went to work on it, and within a year or so came back with a report. We found that we had to completely change the internal revenue set-up. All the appointments, from the commissioner on down through all the local men in charge, were political, and some of these people had failed to live up to their responsibilities. But there always was a man in Congress who would back them because the appointment had been part of his patronage. We were going to stop that.

I went to see Mr. Truman and outlined a plan for a complete reorganization of the Internal Revenue Bureau. It was a hard decision for him to make. Internal Revenue had been set up and run in the existing, political fashion since its beginning. It was a political operation because of the opportunity for congressmen and senators to get their friends into well-paying jobs. But we rewrote the act entirely, and it took us some months to get it through Congress. Fortunately, before the Truman administration went out of office, we had the reorganization in full operation.

KOENIG: Justice Clark, I have a two-part question for you. One has to do with the naming of federal judges and United States attorneys and the selection procedure during your term as attorney general. Second, on the matter of initiating major law suits, did you consult with the president or with members of the White House staff? Would you comment on these two points?

TOM C. CLARK: Taking them in reverse order, the only suit that I remember the president and I talked about was the one against John L. Lewis [*United States v. United Mine Workers and John L. Lewis*, 330 U.S. 258 (1947)]. Frankly, I was not enthusiastic about the suit. So the president suggested that I talk to Clark Clifford, which I did, and then we filed a suit to get an injunction against Mr. Lewis. You remember he had refused to let his men work in the coal mines. We won the case in the trial court and then went directly to the Supreme Court.

Mr. Truman and I were in Waco, Texas, where he was receiving an honorary degree from Baylor University, when I got a telegram from my deputy saying that the Supreme Court had decided the case in favor of the government. I put the telegram on the lectern while Mr. Truman was speaking, and he read it to the audience.

He used to kid me about that case. He said, "Well, you won the case, in spite of the fact that you did not have your heart in it."

I have been accused of filing cases against Communists in order to bolster the president's image in that regard, but there is no truth to this. The president never talked to me about it at all.

Sometimes I would take up a case with him—for example, when we indicted the congressman from his district. I told him about that before we did it, but he never expressed any view about whether we should indict or not. He said, "If you have the evidence, why, go ahead."

ACME Newspictures

Treasury Secretary John W. Snyder and President Truman discuss the reorganization of the Internal Revenue Bureau, November 2, 1952.

Discussion

We also indicted several other congressmen, mostly on income tax charges, and I never even consulted him about those cases although they were full of dynamite. And he never told me that I should have consulted him.

As you know, before he was president, he was the chairman of what was known as the Truman Committee. I was the chief of the War Frauds Division in the Department of Justice at the time. Senator Truman would send his reports, including the testimony before his committee, to the attorney general, and from there they would go through my boss (who was Thurman Arnold) to me. I would sift through all the material and then go over and confer with Mr. Truman. Many times, as a result of our talks, he would reopen his hearing, bring out points that we thought were appropriate, and in that way, enable us to get things off the ground pretty quickly.

So when he first appointed me, we knew each other fairly well; by that time I was the head of the Criminal Division in the Department of Justice, appointed by Mr. Roosevelt. Mr. Truman called me over to the White House and said, "Tom, I want you to be attorney general." We talked about it a while, and then he said, "Now, you go on back over there and do whatever you think is right."

From that day on, he never talked to me about any cases other than this John L. Lewis matter.

On the other point, the appointment of federal judges, I had a practice of sending Mr. Truman three names whenever a vacancy occurred. An attorney general should always attempt—and do his best—to find out in advance when there is going to be a vacancy, because the minute one does occur, terrific pressures set in on him from senators and congressmen and governors and everybody else to get a particular candidate appointed. When I went around and talked to the judges at their conferences, I would always try to get them to send their letters of resignation directly to me or to let me know of their retirement, but quite often they would send the notice to their senators. Senator [Alben] Barkley, for example, would call me up and talk to me about a vacancy from Kentucky on the Court of Appeals. I would say, "There is no vacancy there, Senator." And he would come right back: "Oh yes, there's a vacancy. I have the retirement papers right here," and he did.

Among these three names of judicial candidates, I would try to include one senator or congressman. Mr. Truman, of course, knew all the senators and most of the congressmen. Presidents often do, and as a result there is always quite a percentage of former congressmen and senators on the federal bench. So, I would include one. For example, on the first vacancy which happened on the Supreme Court, one of my three candidates was Harold Burton, another was Bob Patterson, and I have forgotten who the third one was. At first, I thought Mr. Truman was going to select Patterson, but over the weekend he changed his mind. He called me on Sunday and said, "Get up the papers on Burton."

The second appointment to the Supreme Court was Chief Justice Vinson. You remember, Chief Justice [Harlan] Stone died quite suddenly in 1946 and there had been a rift in the Court. Justice [Robert] Jackson was in Nuremburg [as chief prosecutor in the war crimes trial] but he heard pretty quickly of Chief Justice Stone's death and guessed that Justice [Hugo] Black was going to be appointed. Jackson held a press conference in Paris, in which he blasted Justice Black for not having withdrawn from some cases that his former law partner had argued before the Court.

Justice Black had been in Washington for nearly twenty-five years, so there could not have been much to the charge, but it eliminated him from consideration.

The president suggested that I talk to retired Chief Justice [Charles Evans] Hughes. So I called the chief justice and told him what I had in mind. He said, "That's an official matter: I'll come to your place, I wouldn't let you come to my place."

So he came down to the department, and he thought a while and named three or four names. Then he said, "You know, one name comes to me—there is a former judge that I have a high respect for—Fred Vinson. I designated him as head of the OPA Court [the Emergency Court of Appeals]." (The chief justice could designate sitting judges—and Fred, at that time, was on the Court of Appeals—to any court and so Hughes had designated Vinson to the OPA Court, which was an expediting court.) Hughes said Vinson had done a wonderful job there. I, of course, knew of the warmth that Mr. Truman felt for Fred Vinson and so it was a simple matter after that: he appointed Vinson chief justice.

I was the president's third Supreme Court appointment. He called me up one day and asked me to come over. He seldom asked me to come over unless it was something important that he wanted to discuss—not always just matters assigned to the department. For example, he had talked to me before he appointed his Committee on Civil Rights. I thought something like that was on his mind. But when I came into his office, he said, "I have a package job for you. Remember, when you came down here and I talked with you about being attorney general, I told you to select your second person so that if I decided to put you somewhere else, you would have somebody who would not have to start from scratch?"

Discussion

I said, "Yes, I remember that and I remember that my retort was that you must not expect to keep me very long. You were going to have a successor real quick."

He laughed and said, "Well, now that was Howard McGrath, and I've been thinking about it. We have this vacancy on the Court, and I thought that I would put you on the Court and put Howard in your place, and I'd like for you to talk with him about it." So I did and Howard agreed. We went to the White House together and talked to the president, and those appointments were effected.

Justice [Sherman] Minton was appointed when Justice [Wiley B.] Rutlege died, soon after I went on the Court. That was Mr. Truman's fourth appointment, but because I was on the Court by that time, I had nothing to do with it. Mr. Minton was on the Seventh Circuit at the time and had served President Roosevelt—as one of those assistants who love anonymity—after he had been defeated in his own bid for reelection in Indiana. But, before that, he had also been on the Truman Committee; evidently the president had had Judge Minton in mind before.

As attorney general I would usually select as one of my three candidates one person out of the Senate or the House, one sitting judge from either the federal or the state system, and one practicing attorney. I have been accused of putting my name down for all three slots when I was appointed. The story goes that the first name was Tom Clark, the second name was Tom C. Clark, and the third name was Brother Clark. But the president moved on my appointment before there was any list.

KOENIG: If we can switch the discussion a bit, I was wondering about the kind of clearance process involved in the development of plans and programs?

CHARLES F. BRANNAN: I hope my experience in this connection may be helpful. Perhaps the most controversial proposal to come out of the Department of Agriculture was the so-called Brannan Plan. It was discussed during its formative stages with the White House staff, whose comments were constructive and helpful. Development of the plan extended over a two-year period. It started during the time that Clinton Anderson was secretary. He had assigned me, as assistant secretary, to the task of developing a long-range program for agriculture following the close of World War II. A series of subject-matter committees were created not only from the staff in Washington but also from all of the department's major field offices. When the studies and deliberations of these committees had produced a series of recommendations which we thought were worthy of presentation to the Congress, they were submitted to Secretary Anderson for his review. The recommendations included all phases of the department's activities, from agricultural research to soil conservation. But the areas of highest sensitivity were the proposals dealing with farm income and prices.

After Secretary Anderson reviewed the recommendations and made his own modifications, he took them to the Congress for presentation in separate hearings before the House and Senate committees on agriculture. He did not adopt the price and income recommendations but submitted his own views which generally paralleled the existing programs.

Shortly after the hearings Secretary Anderson resigned and went back to New Mexico to run for the Senate.

The Congress, in general, was also concerned with fall elections, and little attention was given to the department's recommendations. Most everybody expected that a new Congress would be dealing with the department in 1949 under President Thomas E. Dewey.

Hence, it was with some surprise that we found ourselves confronted after the election with a request from Congress to offer another set of proposals.

The proposals submitted by Secretary Anderson were reviewed once more by the same department committees and discussed with the White House staff. Few changes were made except in those proposals dealing with farm prices and income. The revised recommendations were then taken to President Truman and discussed one by one. When the president and I came to the very last price and income proposal, I advised the president that, in my opinion, it would subject the department and, by inference, the administration to a great deal of criticism. The plan provided for a payment to farmers of the difference between a fair price, as determined by a revised parity formula, and the average price received by all farmers for that commodity in the marketplace during that marketing season; it also provided that there would be a top limit on such payments paid to any one farmer. I said I thought it would be characterized as communism and socialism and all the other taboos.

The president studied it for a few minutes, then looked up at me and said, "Charlie, after all, it is right, isn't it?" I responded that I believed the plan was right and also that it was the only way a fair income for farmers could be assured at an acceptable cost to taxpayers.

Without further hesitation, the president stated, "It stays in." He was thoroughly aware of the political problems, including the charges of communism, and had made his decision solely on what he considered to be right.

Well, I presented the proposals to a joint meeting of the Senate and House committees on agriculture on April 7. I remember telling Mrs. Brannan, "We have worked like the dickens on this, but after this is over

Discussion

I am going to get a rest." Well, as many here will remember, there was anything but a rest after that day, and in the end the Brannan Plan was defeated. As expected, all the charges of communism and socialism and the like were indeed leveled. But there were two factors that I think were more important than anything else in the defeat of the program. The first was the charge that it would be tremendously expensive. And then, the Korean War broke out and farm prices began to go up, so that farmers worried less about their problems and quit communicating with their congressmen. If I had to put my finger on what really knocked us off, I would say it was, first, the Korean War, second, the charge of excessive cost, and only third, the charge of communism or socialism.

But the point is that the president himself made the decision to go ahead. He made it quickly after having gone through all of the material. I don't know how much he was briefed by the White House staff in advance of that meeting, which lasted maybe an hour, but I do know that he made the decision promptly, and he was not deterred by the possibility of further attacks as being "soft on communism." It was, in my judgment, a very courageous and forthright decision.

PHILLEO NASH: I am curious about the relationship of Secretary Anderson to the Brannan Plan. I had the notion that this was not something that he favored, that he was essentially a nonsupport theorist in agriculture.

BRANNAN: You are right. Although Secretary Anderson initiated the studies out of which the so-called Brannan Plan proposals evolved, he never accepted the concept of "differential payments" and refused to present such views to the Congress in 1948. Furthermore, after his election to the Senate, he openly criticized the department's new proposals at numerous Farm Bureau meetings—notwithstanding the fact that the president had strongly endorsed them.

FRED I. GREENSTEIN (Princeton University): I would like to ask Justice Clark, in pursuit of this matter of Mr. Truman's seeking and getting a good bit of advice from many sources before making decisions, did he ever seek advice from you or, as far as you know, from Mr. Vinson after you were on the Court?

CLARK: No, he never asked me any questions after I was on the Court. I think he thought that that would be inappropriate. There is some rumor that he did talk to Fred, but I rather doubt it.

While I was attorney general, he talked to me quite often about a variety of matters. One that comes to mind is when we were having trouble in Italy, he asked me to make some speeches that would be

33

The Cabinet

recorded and played in Italy—in Italian—telling the Italians that they would not be allowed to come to the United States if the country went Communist.

Then he talked to me one time about the Civil Rights Commission that Charlie Wilson chaired. If you read the report, *To Secure These Rights,* which Mr. Truman signed, it laid down a blueprint on civil rights in 1945–46 that has now been adopted by the Congress and the courts. Mr. Roosevelt, whom I admired but did not know very well, did not integrate the armed services; Mr. Truman did. And while Mr. Roosevelt had set up the Fair Employment Practices Committee [FEPC], Mr. Truman was more realistic on race questions.

I found Mr. Truman to be one who would make decisions not on the spur of the moment, but after talking with many people. He used to have a little luncheon over there on Tuesdays, with two or three cabinet people, and we would talk about the problems he had on his desk.

I remember at least two occasions when he went down the line in the cabinet. One was when General Marshall came back from China with his report on what the Chinese were doing with our munitions, and

Harris & Ewing
Cabinet meeting, February 11, 1949. *Clockwise from bottom left:* Julius A Krug (Interior), Charles Sawyer (Commerce), Alben W. Barkley (vice-president), Maurice J. Tobin (Labor), Charles F. Brannan (Agriculture), Jesse M. Donaldson (postmaster general), James V. Forrestal (Defense), Dean G. Acheson (State), President Truman, John W. Snyder (Treasury), Tom C. Clark (attorney general).

Discussion

Mr. Truman asked each cabinet member about it. Another time was when someone had proposed that we give the atomic bomb secrets to the Soviets, and we talked that out in a cabinet meeting. Things like that he would quite often bring up in a cabinet meeting, but he had a habit of consulting people either in his office or on other occasions.

His greatest attribute was that he made decisions and then he put them aside; he did not worry about them. He had enough problems to decide tomorrow, so he put today's thinking on tomorrow's problems not on yesterday's, ones he had already decided. And that is why he was a great president. Most presidents are not able to do that. That's why he was able to make so many decisions that were needed, and were right, and came at just the right time.

ROGER W. TUBBY: Along these same lines, I was going to ask Governor Harriman about his recollection of Prime Minister Churchill's judgment of President Truman.

HARRIMAN: I know that Mr. Churchill had a very high regard for Mr. Truman. Of course, you remember that Mr. Truman invited him to Fulton, Missouri, where he made his famous speech. After that, Churchill spoke to me in the most glowing terms about Mr. Truman.

I think that we ought to get into the record that President Truman did have a weekly cabinet meeting; other presidents have not. It was very useful for members of the cabinet to hear each other bring up with the president the subjects they wanted to have raised. The cabinet never voted on any matter; the cabinet never made the decisions; it was always Mr. Truman, but it was very informative for all of us to know what was going on and to know the president's mind on matters which were overlapping.

I had a very close relationship with both Mr. Anderson, who was then the secretary of agriculture, and with the secretary of labor [Lewis B. Schwellenbach], and I used to have many discussions with them before going to Mr. Truman. Sometimes we went together and talked about our mutual problems. The president was always ready to see cabinet officers, but he did not very often call us to his office. He would sometimes telephone, but he expected us to come to him if we needed some assistance. Otherwise he counted on us to do our jobs. He allocated to the secretaries of the departments the direction of their departments, and he did not interfere. Of course, the staff of the White House did play a role and so did the director of the budget. President Truman used the director of the budget to see that each department was carrying out the programs assigned to it. The control of the purse was one of the ways he controlled the departments.

The Cabinet

SNYDER: It was very important that the cabinet meeting gave you an opportunity, every week, to bring up what was important to you. President Truman would bring up any matter that he had and then ask each one of us, "Did you have something to say?" And he also gave us the opportunity to come to talk later with him if the subject was not germane to the whole operation.

The budget was indeed very important to Mr. Truman. President Truman understood the budget better than nearly any other president. He dug into it carefully, and he wanted to know what was necessary and how it was going to affect the people, more than how it was going to affect him or the party. He would hold a press conference on each budget and spend hours with the press going through it. Of course, the budget director and I were there to back him up, but it was rare that he had to call on us for help on a budget matter.

DOROTHY JAMES: Following up on the point that Governor Harriman made: Stephen Hess, in his book *Organizing the Presidency*, asserts that the problems of the more recent presidents were present in small form, in seed, during the Truman administration. He asserts that there was the beginning of the development of a staff that would interfere or intervene between the president and the cabinet members; this, of course, has become a very major problem for the presidency. Did you gentlemen have a feeling that this was occurring when you served in the cabinet?

SNYDER: Since I was in the cabinet longer than any one individual, I will say that that never occurred insofar as the Treasury Department was concerned. President Truman wanted to get his information straight. I do not know of any staff member interjecting himself between a cabinet member and Mr. Truman. Of course, he would use all sorts of outside help and he would rely on a great deal of the staff work, but he would always go back to the cabinet member.

HARRIMAN: But President Truman also developed staff work in the development of policy. I think the classic example of the White House staff developing policy for and with the president was the Marshall Plan. That program was thought out by the staff, and the White House staff played a very major role in its development.

SNYDER: But that was not a case of the staff coming between a cabinet member and the president.

HARRIMAN: The president never used the staff to interfere with cabinet members' operations.

BRANNAN: I certainly agree.

Discussion

CLARK: I was in the cabinet before any of the others here tonight. I came in soon after Mr. Truman became president, on July 30, 1945, and during my period in the cabinet I suppose I was over at the White House as much as any cabinet member. At no time did I ever have any staff member—and I knew them all fairly well—try to impose any view on me or dictate any decision I should make. Indeed, I found just the opposite: I would call on them to give me their views, particularly Clark Clifford, who was the special counsel. There had been quite a rift between the counsel of the president and the attorney general during Mr. Roosevelt's time: the attorney general did not think that the president should have a counsel—after all, the attorney general was his counsel. But I found that Clark Clifford worked with me 100 percent; he never asked me to do anything that I regarded as an imposition or an interference with my job.

CHARLES MURPHY: I would like to comment in response to Professor James's question. There was not only a lack of interference by the White House staff between the president and his cabinet, but, to the contrary, there was an extraordinary degree of cooperation between the White House staff and the staffs of the various departments. I participated in this in a good many different ways and one of my functions, after I succeeded Clark Clifford as special counsel, was to oversee the staff work on messages to Congress and on speeches. We had a regular operating practice to permit any department with a legitimate interest in the subject of a message to have a staff person participate in the work on that message. Sometimes this got to be quite cumbersome, but it was always done.

KOENIG: Since Stephen Hess's book has come up, let me raise another point that he makes. He says that within the Truman administration there was a group that might be called liberal and another group that might be called conservative. The names given by Hess on the conservative side are Dr. Steelman and Secretary Snyder; and on the liberal side, Mr. Murphy, Mr. Clifford, Mr. Keyserling, and Mr. [Oscar R.] Ewing. I was wondering, Secretary Snyder, if you have any comment? Are you satisfied with that conclusion?

SNYDER: I am perfectly satisfied to say that I was a conservative. We must remember that a president has a large group of counselors and advisers; and he is entitled to have at least one or two on the conservative side when there is always such a willing and anxious group on the progressive or liberal side. If something was important for the people, President Truman was as liberal as anyone could be, but he did not want extensive expenditures or plans that would not be productive or good.

There are many historians who contend that Mr. Truman should have sponsored more programs for the welfare of the people while he had control of the Congress. But Mr. Roosevelt, in his last years, did not have control of the Congress and Mr. Truman certainly did not have control. The revisionists who try to make this look like a failure on the part of Mr. Truman simply do not know their facts. He came forward definitely and at all times for the things that were for the good of the people—even with conservatives sitting on the side, occasionally raising a question or two.

HARRIMAN: I would like to go back to something very important that Charlie Brannan said. The president always wanted to know what the *right* thing to do was. He never asked you what his *options* were.

SNYDER: When I would go to him with my kind of problems, the first thing he would say was, "Now, let's get at how this is going to affect the people, not how it's going to affect your budget, not how it's going to affect the Democratic party, but how it is going to affect the people." That was the first thing he wanted to know about any new proposal that you brought to him.

CLARK: As I said, when he appointed me he told me, "Go on back over to your department and do what you think is right." R-i-g-h-t. And he always stuck by that.

BRANNAN: Just to reiterate: on almost every occasion when I had a specific problem on which I wanted the president's advice, the paramount factor in his decision was whether or not the proposed solution was right.

KOENIG: Dean Acheson, in his memoirs, *Present at the Creation*, puts a great deal of stress on Truman's procedures. Acheson thought that for the first time among modern presidents, Truman established the written decision as an aspect of doing business. Acheson also commented on the procedure by which decisions were made known—that is, a basic equality among the members of the cabinet.

HARRIMAN: I think that is quite true. Churchill spent his entire day writing memoranda to different departments or to people he wanted to communicate with. Mr. Churchill started at 7 o'clock in the morning, and he used to write an infinite number of letters, sign them with a red pen, make certain corrections with red ink; and then he distributed twenty or thirty sometimes between 7:00 and 8:00 in the morning. But that was his way of communicating. Truman very frequently telephoned, I rarely got a written message from him; he did not operate like

Discussion

Churchill. But I think Acheson's point was that Truman wanted his decisions recorded.

BRANNAN: I would just like to say that Mr. Truman once made a decision and gave me an oral directive on the basis of which I spent $2.5 *billion* in the course of forty-eight hours, and there is not one written word giving me authority or showing that he ordered, directed, or permitted the action.

HARRIMAN: That raises a serious question about the Acheson statement.

CLARK: I never got a memorandum from the president on any matter the whole time I was attorney general, which was about four and a half years.

SNYDER: I got plenty.

KOENIG: I want to ask about the weekly luncheons. I understand that the president would meet at luncheon with three or four members of the cabinet on a rotating basis. Is there anyone who could speak about that experience?

SNYDER: I think every one of us can, because that was one of his standard procedures. He would bring together cabinet members who were acquainted with the particular subject that he had on his mind. He also frequently used his trips down the Potomac that way. Many times he'd call people over not for a meeting, but just to sit around and talk for a while; he was careful, however, to select those who could contribute to the subject that was puzzling him at the time.

CLARK: That is my understanding too. Of course, when I went down the river or to the White House or other places, and played a little poker with him, he never discussed any business at all.

BETH CAMPBELL SHORT: David Halberstam in his book [*The Best and the Brightest*] says that Acheson really did not respect President Truman. The only experience I had was that Secretary Acheson had tremendous respect for President Truman. Was that your experience, you who knew him so much better than I?

BRANNAN: Definitely.

SNYDER: Yes.

HARRIMAN: Acheson was in real trouble in 1950. Almost every Democrat who was running for public office wanted the president to relieve Acheson because of his unpopularity, for reasons which we don't have to go into here. Acheson said to me at the time that Mr. Truman was his great friend, a man who supported him and saw him through that trouble. In that day, he never looked down at President Truman. President Truman saved him from a great deal of difficulty; and anyone who thought that Acheson looked down on Mr. Truman did not understand the relationship between the two men. Acheson would not have survived had it not been for President Truman, and I think that Mr. Acheson understood that thoroughly because he told me so during the summer of 1950.

SNYDER: Acheson says so in some of his books. He speaks very positively about how fortunate he was to have had a chief like President Truman, a man who could make decisions and would back them up. And you have respect for a man if you make a statement like that.

HARRIMAN: Acheson did have a good deal of contempt for certain people that he did not think were his equals.

SNYDER: We were not talking about *all* the people, we were just talking about Truman.

HARRIMAN: But as far as President Truman was concerned, I know what I am talking about in the statement that I have made.

ROBERT L. DENNISON: One time I asked Dean Acheson why he had not written a book about President Truman (this was before *Present at the Creation*), and he said, "Well, I have such a high regard for him, and I am so fond of him, that I feel I could not possibly be objective." I have talked to Dean through the years a number of times, and I can promise you that he had the highest regard for the president, regardless of their different personalities.

EDWARD HOBBS: I believe the record shows that Dean Acheson said that President Truman was the most remarkable man that he had ever known.

II

THE WHITE HOUSE STAFF
EARLY PERIOD

Until just a few days before the conference, Clark Clifford expected to attend; he would, of course, have been a prime contributor to the discussion of the White House staff's work in the early period of the Truman administration. Quite unexpectedly, however, he was asked by President Carter to undertake a special diplomatic mission abroad—a request he could neither decline nor postpone.

The principal discussants, therefore, in the second segment of the conference were—again in alphabetical order—Donald Dawson, William J. Hopkins, E. A. Locke, Jr., Philleo Nash, and Robert C. Turner. All but Mr. Locke are also represented in this section by written statements prepared in response to the conference organizers' call.

William J. Hopkins looks back over a lifetime of service in the White House. He succeeded to the position of executive clerk in 1943; in 1949 his title was changed to senior executive clerk, and in 1966 President Johnson designated him executive assistant to the president, a position he retained during the Nixon administration until his retirement in 1971. In his statement Mr. Hopkins stresses the importance to the effective functioning of the White House of the morning staff conference, which he describes in some detail. He also underscores the importance of President Truman's personal work habits and of his trust in people.

Donald S. Dawson served from 1947 to 1953 as administrative assistant to the president, his special assignment being personnel matters. His essay describes the scope of these responsibilities and the manner in which he interacted with the president. Mr. Dawson is now a practicing attorney in Washington, D.C.

Philleo Nash's statement recounts his particular duties which related to minority groups. Although his relationship to the president was rarely direct—for much of the time David Niles was Nash's immediate superior —Mr. Nash supplies insights about Mr. Truman's attitude and actions on minority problems. Mr. Nash later served as lieutenant governor of Wisconsin and as U.S. commissioner of Indian affairs. An anthropologist by training, he is now on the faculty of American University.

Robert C. Turner, who until his death in December 1978 was distinguished professor of business economics and public policy at Indiana University (where he also served as vice-chancellor), had two opportunities to learn about White House operations. He served as an assistant to John Steelman from 1946 to 1948 and, four years later, as a member of the Council of Economic Advisers. In between, he was a frequent White House consultant. From this vantage point, he discusses the staff's functioning, with special emphasis on Steelman's role and the importance of the speech-writing process. One question that emerges here is whether there was a chief of staff in the Truman White House, a matter which recurs—and more than once—in the discussion.

Edwin A. Locke, Jr., after an assignment in postwar China, was special assistant to the president in 1946 and 1947. His duties involved liaison and "trouble shooting," some of which he describes in the course of the discussion. Mr. Locke is now the president and chief executive officer of the American Paper Institute.

WILLIAM J. HOPKINS

As one who was privileged to work in the White House Office during President Truman's administration, I want to devote my comments to his outstanding strengths as an administrator and as a human being. In my nearly forty years of White House experience no one set a comparable tone. His leadership produced efficient and effective operations with less confusion, fewer false starts, less overlapping, and other demoralizing procedures. President Truman was a man of compassion. He liked people, he trusted people, and in turn he engendered a feeling of unqualified loyalty and devotion among his staff.

To my mind, President Truman's most effective tool in interoffice administration was his morning staff conference. I have often wondered why political scientists studying the presidency have not placed more emphasis on the effectiveness of this device. Keeping in mind that each president must operate in a manner with which he feels comfortable, to my knowledge no other president has used this system. The opportunities this device presents for coordination and the development of good staff relations are without limit. While it is true that the staffs of other presidents have held regular staff conferences, they have not been presided over by the president himself and therein lies their defect.

President Truman convened the staff conference each morning at the same hour in the Oval Office. He sat at his desk and the staff sat in chairs and on a sofa in a semicircle around the desk. Just prior to the conference each morning he completed his dictation to his personal secretary. In keeping with his consideration for others, after some months of holding the meeting at earlier hours, the time was changed, as I recall, to 9:30 A.M. to accommodate those members of the staff who found it hard to make the earlier time. The conferences lasted for approximately one half hour and were carried on in a relaxed atmosphere. Customarily each one was attended by the dozen or so top staff members housed in the West and East wings. The president gave everyone in attendance an opportunity to bring up matters of concern in their particular fields of operation. The press secretary would discuss his dealings with the press. The appointments secretary would run over the schedule and possibly make recommendations and secure commitments for future appointments. The staff member involved in presidential personnel matters would cover this area and might make recommendations and receive commitments for pursuing a particular course of action in recruitment. The staff official concerned with labor-management relations might have ready for consideration and signature by the president a proposed Executive Order. Those engaged in the preparation of presidential speeches or messages would have topics for discussion, since policy decisions were so closely entwined with speech preparation. Each participant was encouraged to express his views, whether or not the specific matter under discussion was in his specialty. And during all this the president would interject his thoughts, his directives, and his philosophy.

The president maintained two desk files. The one on his left, with tabs for each of those attending the daily conference, was his receptacle for accumulating documents that he wished to hand out to the staff at the morning conference. These ordinarily covered a great panorama of presidential activity—letters to be answered, personnel recommendations, suggestions for public appearances, proposals for speech subjects, ideas that needed study and consideration by the staff or by the appropriate department or agency. It was a simple way for the president to turn assignments over to his staff and to help dispose of his mountain of paper work. It was an excellent opportunity for the staff to absorb in some depth the president's philosophy, his concern for all citizens, his desire for staff cohesiveness, and his general attitude toward the presidency and its relations with the other branches of government. Receiving guidance and instructions as a group directly from the president each morning made it possible for each participant to know more of what was going on and tended to encourage good feelings among the individual members of the staff.

Of course, on many issues and on many occasions the president had to see particular staff members on a one-to-one basis and for a more protracted time on complex matters of policy, speech preparation, and the like, but the work accomplished in the morning staff meeting was a great timesaver for the president as well as for members of the staff. It gave the staff a feeling of being on the team. It acquainted each member with the type of material and the type of assignments the president was passing along to his fellow staffers. It fostered cohesion and cooperation rather than competition and combativeness. It helped decrease duplication of effort, the confusion, and the lack of direction that results from working at cross purposes.

The executive clerk, first Judge [Maurice] Latta and later myself, was privileged to attend the morning staff conference. It helped us tremendously in keeping track of documents, in establishing better relationships with members of the staff, and in absorbing the basic philosophy of the president and the staff and allowed us to provide better guidance to the civil service personnel, whose job it was to serve the president and the members of his staff loyally and to the best of their abilities.

The flow of paper in the White House office under President Truman was probably the best I have experienced, and that was due principally to his working habits and his trust in people. Except for those documents that a member of the staff felt ought to be discussed with the president personally, a great percentage of the documents ready for signature were carried in to the president by the executive clerk. This encompassed a wide range of documents—enrolled bills, Executive Orders, proclamations, executive clemency cases, treaties, directives to the departments and agencies, nominations, commissions, messages to the Congress, and so on. These documents constituted the signature folder. In addition, the executive clerk brought the president the reading folder. This contained primarily gleenings from the mail—letters from members of the cabinet, the Congress, state and local officials, important personages, and the general public. These folders were delivered to the president routinely twice a day, in the morning and right after lunch. Customarily he would dispose of the material for signature in my presence, so that it could be processed immediately. This system made it easy to keep track of documents and to answer with dispatch queries from responsible officials in the departments and agencies as to the status of documents in which they had a legitimate interest. An inability to respond promptly and in an informative way to such queries is the surest way I know to engender in the departments and agencies the feeling that the president's office is inefficient, and such a feeling can only be harmful to the president.

The material in the president's reading folder customarily reappeared the next morning in the form of dictation to his personal secretary or in the material the president distributed from his desk file to the staff at the morning conference. Thus, it was relatively easy to know the status of documents without an elaborate and wasteful system of coordination. It was not always thus in other administrations. Undue delays in acting on documents when all the necessary preliminary work has been completed can lead to all kinds of complications. Pressures build from the departments and agencies when time is of the essence, and press leaks frequently occur when action is not taken on a timely basis. Such problems were held to a minimum by President Truman's orderly way of handling office procedure.

Having worked under seven administrations, I must admit that memory is a fallible thing; and as I try to recall the happenings of forty years in the West Wing, many events of various administrations tend to blend and merge together. But some things about President Truman do stand out.

I remember President Truman as a decisive man. He could make an important decision and get a good night's sleep without rehashing it and being overtaken by doubts. In fact this quality was so well recognized, even by the opposition, that very early in the Eisenhower administration the staff was urged to be decisive.

I remember President Truman as a man who was gentle and kind and considerate of his staff. In spite of his press image as a profane man in the "Give 'em Hell Harry" style, I never heard him utter an unkind word to or about any member of his staff. In other times, this too was unusual.

I remember President Truman as a thoughtful man. For example, in his desk he kept cloth swabs to wipe off the pens used at signing ceremonies before the pens were handed to recipients, thus avoiding any possible ink stains on clothing.

I remember President Truman as a punctual man. You could set your watch by his coming and going. When he went to lunch, if he left word that he would return at 2:00 P.M., he was back without fail, not at 2:05, not at 1:55, but at 2:00 P.M.

I remember President Truman as a man who could not be influenced by pressure groups. Once, walking through the office, he spied a collection of pressure mail, letters numbering in the thousands, on a subject of current interest. When told what they were, he said, "You can light a match to that so far as I am concerned."

I remember President Truman as a man with a great knowledge of history and a keen sense of history as it related to the country and to the presidency. He was probably the most avid student of history ever to occupy the office. With this knowledge he consistently analyzed current problems in their historical sense, bearing in mind how other leaders had responded through the ages. On more than one occasion I heard him say, in effect, that if there was a clean break with all that had gone before, we would have chaos. This sense of history was one of his great strengths and provided unusual insight in handling many of the problems he faced.

I remember President Truman as a man who insisted on having all the facts before making a decision. This was evident on many occasions —for example, in the steps he took in governmental reorganization to assure that he was aware of all facets of a problem. Speaking of his staff in *Mr. President*, Mr. Truman said:

> To make sure I get the facts I need, I had to reorganize the office and staff of the President. A staff has been set up in the White House which consists of the press secretary, the assistant to the President, the secretary who makes appointments, the legal counselor, the personal executive, the correspondence secretary and the aides representing the three defense services. The staff reports to me every morning and gets its instructions for the day.

He went on to say that he set up his cabinet on the same basis that his staff was set up and that his purpose in setting up the Central Intelligence Agency was to get the facts he needed on a coordinated basis.

I remember President Truman as a diligent man. To the best of my recollection in all his years in office, with the exception of a few days he spent at Walter Reed Hospital during the final year, he was at his desk in the Oval Office every working day that he was in Washington, morning and afternoon. I know of no comparable record.

I remember President Truman as a discerning man. While he liked people and trusted most of them, he had disdain for those who developed "Potomac fever" and for the "cookie pushers" and some of the "striped-pants boys."

I remember President Truman as a sentimental man. After the Blair House shooting incident, the president received more than seven thousand letters expressing regret over the incident and gratitude that he was unharmed. A great many of these letters were from ordinary people in Puerto Rico. President Truman insisted that a word of thanks be sent in response to each one, and he signed each of these more than seven thousand letters of acknowledgment personally.

I remember President Truman as a good judge of people. In my view his presidential appointees throughout the government, including his White House staff, were at least equal to the best in our times.

I remember President Truman as one who supported his staff. During the 1953 transition, the gentleman who was designated as office manager of the White House for the incoming administration was making certain demands on some of the Truman staff that might be considered premature. President Truman happened to see him one day at the receptionist's desk in the West Wing and said, in effect, "I hear you have been pushing some of my people around. I don't like it!" With that, the president turned on his heels and walked away. Things were on a better footing after that.

The White House Staff: Early Period

I remember President Truman as a man who carefully guarded the constitutional prerogatives of the presidency. By his use of the veto he insured, on several occasions, that such powers were not eroded by legislative action.

In his recent book Stephen Hess intimates that during the Truman administration the White House staff first began to interpose itself between the members of the cabinet and the president. If such was the case, it was not evident to me, for I heard the contrary philosophy expounded throughout the office on many occasions. Likewise, I would take issue with Hess's premise that there may have been more dissension among the Truman staff than among the staffs of other modern presidents. That was not my impression. By and large I remember it as a cohesive staff whose loyalty to the president was the glue that held the team together.

My first boss in the White House, an astute observer whose service there began in 1909, used to say that what any president needed on his staff were generalists with political instinct of the highest order. In large measure, I believe that President Truman's top staff met that criterion.

The human instincts of the president, coupled with the qualities of his staff, combined to make the Truman years pleasant for me.

DONALD DAWSON

I was appointed administrative assistant to President Truman on August 6, 1947, and remained in that post until January 20, 1953, when I resigned at the end of his term as the thirty-third president of the United States.

In that capacity I was responsible to the president for personnel management within the executive branch of the federal government and for the recommendation of all those to be considered for presidential appointments—as well as termination—in the executive and the judicial branches. I was the president's direct liaison with the U.S. Civil Service Commission and all departments including the FBI, the members of Congress, the Democratic National Committee (DNC), and others. Approximately two hundred appointments to the highest level were made annually and a far greater number of such appointments as federal district and appellate court judges, postmasters, collectors of internal revenue and customs, U.S. marshalls, and others. (Full field investigations by the FBI were first initiated by me as a requirement for all presidential appointments.) It was my responsibility to assemble and recommend appointees to boards, commissions, and courts established by law or Executive Order. In addition, at that time all appointments and promotions of regular officers in the military services required Senate confirmation, and these lists were also cleared through my office before being considered by the president.

Included in my responsibilities were those of director of the Liaison Office for Personnel Management, established by Executive Order; thus, I coordinated planning and policy in the personnel and personnel-management field for the executive branch (as distinguished from the examination, recruitment, and classification of employees subject to the Civil Service Act).

In my work with the Civil Service Commission, among other matters, I was responsible for the complete revision of the Classification Act in

1949, which set the grades and compensation of federal employees. The revision was the first in many years and encompassed the establishment of new grade schedules, the upward revision of salaries to $15,000, and the addition of some two hundred new "super-grade" positions with a top salary of $20,000. Designation of those positions was subject to my approval.

I recommended—and by Executive Order President Truman provided for—the appointment of career administrative assistant secretaries in certain of the departments to provide administrative continuity on a nonpolitical basis.

Messages, Executive Orders, and addresses of the president relative to the Civil Service and to employee organizations were also the responsibility of my office.

The Economic Cooperation Administration and the Office of Economic Stabilization, comprised of the Office of Price Control and the Office of Wage Control, were organized and staffed by me prior to the appointment of the administrators of those offices. This was subject, of course, to their approval and to any changes they might make, thus assuring a completely operational office and a quick start.

I was the president's representative in the acquisition of office space for new agencies and in the transfer of agencies and offices to new quarters insofar as the executive branch was concerned. I performed a similar function for the Executive Office of the President, such as assigning offices and conference rooms and locating the present White House office dining room.

I was in charge of all advance work for the president's election campaign, beginning in September 1948. These arrangements for the president's formal public appearances generally involved close liaison with the Democratic National Committee [DNC] and with local political and civic bodies. An example would be the president's report to the nation from the San Francisco Opera House after his Wake Island conference with General MacArthur or his appearance in Detroit for the celebration of the city's Centennial Exposition or his appearance at Soldiers' Field, Chicago, for the Shrine Convention.

A great part of my duties were in the political field, as the direct contact for the president with the DNC and local political organizations concerning patronage, primaries, general elections, and organization. In this sense, I was representing the president in political matters. I also served as his personal representative to the 1952 Democratic National Convention in Chicago and carried his instructions to Tommy Gavin of the Missouri delegation, designating the president's choice of a presidential candidate; this constituted the first public notification of Mr.

Donald S. Dawson

Truman's endorsement of Adlai Stevenson. During their terms as chairmen of the Democratic National Committee, I worked very closely on an almost daily basis with Bob Hannigan, Howard McGrath, William M. Boyle, Frank McKinney, and Steve Mitchell.

After David Niles's death, his assistant, Philleo Nash, was transferred to my office and continued the work relating to minority and ethnic groups done under my supervision.

I was chairman of the White House Loyalty Review Board, which reviewed any charges of disloyalty or derogatory information affecting any employee on the staff of the Executive Office of the President. General coordination and supervision of the Loyalty Review Program for the executive branch was also my responsibility.

The president called on me for many special assignments of all kinds—for example, to secure the necessary steel in time of shortage for a new municipal stadium in one of our large cities (as requested by the mayor) or to see that Mr. Truman's views were made known in the redistricting of the Missouri congressional districts.

I was exceedingly fortunate to have the assistance of Martin L. Friedman, with whom I had been associated in the Air Transport Command during World War II and who came to the White House from the Civilian Personnel Division of the Office of the Secretary of War. He was ideal for this work because of his broad technical background, practical experience, and unusually keen judgment. The relationship was exceptionally fine and gratifying to me.

PHILLEO NASH

President Truman inherited me from the Roosevelt staff. I had been on detail from the Office of War Information to Jonathan Daniels, administrative assistant to President Roosevelt. My duties were to provide Daniels with a running analysis of racial tensions and of developing situations of potential racial violence. I did this from 1943 until his appointment as press secretary only a few weeks before Mr. Roosevelt's death. At that point, I was assigned to David K. Niles to continue the same work, and that is where I was when F.D.R. died. Thus, Mr. Truman inherited an office and people he knew very little about.

Early in Mr. Truman's term, Niles was asked to prepare a memo outlining the functions of his office, which he asked me to write. As I recall, it was not a very full memo, for Mr. Niles—being very much a telephone type—was never keen on committing his operations to paper. Fortunately the president had his own means of testing us, for very quickly in his administration, the entire appropriations for the war were held up by a filibuster over the continued existence of the Fair Employment Practices Committee. The guts of the Niles operation was close liaison with liberal and labor organizations of all kinds, but particularly those that were influential along the Washington–New York–Boston axis. The FEPC question was eventually compromised with a six-month terminal appropriation rather than one for a full year. In terms of the staffing of the White House operations, what the appropriations budget had exposed was Niles's sense of timing and thorough knowledge of the Left-liberal organizations. But this was also a time of testing the new president who was as unknown to us as we were to him. Would he stand up under the filibuster? Would he accept, as Mr. Roosevelt had done, Niles's "ambassadorship" to the third-party movement in New York? Would he recognize the need to use it as a counterforce to the conservative congressional coalition that was riding high after Roosevelt's death? Some liberals had dared to support the FEPC as long as they could ride on F.D.R.'s coattails, but now they were fading rapidly. It is all history today. Truman did stand up; he refused to be intimidated by the filibuster or panic in the face of a war financed by a continuing resolution. FEPC was saved, though with a shortened life, and Niles and I agreed (between ourselves) to sign up for the duration.

Race relations were my bag. Niles knew the Jewish organizations and the labor-liberal coalition, and we divided up the field. Our method of operation continued without much change from that time until Niles became very sick in 1950 and, after a lingering illness, died in 1952. Don Dawson supervised my work until Niles's death; I was on my own—in the sense of reporting directly to the president—only for the final month.

With reference to the organization of the Truman staff and how it conducted itself and how we related to our colleagues, the style was basically set by Niles. Someone said that while administrative assistants were intended under the 1939 reorganization to have a "passion for anonymity," in Niles's case it was a mania. He conducted direct negotiations with old friends and colleagues in all the major departments and agencies. He visited with the president privately and seldom, if ever, attended staff meetings. He put as little as possible in his files and stripped them annually in celebration of the New Year. He felt awkward as a writer (though I saw nothing wrong with his style) and often asked me to prepare written documents for him. He was always gone from mid week to Monday mornings, attending board meetings of New York-based organizations that concerned his liaison duties, taking in a play on Thursday nights (he was a passionate theatre-goer), and always returning home Fridays for a family dinner with his mother. Weekends he devoted to the Ford Hall Forum, Boston's famous Sunday night lecture-debate on controversial public issues. Mr. Niles had been the forum manager since the Sacco-Vanzetti days, and he kept up his active participation in its affairs as long as his strength held out. The overnight train after the forum on Sunday brought him to Washington and a renewal of his weekly rounds.

Dave's privacy was complete. He took no one with him when he met with the president or any of his colleagues "across the street." (We were housed in Old State—now the Executive Office Building—by Dave's preference; we were out of sight there and he preferred it that way.) Nevertheless, I was aware that Mr. Truman had grown very fond of Dave and that he trusted him completely to deal with the liberal Establishment. Handwritten scrawls by the president on various communications he sent to Dave showed that Mr. Truman felt baffled by New York City's intricacies and machinations. The ideologues troubled him and he relied on Dave to handle them.

Dave's trust in me was also complete within my area of competence. He expected to be kept informed and was most unhappy the few times he was taken by surprise. Generally speaking, trust, confidence, and privacy were the pattern, and success in the program plus a low profile were all that were required.

What was the rule inside our office was also the rule in our relations with others on the White House staff. They had their work and we had ours. We should not try to do "theirs" lest they try to do "ours." Hill contacts, newspaper contacts, agency and departmental contacts were fine; but there was to be no publicity. There were a few times when the preparation of legislation or the drafting of a presidential statement required our help and I was sent for, but only if Mr. Niles was not immediately available.

It should be clear that the Minorities Office (if that is what we were) was a rather isolated operation and, in that respect, rather different from the rest of the White House staff. The one-to-one relation between Mr. Niles and the president meant that assignments and instructions came directly to him and were not necessarily shared with colleagues. This had its obvious disadvantages, but it kept both of us aloof from most staff tensions. It also kept me free, more or less automatically, of the perennial difficulty of the White House staffer: getting caught between a presidential decision and a cabinet officer.

The emphasis on survival came from more than Dave's temperament. He was acutely aware that we were operating in a highly controversial area. One of the reasons why there had never been a permanent race relations agency in government was that none had ever survived very long. In that sense my work for Mr. Truman under Niles's direction was only a continuation of what I had done for Jonathan Daniels during the Roosevelt administration. Daniels had developed a series of low visibility relationships with the necessary departments to deal with the problem of racial tensions and the prevention of domestic violence during the war. Specifically at Mr. Roosevelt's direction, Daniels formed an interdepartmental committee that never met. The members, assigned by the cabinet departments, knew they were to report to him regularly and to be available on call, but they never got together in one room. They had a common function, but no visible structure. I helped put this "committee" together and was able to continue some of its functions in a liaison capacity for Mr. Truman.

Thus, programs of employment, advancements, information, contract compliance, and the like, involving minority groups, were developed in nearly all government agencies during Mr. Truman's administration. I was able to keep in touch with these programs via the special assistants.

These were mostly blacks, both men and women, who served in many departments and independent agencies, reporting directly to the head, with general responsibilities in the area of civil rights. This arrangement originally came into being just before World War II to deal with Negro protests about discrimination in the War Department and later in the Defense Department. In the minority world during World War II these assistants were known as the "black cabinet." Throughout the war years, I was in daily touch with these individuals, and during the Truman years, I worked with them or their successors on their programs. They received no instructions from me, of course, but I kept in touch with what they were doing and saw to it that Dave Niles and, through him, the president were kept informed. Often I could be of help to them in advancing their programs or in bringing additional resources into play. But there was never any question of standing between the department head and his staff or between the department head and the president. If there was, I got out—or was taken out—quickly.

The last two years, 1951 and 1952, were different. Niles became increasingly weaker, but such was Mr. Truman's affection for him that replacing him was out of the question. Mr. Truman indicated, however, that he wanted me to do the work insofar as I was able, and that was the way it was right up to December 1952. But only Dave could go to those board meetings in New York! I could keep track of the rest in a low-key way, and that is what I did. But I still had supervision, and there was a big difference in style between Dave Niles and Don Dawson. Don and I had a visit every morning immediately after the president's staff conference. We discussed plans and problems together, and I executed my part of them on my own, calling for help when I needed it.

As I look back on those years and think of the behind-the-scenes way in which Dave and I worked, I have mixed thoughts. Dave came to the White House staff with Jim Forrestal, Jim Rowe, and Laughlin Currie. They all kept low profiles as long as they were in the White House (though not necessarily afterwards). The days of press interviews, public statements, and declared responsibilities came much later. In my work for Roosevelt and Daniels and for Truman, Niles, and Dawson, only a few people knew what I was doing and how I did it. The story of the Daniels operation under F.D.R., for example, has never been fully described. I continued the same philosophy in my work for Mr. Truman. As far as I was concerned, only Niles, Dawson, and the president needed to know, and my loyalty to them was complete. I was never asked to do anything that would have hurt them or me if it had been made public. But the national shift from segregation to integration, from discrimination against minorities to participation by minorities was just beginning. The forces lined up against Mr. Truman in the area of civil rights were very strong. The legislation President Truman asked for in his special message of February 1948 did not pass Congress until 1964. We took such action as was possible within the executive branch under already existing, but mostly unused, authorities. I do not think we would have made any progress at all if we had gone public. The conclusion is easy to arrive at. The tone of right and wrong is set for the staff and the administration by the president and no one else. (The high visibility of the Nixon staff, after all, did nothing to keep them open and above-board.) We were kept within bounds by Truman's clear goals and by the strict standards he applied to the presidency. That standard of accountability is perhaps the best one.

ROBERT C. TURNER

My service in the Truman administration was relatively brief: two years (1946–48), followed by several summers and briefer stints at economic report season as an assistant to John Steelman, and about six months as a member of the Council of Economic Advisers. As an assistant to Steelman, I was a junior member of the White House staff and hence was not directly involved in the major policy debates. I did brief Steelman on policy issues either orally or by memorandum, but he "carried the ball" from there on. And my service on the council was at the end of Mr. Truman's second term, when few initiatives were being undertaken. During those closing months, the council operated pretty much on its own with very little contact with the president, especially after the election when it was known that he would be succeeded by a Republican.

Although my opportunity to observe firsthand the management of the presidency by President Truman was quite limited, it is my clear impression that President Truman was his own chief of staff. He met with his few immediate staff assistants informally and frequently, and responsibilities were parceled out more or less functionally. It was my impression that no presidential assistant had authority over all other presidential assistants. This was true even though Mr. Steelman had the title "the" assistant to the president.

It is true that Mr. Steelman had primary responsibility for labor-management relations. (Incidentally, there was a tacit understanding between Mr. Steelman and myself that labor-management relations were *not* within my area of responsibility.) But his responsibilities also extended beyond. His role, as I saw it, was that of a coordinator and problem-solver within the executive branch, especially where conflicts among agencies were involved. In general, these coordinating and problem-solving activities were concerned with economic and regulatory matters of a fairly specific character: for example, winding down wartime controls; disposing of surplus property (merchant ships, synthetic rubber facilities, etc.); coping with the shortage of freight cars; and formulating policy with respect to the strategic and critical materials stockpile, the housing program, government loans, subsidy programs, price controls, etc. A complete list would be extremely long and highly varied. It would include a great many, if not most, of the problems that typically arise in the day-to-day functioning of the executive branch, including the activities of the regulatory agencies.

In addition, he served as a conciliator to maintain good working relations both within the government and with outsiders. He had a constant stream of visitors (congressmen, agency heads, business executives, representatives of interest groups) with a point of view or a complaint that they wanted heard by the White House. Mr. Steelman had an amazing ability to listen sympathetically to these visitors, acquire or maintain their good will, and send them on their way, satisfied that they had a personal friend in court—but to do so without committing himself to any particular course of action other than to follow up on the matter. Action would follow, but only after the matter had been "staffed out," checked with the president if it was of enough importance, and a solution worked out with the persons and agencies concerned. Thus, Steelman did not act as an alter ego to the president; he never made decisions in the president's name as Sherman Adams did in the Eisenhower administration. Rather, Steelman tried to negotiate acceptable solutions to problems that came to the White House so that they would not have to go to the president for a decision. Occasional exceptions arose, of course, when there were irresolvable conflicts or when the matter was of such importance that the president needed to be personally involved.

Mr. Steelman considered overall economic policy to be within his area of responsibility, but I do not really know how much of a role he played. I do know that in drafting presidential messages to Congress and certain public addresses that involved economic matters, he usually asked me to serve as his proxy. Charlie Murphy took the lead in drafting most of these papers, and sometimes I felt that I was working for Murphy almost as much as for Steelman—though I made it a point to touch base with Steelman regularly. I do not recall that he ever disagreed with positions I took.

The 1947 and 1948 Economic Reports, drafted by the Council of Economic Advisers, were officially published over the signature of the president in their entirety (in contrast to later reports in which the president's part was the first twenty-five or thirty pages, followed by the fuller report to the president over the signature of the council members). Perhaps for this reason, President Truman wanted those reports to be thoroughly gone over and rewritten as necessary by members of the White House staff. Murphy and Steelman were jointly assigned that responsibility, and they in turn delegated the job in substantial part to David Bell and myself. Bell and I worked in complete harmony on this assignment, even though it involved some conflict with the council members. To the best of my recollection, Steelman never took exception to the work we did. The principal function of the Economic Reports, however, was to provide technical and analytical support for economic policy decisions that had evolved during prior months—decisions in which the council had participated chiefly via discussions with the White House staff. Rarely, as I recall, was the Economic Report used as a launching vehicle for proposing major, new economic policy actions.

One incident, however, may throw a bit of light on a narrow segment of policy-making in this area. The White House staff had drafted a message or speech (I do not recall which) in the field of foreign affairs. Because economic matters were involved, though in minor degree, I was a member of the drafting team. When the draft was completed, following usual procedures (which I will come to), the president called a meeting to discuss the draft with the cabinet members primarily concerned. It was the consensus of those present that the draft was not satisfactory. The president asked Dean Acheson, then secretary of state, personally to supervise the job of redrafting. We adjourned to another room and Mr. Acheson, almost single-handedly, reworked that draft into a far superior paper with quite a different policy tone. I was tremendously impressed with Mr. Acheson's breadth of knowledge and his sheer brilliance. It was obvious to me that the president knew what he was doing when he asked Mr. Acheson to take on that assignment. Mr. Truman had an extraordinarily high degree of respect for and confidence in Dean Acheson and relied on him heavily for policy guidance.

Very often policy decisions were made in the process of drafting presidential messages to the Congress or major public addresses. The immediate presidential assistants would discuss with the president the general position he wanted to take. Then, often under the direction of Murphy, a drafting team would be organized, its composition varying with the subject matter. A day or two of discussion would yield a preliminary outline. The outline would be divided up among members of the team for study and preliminary drafting. Issues would be discussed with top staff people in the agencies concerned. The contributions of the several members of the team would be combined into a very preliminary draft and duplicated. Successive drafts would follow, each a product of group authorship. When the draft was believed to be in fairly acceptable form (or sometimes even before), top staff members of the agencies concerned would be asked to join the team for a further redrafting session. Then the ensuing redraft would be duplicated and circulated for ·comment to the relevant agency heads, who no doubt turned to their top staff people for advice. With these comments, further redrafting was necessary. This method of obtaining agency advice, incidentally, may well have been more effective than a formally collegial cabinet meeting. Agency representatives felt much freer to express their objections forcefully to the White House staff than they (or even the agency heads) would have to the president himself.

When it was thought that the draft was near finished form, it would be submitted to the president. Typically, he would then call a meeting of the cabinet members and other agency heads concerned (often including some of those only peripherally involved) to discuss the draft. If it was a speech, he would sometimes read it aloud. He would solicit comments from those present. By and large, however, agency views had already been reflected—though not necessarily incorporated—in the draft under review. He would referee any remaining disputes and identify changes that he himself wanted to make. The next draft was final if the president found it satisfactory.

Certain very important policy decisions obviously were made without any written documentation. But many were made in the process of drafting messages to the Congress or formal public addresses. My purpose in describing our drafting procedure is to emphasize that policymaking of the latter type was indeed collegial. The White House staff did the work of putting successive drafts together, but hundreds of knowledgeable people, including the relevant agency heads and their top staff, contributed to the process. Although the president made the final decisions, he had the benefit of the views not only of his own staff, but of virtually all of those legitimately concerned with the subject at hand.

Although the president did not call many cabinet meetings, the notion that he did not involve the cabinet and other agency heads in the policy-making process is, I believe, incorrect. Clearly, he listened to some advisers with more respect than others, but much, if not most, of the "non-crisis" decision-making in the Truman administration was genuinely, if not overtly, collegial in character.

DISCUSSION

DOROTHY BUCKTON JAMES (chair): In our first session cabinet members indicated that they never felt the White House staff intruded or acted as a buffer between them and President Truman. I would now like to ask the members of the White House staff if from your positions in the White House you shared this view of the process?

EDWIN A. LOCKE, JR.: I am sure this applied to members of the cabinet, but I do not think it applied to a good many of the agencies. At least that was my experience. One of my assignments was to handle matters with the Civil Aeronautics Board [CAB]. First Welsh Pogue and later Jim Landis used to call me whenever they had something that required the president's approval. I would spend a good deal of time not only going over the situation with them, but also doing some independent checking on my own. For example, on these international route cases I frequently would consult the heads of the airlines involved. To the best of my knowledge, the chairman of the Civil Aeronautics Board rarely, if ever, saw the president.

CHARLES S. MURPHY: If I may, I would like to tell a little story that is perhaps not directly responsive to the original question. Eventually I inherited Eddie Locke's assignment of keeping up with the Civil Aeronautics Board decisions. Now, CAB decisions relating to international matters require presidential approval; those relating to domestic matters do not. There was an occasion when the CAB sent over a case that involved some domestic authority and some international authority, and the board had recommended that the whole thing be denied and that no authority be granted.

The president decided that he wanted the authority granted, and he told me to call the chairman of the Civil Aeronautics Board—Joe O'Connell at the time—and tell him that that was what he wanted. I called Joe O'Connell and we talked about it, and Joe said, "Charlie, you tell the

61

president that so far as the international authority is concerned, he is entitled to say what can be done about it, and we'll very happily do what you tell us he wants done. But so far as the domestic authority is concerned, that's for the Civil Aeronautics Board to decide, and we're going to decide what to do about that. But we'll take the case back, and we'll take a look at the whole thing in light of the fact that the president wants the international part granted. It may then make sense to grant the domestic part as well."

I reported this conversation dutifully to the president and he thought that was just fine, that was what the law said, that was the way it ought to work; the Civil Aeronautics Board had its function and they ought to perform it.

The Civil Aeronautics Board did take another look at the case; they decided that the domestic authority ought not to be granted and sent the case back that way. That applicant got its international authority and never did get the domestic authority.

DONALD DAWSON: I might add a little bit from my position in dealing with the Civil Service Commission. I had almost daily contact with the members of the commission, under Chairman [Harry B.] Mitchell in the beginning and Bob Ramspeck later. We had a great many problems that had to be dealt with continually. They did not *ask* to see the president very often; as a matter of fact, they preferred to deal with the staff in ironing out a lot of the day-to-day problems. But whenever they wanted to see the president, it was my responsibility, and my duty by assignment from the president, to see that they got to see him *as soon as possible.*

ROBERT C. TURNER: I would confirm what Mr. Dawson just said because the function of the White House staff, as I observed it, was to handle a good many of the problems which might definitionally have gone to the president. Agency heads, or more particularly the top staff in the agencies, discussed innumerable matters with the top White House staff people, who in turn, no doubt, consulted with their superiors. Thus, resolutions were worked out so that it was not necessary for the agency head to take the matter up directly with the president.

Now, if the problems were not worked out, agency heads did go to the president, and no member of the White House staff ever attempted to put himself in the posture of being an alter ego for the president, of making decisions on the president's behalf. Rather, what they were trying to do was to negotiate solutions to problems at a level below that of the president so that any particular matter would not have to go to the president for a decision; an enormous amount of such staff work was

Discussion

done. John Steelman, for example, was in constant touch with agency heads, particularly those of the regulatory agencies and the carryover of the war agencies and the like, so that 90-odd percent of the issues that might have gone to the president were worked out without having to be taken to the president.

PHILLEO NASH: I would like to add another perspective: I was a legacy as far as Mr. Truman was concerned. He inherited me as an assistant to Dave Niles (whom he also inherited), and we were charged with what was then called "race relations"—the term "civil rights" didn't exist as such until President Truman's commission. Since the area of race relations was everybody's business and yet nobody's business, we were always in serious danger of interfering with cabinet duties and cabinet responsibilities as well as crosscutting other White House staff responsibilities. It would have been very easy to get everything into a terrific bind by overacting—thinking that this pervasive, sensitive, and controversial problem should be the basis for interfering in every single decision. So I see the question of interference somewhat differently than it was described in the previous session. I like to think that the cabinet officers were not interfered with because some of us staffers were very careful about not interfering and yet were aware of the fact that there could often be substantial differences of opinion even between the president and his cabinet. Of course, our method of operating, going back to the last three years of the Roosevelt administration, involved a series of networks at inside agency levels, much below the cabinet level, simply to keep track of what was going on, and that was a very delicate operation.

JAMES: Yours may well have been among the last group of staff members that had a passion for anonymity.

WILLIAM J. HOPKINS: The mail from members of the cabinet addressed to the president came to the executive clerk's desk. It was the practice in those days, with very few exceptions, that letters from cabinet members went directly to the president. He then parceled out the letters at his morning staff conference unless they involved something he wanted to handle himself. In other words, there was no attempt to interpose any of the staff between the president and members of the cabinet. If a cabinet member addressed a letter to the president without marking it for the attention of any particular staff member, it would, with rare exceptions, go directly to the president.

MURPHY: It seems to me that this question of possible intervention of a staff between the president and his cabinet comes up in business flowing in two different directions. The first is business flowing from the cabinet members to the president in the White House. It is, I think, normal in the course of government operations for departments and agencies to want to get something from the president. It was my observation that different members of the Truman cabinet went about this in different ways. Some went fairly directly to the president in all cases. Others frequently, if not always, went first to the White House staff to see whether they could get what they wanted, and only if it wasn't possible did they then go to the president. I must say that the latter always seemed to me to be a pretty smart technique because it gave them two cracks at it. But there was no effort—ever, so far as I know—on the part of the White House staff to keep cabinet members away from the president.

Now the other direction in which interference might occur is in the White House undertaking to control the operations of the various departments and agencies. I think it is fair to say that during the Truman administration there was virtually none of that. In the first place, the president regarded it as highly improper; and in the second place, I do not think the staff had any such ambitions or desires. The president did regard it as his responsibility to exercise some control over the spending operations of the departments, and he used the Bureau of the Budget for that purpose. I think it is also true that during this period the White House did not look with suspicion upon the departments and agencies and the career service. We did not regard them as enemies or feel we had to be particularly on our guard. At the same time, there were certain of the president's policies that we thought we should encourage the departments and the cabinet members to follow; we worked at that, but we did it in a perfectly open and aboveboard way and usually maintained excellent relations with the cabinet members.

DAWSON: Dr. James, let me comment on your statement regarding a passion for anonymity and the president's staff. I think it is a very good principle. If the staff serves the president and responds to his wishes, they have enough to do. If they are continually appearing on radio and in the press, then they have their own programs to defend and work up. A man with anonymity is not under that burden.

LOCKE: Of course, Don, you know that some people said all we had was passion.

DAWSON: Well, some said it was only anonymity.

LOCKE: I would like to underline a point that Mr. Turner made a few minutes ago, which Charles Murphy alluded to: you never made a decision for the president if you wanted to survive on the White House

Discussion

staff. Hugh Fulton, who had been the general counsel—and a very excellent general counsel—of the Truman Committee, did not learn this and within two or three weeks he was out quite abruptly. When we brought things to the president we tried to point out the consequences of our particular recommendation, but we never—repeat *never*—made a decision for him.

TURNER: I think the objective of the White House staff operation was to find solutions to problems so there would not be an issue to take to the president. A lot of relatively routine or less important decision-making has to take place in the White House; by no means can all of it go to the president for decision. A lot of it has to be worked out somehow, especially when there is a difference of opinion between agencies as to what policy ought to be adopted. There has to be a resolution of those conflicts, and very frequently that can be done at the staff level, without having to take the issue to the president for decision, and the agencies are perfectly satisfied.

HOPKINS: I might say, too, that in those days when you saw a document leaving the White House signed "Harry S. Truman," it was the president's act, it was not an act of some staff member using his name.

JAMES: It might be useful to probe how President Truman used his staff by dealing with some of the individual positions. John Steelman's title was a very elevated one, but its functions have never been completely clear. I would like to ask: As you saw the relationships within the White House, what would you say Steelman's role actually was?

MURPHY: Elmer Staats had a good deal to do with the arrangements for setting up the Steelman office, "the assistant to the president." Bob Turner and Dave Stowe worked with Dr. Steelman a good deal, and I am sure that they are familiar with his operations. I will make just one comment: They did an awful lot of things. When I first went to the White House in January 1947, the first thing I tried to do was to find out who did what, and I found that Dr. Steelman had a staff meeting—daily, as I recall. He had a professional staff of high quality, some six, eight, or ten people; and I discovered that they were doing a lot of interesting things. I asked Dr. Steelman if I could come to his staff meetings and he readily agreed. I think he was pleased and flattered. I went to Dr. Steelman's staff meetings, and I learned quite a lot in that way, but I won't undertake to describe his operations if you can get these other people to do it.

ELMER B. STAATS: I would be happy to comment on this. I was

involved partly because of the role I was playing in winding down the civilian war agency programs. President Roosevelt had set up the Office of War Mobilization, which after the end of the war became the Office of War Mobilization and Reconversion, headed by John Steelman. There also were a large number of other civilian war agency programs—the Office of Economic Stabilization, the Office of Price Administration, the War Production Board, and many others. These were eventually combined into the Office of Temporary Controls as one way of winding down the control period.

During this period I did a great deal of work with John Steelman. Then the question arose of where to locate the residue of these functions and what should happen to the OWMR staff. I was given the job of trying to work out a charter for John Steelman and his staff in the White House. Technically, before that time they had been part of the Executive Office of the President but not of the White House.

We worked up a draft based on conversations with various people in the White House, including the president. I went over one day to check out the draft with John; I had written on it, "assistant to the president." He looked it over and said he thought the substance was pretty good, but he penciled in the word *the* in front of *assistant*. He said, "My understanding is that I am supposed to be the chief of staff of the White House." I said, "Well, that's news to me, but I am afraid I cannot really make that judgment." But President Truman allowed it to stand.

The practical situation was, of course, somewhat different. My impression from where I sat during this period was that the staff tended to gravitate around two focal points. One was John Steelman, and the other was Clark Clifford (and later Charles Murphy), with most of the staff being assigned to work with the latter. Then Bob Dennison's role went well beyond that of merely a military officer in the White House, because President Truman had a lot of confidence in him. Dennison was able to do a lot of things, but I never was quite sure where he fitted into this structure. The fact is, of course, that there was not any effort to structure things too much. The White House staff was small enough so that this did not present a great problem for those of us who were in a support relationship to the White House staff and to the president.

HOPKINS: With reference to the commission of Dr. Steelman, his first commission in the White House was as "assistant to the president"; the second commission was as "the assistant to the president." I know a certain number of the White House staff were a little unhappy when they learned that the word *the* had been added to the commission.

MURPHY: Spelled with a capital *T*, by the way!

Discussion

HOPKINS: Dr. Steelman probably received more presidential commissions than anyone who ever served on the White House staff. He had a number of jobs—in the National Security Resources Board, OWMR, and others. I think he received either six or seven presidential commissions in the whole process.

JAMES: But, practically, as the other members of the staff viewed it, what significance did that definite article have? It might be a point of pride for a gentleman to call himself "the assistant," but did you see any significant difference between Steelman, assistant, and Steelman, *the* assistant?

TURNER: I don't think there was a significant difference.

JAMES: It has been said here that there was no chief of staff in the Truman administration. Certainly there was no Haldeman or Ehrlichman or Sherman Adams in the Truman White House, but wasn't Clark Clifford's role a start in that direction?

JOHN W. SNYDER: I think that you will find that the cabinet considered Mr. Clark Clifford and subsequently Charles Murphy to have been the two people who really shaped up affairs over in the White House for the president.

W. AVERELL HARRIMAN: They had to do with the formulation of the speeches and consultation with the cabinet members, and they were, I would think, the focal point. But in no sense was either of them a chief of staff. I was special assistant to the president during the Korean War, and my job was to try to coordinate State and Defense; the secretaries of state and defense were not getting along very well at that time. I tried to bring the cabinet members closer to the president and to defuze the battles between them rather than to superimpose myself as an individual between them and the president. But I can assure you there was *no* chief of staff. I naturally consulted Charlie Murphy and other members of the staff as I thought they might be of value. But it was the *president* we all looked to, nobody else. We never went to a member of the staff in order to get to the president. In order to get action from the administration we went to the president of the United States.

CHARLES F. BRANNAN: I think one significant method of operation which supports this is that at cabinet meetings *only* cabinet members were present. Except for Matt Connelly, who sat off on the side and made notes of appointments the president set up with cabinet members to talk about some specific thing, there were never any staff members in the room.

The White House Staff: Early Period

MURPHY: It was my recollection that John Steelman went to cabinet meetings.

HARRIMAN: I don't remember Mr. Steelman being present.

BRANNAN: Neither do I.

TOM C. CLARK: I think I have a picture with Steelman there.

SNYDER: On some labor problems, I recall Steelman was invited in. Generally, I do not recall his being there.

CLARK: He was not there every time. I never heard of a chief of staff at the White House. I always thought of Mr. Steelman, as John indicated, as being a labor man. I dealt with him on our problems with John L. Lewis and in other areas of labor relations. But when it came to other matters, I would deal with Don Dawson or with Clifford, whom I looked upon as being not "the" assistant or the chief of staff, but just as a man who handled quite a few matters for the president.

LEON H. KEYSERLING: I would like to comment on two points that have been made. It is certainly correct that it was the general policy of President Truman to have only cabinet members at cabinet meetings. But to illustrate how Truman organized the presidency and his concept of who should be at and participate in cabinet meetings, I might say that at least from the time of the Korean War, I attended most, if not all, of the meetings of the cabinet and of the National Security Council. I was treated by the president in the same manner as the appointed members of the cabinet. In other words, the president recognized that the structural form of cabinet meetings as determined by the old-line departments under statute was inadequate, that there were some government officials who had far more important roles than did some of the cabinet members. The president exercised the initiative and imagination to adjust to that fact.

BRANNAN: I have to acknowledge that exception. During the Korean War, there were additional people brought into the cabinet meeting.

HARRIMAN: I was asked to be present during the war.

BRANNAN: And so was Stuart Symington, wasn't he?

STAATS: I think you have a semantics problem in defining a cabinet meeting. I was at many meetings myself where a majority of the members of the cabinet were present. It was not called a cabinet meeting, but in fact it served much the same purpose.

KEYSERLING: The meetings that I attended *were* called cabinet

Discussion

meetings; they were held on the regular *days* of cabinet meetings; there was no distinction made by the president between my attendance and the attendance of other members of the cabinet. In that sense during the perilous period of the Korean War the president *did* enlarge the structural concept of the cabinet, and he did the same with the National Security Council.

I also want to comment about the first statement which had to do with the Economic Reports and the role of Mr. Steelman. My recollection is that the Economic Reports were written twice a year during the Truman presidency, which meant that throughout the administration there were twelve. It was only for the first, issued in January 1947, when the Council of Economic Advisers was new and untried and its position not clearly defined, that Mr. John Steelman, in my view, sort of tried to take over the council and subordinate it to the Steelman operation. When our Economic Report went over to the White House, it was thoroughly rewritten—mangled—by the Steelman office. But we succeeded in getting it brought back to the council through meetings in the council offices, which I recall very well. Without going into the question of compromises over phraseology, we did reassert our responsibility for serving the president in the preparation of those reports.

Now after mid 1947—quite independently of our decision to separate the president's reports from the council reports—from that point forward the council was not interfered with in the sense described. It was our practice, and my practice when I was chairman, first to conduct a thorough submission and consultation process with the basic cabinet officers concerned with economic policy. Then, after the reconciliations were made, the drafts were prepared—both the draft of the president's report and the draft of the council's report, which really had to be consistent and part of the president's program. Whether you call it one document or two, they both went to the Congress in the same book, and one (although much longer) was an appendage of the other. They were part and parcel of the same thing. After this kind of clearance with the cabinet and the Budget Bureau, which really was a year-round process with intricate interagency relations at both the top and the staff levels, we worked very closely with the White House staff. Not that they intruded or interfered with our relations with the president or substituted their judgments for ours, but we did work very closely with them in the final development of the reports. We usually would meet with the president and some of the staff people to discuss at least the president's shorter report before it went to Congress in its final form.

TURNER: You are right, after we switched to the technique of having two different reports—one, the president's report, and the other, the report of the council to the president—the White House staff had no assignment to review the work of the council's report. Our assignment was only to review the report which the president signed.

MURPHY: I would like to return to the original question about a chief of staff and comment on several more or less relevant matters that have been mentioned. It is certainly true that in Truman's White House there was no chief of staff other than the president. Clark Clifford was not chief of staff, never undertook to be and never purported to be. He was an extremely able person; for reasons that were never clear to me he did not want any staff of his own. When I first went there to work, he had only one assistant, an extraordinarily able person, George Elsey, who is now the president of the American Red Cross and who unhappily could not be here at the conference because he has to attend the annual meeting of the International Red Cross in Europe.

I soon found out the kind of work that Clifford did. It was the kind of work I wanted to do, and so I went and asked if I could help, and he said he would be glad to have me. So I helped Clifford with his work from then on as long as he was on the White House staff. It seemed to me that he needed additional assistants and from time to time I would pick at him about trying to get some more help, but he just would not do it. I finally did manage to get one, or perhaps two, people transferred from other departments to the White House staff as Clifford's assistants. But I must say that if he worked with them, it was through me.

I had a somewhat different point of view about getting people to help; and later when I became special counsel I latched on to Dick Neustadt, Dave Bell, Dave Lloyd, and Ken Hechler, and then we did pretty well.

Something has been said about just who attended cabinet meetings. It is my recollection that when there was a vice-president, the president asked him to attend cabinet meetings regularly.

CLARK: The vice-president was always there—

BRANNAN:—and he was the first person the president called on.

MURPHY: That was my recollection. And my recollection is that he did that for a reason. When Mr. Truman succeeded to the presidency very suddenly, he felt that he was not as fully informed as he might have been and should have been; and I think he took this as his one method of keeping the vice-president informed about what was going on. It also is my recollection that there were two major independent agencies that were not cabinet departments, but whose heads he treated as members

Discussion

of the cabinet and invited to regular cabinet meetings: these were the Federal Security Agency (which is now Health, Education and Welfare) and Housing and Home Finance.

To jump to another subject, let me add to this business about the work on the Economic Reports. My recollection is clear that in the latter years of the Truman administration we, on the White House staff, *did* revise the language of that part of the Economic Report that went out

Thomas D. McAvoy, LIFE

Clark M. Clifford, special counsel, December 21, 1948.

over the president's signature. The staff worked on this with the council and then, of course, with the president. The first draft of this part of the report was always prepared in the council. So when we (the White House staff) worked on it, we were revising what had already been prepared over there and worked with Dr. Nourse, with Leon Keyserling, and with the third member of the council—at that time, John Clark. John Clark and Leon Keyserling never seemed to me to be particularly sensitive about having their language changed. They would disagree with us, sometimes vigorously, but it always seemed to me that they were willing to argue a point on the merits. Dr. Nourse, on the other hand, seemed to me unduly sensitive about having these "young whipper-snappers" at the White House change any of the language that had been prepared by the council. The result was that our labors went very slowly. But after this happened a time or two, we realized that Dr. Nourse, who was a good deal older than the rest of us, began to tire late in the evening. We made it a practice to start on this project about 3 o'clock in the afternoon, on the last day when it could be done—when the report had to be finished that day—and we found out that after midnight Dr. Nourse got to be very much easier to deal with.

JAMES: Would any others wish to comment on the role of Clark Clifford?

DAWSON: I did not want to respond specifically to that but to give my view, as a staff member, of who was chief of staff. I do not consider that there ever was a chief of staff other than the president himself. I reported *only* to the president; I did not report through Clark Clifford or Charlie Murphy or Dr. Steelman. I worked with them every day. I would, in my simple way, define their duties in two fields: the counsel's office—that is, Charlie Murphy and before him Clark Clifford—was mainly responsible for policy and planning; Dr. Steelman's office was the operations office. Both sort of overlapped on occasion: sometimes Dr. Steelman would get into policy and sometimes Charlie Murphy would get into operations. But generally it worked very smoothly.

HOPKINS: Remember that from the administrative standpoint, there was Matt Connelly. During the Roosevelt administration the appointments secretary was more or less in charge of administrative matters within the president's office. Just as an example, I remember Charlie Murphy had these bright young fellows working for him and he tried for some months to get some recognition of their efforts, which they certainly deserved. His solution was to have them commissioned as administrative assistants to the president. That dragged on for several months until I

Discussion

finally got instructions from Matt Connelly to have the commissions prepared.

DAVID H. STOWE: I would like to comment on the original question of Steelman-Clifford. I was with Dr. Steelman for a year in 1948. The first assignment I had was to move the remaining OWMR staff completely and totally out of the White House; that took a little time. Then, as I recall, Dr. Steelman went over to the NSRB [National Security Resources Board], and I spent about six or nine months over there. But I think the description that Bob Turner gave was the one that I would have given of Dr. Steelman's role, with perhaps a little more emphasis on one thing. Dr. Steelman was probably one of the best known labor mediators in the country. He was able to bring that talent to bear on many day-to-day little problems that came up between independent agencies, between segments of departments, between others. So his role was not just that of a labor mediator, although we did, as you recall, get into many labor disputes that some people thought we shouldn't. But in disputes within the government itself, he was quite an artist. As a good mediator, he never imposed his judgment; he was always trying to get the parties to agree, and he was eminently successful in that field.

On the other hand, messages to the Congress and the president's public addresses—often the point where great policy decisions are made —those were formulated in the counsel's office in the West Wing of the White House, not in the East Wing at all. While I was at the NSRB I heard about the struggle between the East Wing and the West Wing. If there ever was such a thing, it came to an end when Charlie Murphy became the legal counsel, because at that point the East Wing and the West Wing became one.

JAMES: Since we are interested in probing the roles of the staff, might we follow that up with a direct question for Mr. Murphy, as to what he perceived the role of the special counsel to be?

MURPHY: The most important function, I suppose, of the special counsel was built around the staff work on messages and speeches. The way it worked during the Truman administration meant that the special counsel was involved in the formulation of policy. It has been my impression that in later administrations there has been a system under which policy was formulated in one place and when that was all done, the package was turned over to speechwriters. It was not done that way during the Truman administration. I think the president had a view— which I certainly shared—that if people were going to write about something, it would be a good idea for them to understand it as thoroughly as possible. He said many times that his idea of a speech was to say what you had to say as simply as you could say it.

This responsibility for speeches and messages lead to relationships with the departments and agencies and particularly with the other units of the Executive Office. For example, in the Bureau of the Budget there was a Legislative Reference Division, and its function was to monitor and help formulate the legislative program of the president. The division collected recommendations from the various departments and got them in an orderly fashion so that the president could decide what his legislative program would be. When Congress acted on legislation, the same Legislative Reference Division was responsible for making recommendations as to what the President should do about signing or vetoing the bill. This involved collecting recommendations from all of the interested departments and agencies and synthesizing the recommendations in a report that was sent, along with the departmental recommendations, to the president.

That function was very closely related to the work of the special counsel on messages to Congress. So we developed a system whereby the Bureau of the Budget would request the departments to send in—well in advance as I recall, about the middle of the summer for the session of Congress that began the following January—their recommendations for legislation, indicating which portions they thought should be part of the president's program and which should be part of the departmental programs. The departments were asked to draft these recommendations in three versions: one for the budget, one for the Economic Report, and one for the State of the Union message. When they came in, the bureau would take the budget version, the Council of Economic Advisers would take the Economic Report version, and the White House staff would take the State of the Union version. Then we would talk with each other and with the president about what we were going to do with all of the recommendations.

One particular responsibility of the special counsel's office was to see that when these three big messages went to Congress—the State of the Union message, the Economic Report, and the budget message—that they were not in conflict with each other. That was a very sizeable job which we accomplished in various ways. At least one year we asked Dave Bell to go back to the Bureau of the Budget and act as a principal draftsman of the budget message, and we kept that straight.

The special counsel had various and sundry other assignments. Most of them do not occur to me at the moment. I retained this business of liaison with the Civil Aeronautics Board; we had some responsibility for Executive Orders. We did virtually none of the kind of business that you ordinarily think of as "legal" business. When we had a legal problem we went to the Department of Justice; they had a unit that later became the Office of the Legal Counsel. The head of the unit when I first went to the White House was George T. Washington. That is where we took all our legal business, and that is where we got our legal advice.

HOPKINS: During the early days, when President Truman first came in, George Allen made a study of the so-called operating units of the White House office. Up until that time there had been a detail program at the White House: more than half of the people working there were on detail from various departments and agencies. Mr. Allen recommended that everybody be brought onto the White House rolls, the theory being that if you were on the rolls of one of the departments and agencies but worked at the White House, you had divided loyalties. So everyone, with the exception of the postal unit in the mail room, was brought on the White House rolls. That doubled the budget for the White House office. Some of the commentators, like Drew Pearson, made a great play out of that and took great delight in saying that it was costing President Truman twice as much to run the White House office as it had President Roosevelt. We tried to refute this in replying to correspondence that came in, but every once in a while the issue would flare up again.

At that time the president had the authority to appoint six administrative assistants "with a passion for anonymity." The title of special assistant was not used much during the Roosevelt administration—only when the president needed a special job done or brought somebody in for a special purpose. Of course, the titles in the White House office have changed tremendously over the years. In President Truman's time, of course, we had the assistant to the president, but in Roosevelt's time, the top job was considered to be the man whose title was secretary to the president. That is used hardly at all anymore, and if you look in the present-day registers, you will see more special assistants than anything else.

NASH: I had a hard time getting used to the idea of special assistants with direct access to the president. I knew just the last two or three of the anonymous administrative assistants who had worked with Roosevelt. They were generalists, but some of them, like Dave Niles, had special areas and people with whom they were supposed to keep closely in touch. Our picture of the organization at the White House was, as Bill Hopkins has described it, that the secretaries and the counsel to the president were more or less the top people, the "inner circle," with direct access to the president. At the next level were those such as myself who did their jobs but reported to somebody who in turn reported to the president.

We were united by our loyalty to Mr. Truman, and by the easy and informal way of working with each other. For example, Dave Stowe had an assignment that somebody might have said involved minority affairs, which was my task. He handled the movement of large numbers of minority groups across the border from Mexico, a major labor and economic problem. There was no difficulty in recognizing that Dave had a special competence and that this was a different kind of a problem; and we worked together with the greatest of ease. It did not require any chief of staff to coordinate the effort, merely the fact that we all recognized that we were working for one man and we wanted to do everything possible to help *him*.

HOPKINS: Referring to the title of special counsel, I have always felt that that was sort of a misnomer. Ordinarily, as Charlie Murphy indicated, if the special counsel's office had legal problems, they looked to the Department of Justice. Back in the Roosevelt administration, Judge Samuel Rosenman had been very helpful to President Roosevelt in the preparation of speeches and that sort of thing. He was on the New York Supreme Court and would come down from time to time to be of assistance. Finally President Roosevelt convinced him that he should devote his full time to that operation, and he came on the White House rolls. I always felt that the reason the title *special counsel* was used was because Mr. Rosenman had been a judge and that it was appropriate from that standpoint. But the Department of Justice had some feelings that there was no need for a special counsel since they provided legal advice to the president. It always seemed to me that the title *special counsel* was tailored to fit Judge Rosenman, but it has been carried on since.

HARRIMAN: I was special assistant to the president during the Korean War, and it was for two specific purposes: to deal with the special problems of the Korean War and also, as I said, to try to coordinate the activities of the secretary of state and secretary of defense.

I would like to comment also on the manner in which Dr. Keyserling got into the cabinet meetings. There was a discussion as to how much of a burden the economy could take in the way of increased munitions production. Dr. Keyserling took the position—which I shared—that the economy could stand a great deal more. The president brought him in to persuade the Pentagon and other members of the cabinet that if we all did our jobs, the economy could produce substantially more for the war effort. Thus the president used his economic adviser to influence the members of the cabinet and the decisions of the government. It was

Discussion

a very unique situation. Of course, with the problem of inflation, I know Dr. Keyserling participated in a number of the meetings of the cabinet. I do not remember the other two gentlemen who were referred to as attending all of the meetings, but the president did call on men whom he thought would make a special contribution to the cabinet deliberations.

JAMES: Mr. Nash spoke of minority rights and of working for them. During recent administrations there has been a great proliferation of individuals dealing with various subelements of what might be called minority rights. How did you function in relation to them all?

NASH: When I came to the White House staff, during the last three years of the Roosevelt administration, what we would generally call minority relations was, as I said earlier, everybody's business, and therefore nobody's business. It was an area that was of obvious importance and yet so difficult and so touchy, so threatening to national unity. If you did something, it was liable to be wrong, and if you did nothing, it was most certainly going to be wrong. The administrative assistants to the president whom I reported to—first Jonathan Daniels in the Roosevelt administration, then Dave Niles and still later Don Dawson—were all acutely aware of the fact that we had a problem of great complexity and great difficulty but lacked a clear indication that any particular unit of government should (or did) have overall responsibility. Bill Hassett with his marvelous sense of humor used to send memos over to us addressed to the "Department of National Headaches."

During the war, at President Roosevelt's direction, we had developed a network of interagency information exchanges on the general subject of racial tensions as they might relate to war production. Once the War Powers Act had expired, of course, we could not continue in this particular format since the reason for these activities was that it might be necessary for the president to take possession of a plant—something he could not do under peacetime conditions. We began, therefore, to prepare the idea of a commission or committee to look into the problem. Eventually three different committees were formed as an outgrowth of the President's Committee on Civil Rights, each one of which became in subsequent years a part of the executive branch with different duties. Today, the work that one administrative assistant, with the help of another assistant, did for a great many years and under very difficult conditions, is being carried forward by a half a dozen agencies, operating out of two or three cabinet departments and with much more specific powers. Of course, we have today something we did not have then, and that is the legislative breakthrough, because the powers we had to operate under were very general. In 1964, when there was a national sentiment and a legislative breakthrough, all of a sudden Congress handed the executive branch a broad spectrum of powers.

JAMES: It might be useful to move from individual, specific staff roles to consider aspects of President Truman's administrative style and process. What was the nature and role of President Truman's staff meetings?

HOPKINS: President Truman started these staff meetings early in the administration, and they were a very helpful tool.

As you know, President Truman was an early riser. Usually he went out and had a morning walk and then came to the office around 8 o'clock. The first thing he did in the morning was dictate to his private secretary, Rose Conway.

After that he held his morning staff conference which was attended by a dozen or so of the top staff in the East and West wings. He was seated at his desk in the Oval Office, with the staff assembled in a semicircle around his desk, and much of the day's business was gone over. He usually started with Matt Connelly, who would bring up matters relating to presidential appointments, what was on the agenda for the day and upcoming commitments; he would also bring to the president's attention requests for speeches throughout the country, getting the president's reactions and (in some cases) commitments. The president would then turn to Charlie Ross and see what problems might arise during the day in his relations with the press. Many matters were discussed in terms of how to answer press questions and deal with certain problems.

Dr. Steelman, of course, was there, and Clark Clifford (and in the later days, Charlie Murphy), and they brought up matters in their areas of responsibility. It was an opportunity to listen to the president's philosophy and get his directions for the day.

President Truman was a prodigious reader, and each night he would carry home a portfolio, often six or eight inches thick. The next morning, he would have gone through all that material and taken such action as was needed. He had a desk folder labeled for each of his staff members; and at this staff meeting, he would pass out to them documents in their areas of responsibility, or on which he wished their advice or recommendations, or on matters he wanted raised with the various departments and agencies. In this way each staff member present knew basically what the others were doing, knew to whom the president had given which responsibility—whether it was to respond to a certain request, or to follow through on the preparation of an Executive Order or a speech, or things of that nature.

In the early days, Mr. Latta, who was my predecessor, sat in on these meetings, and after his demise I was privileged to sit in on them. This was a tremendous advantage for the executive clerk. In the first place, it developed our relationship with members of the staff; it gave us an opportunity to learn something of the president's philosophy, which we could pass on to those in the operating units for whom we were responsible; and it provided the greatest help from our standpoint—the handling and movement of documents. That was one of our responsibilities: to keep documents moving, to get them to the proper place after the president had taken action, and to know where they were. During the previous administration the system that developed was for most of the material for signature to go in through the president's private secretary. That system had many disadvantages from our standpoint, because Executive Orders, proclamations, nominations, and that sort of thing would go in and sometimes they would not come back to us on schedule. The departments interested would begin calling up and asking, "When is this nomination going to move to the Hill?" Well, all we knew was that it had gone to the president, and we had seen no more of it. So it was a matter of inquiring of the private secretary: if she remembered who it had been farmed out to, fine; if she did not, it meant checking with each of the staff members to see where it was. The end result was that there were many delays.

But having the opportunity to sit in on these staff meetings, having the opportunity to carry personally to the president a great percentage of the more routine material requiring his signature—the type of thing that did not require any particular staff member to take it in personally and discuss it with the president—made it possible for us to keep track of this material in a very simple fashion, without having an extensive system of follow-up coordination. Fewer papers got lost or were delayed; we were able to move them to the departments and agencies in a timely fashion; and when the responsible officials in various departments and agencies would call up asking about a particular document, we felt it our duty to give them a good answer. Under the system provided by President Truman for the handling of papers, in most cases we could do it.

I think one of the greatest detriments to the president from the standpoint of relations with the departments and agencies is to have the opinion get around town that the president's office is inefficient. If you are not able to respond in a timely fashion to queries of this kind from the departments, the word spreads very easily. In so many of these matters, time is of the essence. An Executive Order relating to a National Mediation Board case where a strike is pending or matters relating to nominations which are about ready to leak and should get up to the Senate—papers of that kind must be moved in a timely fashion, otherwise you are just in trouble and that all works to the detriment of the president.

JAMES: How partisan was President Truman in his appointments?

DAWSON: I think I can say objectively that he was both partisan and fair, at the same time. If he thought one man could do a job better than another, he did not let partisanship interfere. There were many cases in which some of us thought that political advantage could be gained if he went the Democratic party route, but he decided to go the other route, and he did so, as the members of the cabinet said earlier, on the basis of "what's best for the country."

One of my favorite stories about President Truman concerns the time I went to see him with several appointments. I put the papers before him and stood behind him and was saying that if he did this, he could get certain advantages and if he did it the other way, he could get another advantage. I kept going on and finally—I suppose he had had enough—he looked up at me and said, "Don, what's best for the country?" And I think that is the basis on which he made all his decisions, without any reservation or doubt.

JAMES: Do others wish to comment on the appointments process?

MURPHY: I would like to comment on the president's staff meeting, before we get too far away from that.

I think this is probably the most important institutional arrangement in connection with the organization of the White House staff. If I were to say how the White House staff ought to be organized, I would be inclined to say that if the president has a daily staff meeting, it does not make too much difference what he does with the rest.

This is not a snap judgment. I said the same thing in a talk here at the Truman Library a number of years ago; and the more I think about it, the more I am sure this is true. I have had opportunities to make this recommendation to subsequent administrations, but none of them have followed it and they all have gotten in trouble. It is my firm belief that they all would have been better off if they had followed this arrangement.

It is important, I think, for the president to have direct access, very frequently, to a number of his White House staff. One or two or three or four will not do; I think it needs to be eight or ten or a dozen. But the president cannot go around every day having a half-hour visit with a dozen different staff people; the days are not long enough. But he can get a dozen staff people in the room at the same time, and he can talk with them for a half an hour. Then they will all know what he is think-

Discussion

ing that day, and he will have some opportunity to find out what they are thinking. I just cannot overemphasize the importance I attach to this and the benefits I think it brought us as members of President Truman's staff.

HARRIMAN: I want to second strongly what Charlie Murphy says. There is one point, though, that I want to emphasize, and I feel rather strongly about it. I understand that the Carter White House staff meetings at the present time take place at 7:00 or 7:30 in the morning. President Truman, it has been said, had the staff meeting at 9 o'clock—I was under the impression it was 9:30. That gave the staff member a chance to get to his own office and understand what was going on in the immediate matters that were before him. I think it is important for members of the staff to go to their offices and see what is on their desks *before* the staff meeting. These very early staff meetings have nothing like the value that President Truman's had. And he set the 9:30 time even though he was one of the earliest risers of the presidents.

MURPHY: I agree. Most of us were awake by 9:30. If you go to a staff meeting before you are awake, it is not nearly as helpful. But President Truman was extraordinarily kind to the people who worked for

White House staff assembles for its morning meeting with the president. *Left to right:* Donald S. Dawson, Matthew J. Connelly, George Elsey, William Hopkins, Charles S. Murphy, John R. Steelman, President Truman, Adm. Robert L. Dennison, Gen. Harry H. Vaughn, Joseph H. Short.

him, in every way; and I think among other things, the reason he set this staff meeting at a reasonable hour was out of consideration for his staff.

DAWSON: It is pretty well known in Washington that whether you are in a department or whether you are outside of the government, if you know someone in the White House, one of the games is to call up and try to find out what the president is thinking or doing or try to get your ideas in. To the staff, one great advantage of the staff meetings, in addition to what Bill Hopkins said about the efficiency of the White House, was that in sitting there five days a week for a half hour, listening to all the subjects that were discussed, the staff members were fully aware of things that were going on in other areas. If we had had individual conferences, we would not have known about these matters.

Secondly, we knew the nature of the president's reaction, his philosophy, his directions—it all added up, so that it was probably the most effective coordinating device. Staff members, instead of speaking as individuals around town, spoke with one voice and that was the voice we heard when we listened to the president each morning at 9 o'clock.

Now, let me return to your question about his partisanship in making appointments. I might mention that Mr. Truman chose as the first ambassador to the United Nations Sen. Warren Austin, a Republican; that he placed Paul Hoffman, a Republican, in charge of the Economic Cooperation Administration; that he made Bob Fleming the chairman of the National Capital Sesquicentennial Commission; and that after the '48 election, in which Strom Thurmond ran against him as the candidate of the Dixiecrat party, he nominated Thurmond to be a brigadier general in the Army Reserve. Also, throughout the course of his appointments, Mr. Truman was very much in favor of career civil service in government. He made Jesse Donaldson, who was a career civil servant, postmaster general and named Vincent Burke as deputy assistant postmaster general. I do not know the party affiliation of either; they were career men as far as the president was concerned. And I could go on at length naming the career appointments, the independent and the Republican appointments, that he made—all good men and women.

JAMES: While you were administering, to what degree were you conscious of applying administrative theory, of actually administering government, rather than just trying to cope with events as they occurred and to put out the fires before they got too hot?

NASH: The whole theory and philosophy, in the minorities operation, was that the big problem of civil rights could be handled by dealing with small problems before they got to be big ones and before they got to be presidential difficulties.

Discussion

JAMES: Were others of you aware of applying administrative theory, especially if you were involved in some overarching process?

THEODORE TANNENWALD, JR.: Are you thinking in terms of the day-to-day operations against the administrative process or the concepts of authority and the problems that arose out of the perceived, or potential, lack of authority?

JAMES: They do overlap, wouldn't you agree? That is, the daily operations do enter the context of an overall vision of what you are doing and what appropriate measures should be taken.

TANNENWALD: The reason I ask is that I can think of a very interesting example of the problem of power and authority; Governor Harriman can speak more directly to it than I can because I was only on the fringes. But my recollection is that during the winter of 1947–48, when there was concern about the possibility of the Communists coming to power in France and Italy and we had the problem of sending assistance to the then-established governments, the only power that existed was the president's constitutional power as commander in chief. It was out of this problem of power and authority that the Military Assistance Act had its origin. We were very conscious of the concepts and the basis of power and authority in constructing what we had to do on a day-to-day basis.

STOWE: I interpret your question to mean, did the staff feel that they spent most of their time coping with day-by-day business or was there some sense of administrative planning, in the political science sense, of how are we going to get from here to there.

JAMES: I did not mean it solely in the sense of, did you have rap sessions about what your philosophy would be, but did you have a feeling that as each crisis came up, you could fit it into an overall framework of ideas. In short, at what point were you aware of patterns and principles guiding you? Was it prior to dealing with the individual daily crises of various sorts—minority rights, or foreign policy, or labor, or what not—or did you make your decisions and then slowly see a pattern developing which you could then articulate?

LOCKE: To answer the question on your terms, were we aware of any administrative theory? I had not thought of it quite in this way before, but I would answer it in very simple terms. I think we were aware that there was a single individual who was in charge, *the* chief executive, and that there was not government by committee but by a single chief executive (to be sure, within the checks and balances of our

Constitution). To me, in those circumstances, this was by far the best and most effective administrative concept for this kind of a job.

HOPKINS: I think each administration comes in with the idea that they are going to spend a great deal of time in long-range planning and not just get caught up in details. But as a practical matter, long-range planning centers in the area and the time of year in which the president's program—as represented by the message to Congress on the State of the Union, the Economic Report, and the budget document—is prepared. These set forth the program and provide the guidelines by which people try to operate. But in the day-to-day operation they get caught up in the details so much that sometimes other things go by the board.

MURPHY: President Truman himself was very much interested in administrative management, and I think perhaps, as an individual, he was the leading person in the White House who worked on that. It was not particularly my cup of tea, but the Bureau of the Budget was pretty strong in that field, and he worked quite closely with the Bureau of the Budget. I think it also is relevant here, and important, that President Truman in his personal habits was a very orderly man; he thought in very orderly terms. In terms of thinking ahead, in terms of getting things done and being ready to meet problems as they might arise, the president himself was leading the way.

SNYDER: We ought to bear in mind as we approach these various subjects that Mr. Truman inherited the government of President Roosevelt and that he felt very strongly that he had arrived at the office of the presidency through the platforms and the policies and the plans he was elected under as vice-president. Many of these things he later threw his heart into were things that had not yet been started when Mr. Truman took over. And many of the programs he kept trying to carry out, he considered the obligation of the party in power dating from the election of Mr. Roosevelt.

With his own election in 1948 there came a marked change in Mr. Truman's general attitude because he was then on his own. But I do think we should bear in mind that he did try honestly and properly to carry out the established plans on which he thought that he and Roosevelt had been elected.

HARRIMAN: May I second this very briefly. I arrived back from Moscow eight days after President Roosevelt died. President Truman told me directly, "I was not elected President. It was President Roosevelt who was elected. It is my obligation to carry out his policies, and I want to understand his policies. I know little about foreign affairs, and I want you to tell me about it." But new situations arose almost immediately. I know that he did have a greater sense of responsibility himself after he got elected in 1948, but it was almost immediately upon taking office that he faced new situations and showed the courage and determination to do that.

FRED I. GREENSTEIN (Princeton University): From reading George Elsey's oral history and the private diary of Mr. Eben Ayers in the press office [both in the archives of the Truman Library], I got a sense that the staff meeting was something which evolved during the fire-fighting period of the transition phase in 1945. There seems to be a great deal of description of informal conversations among Mr. Snyder, Mr. Steelman, and Judge Rosenman, out of which the staff meeting then took shape. Was the staff meeting an immediate development or a gradual evolution during the first year or two?

HOPKINS: It is my recollection that it was a very early development. Of course, during those days, Clark Clifford was in the Map Room, as was George Elsey. Admiral Leahy, of course, came over and briefed the president each morning, but he did not attend the morning staff conferences because they were more related to the domestic area. Admiral Leahy was the conduit of most of the very important documents relating to the war coming both from Defense and State, and he briefed the president every morning and, of course, saw him at others times in addition.

SNYDER: But that started under Mr. Roosevelt.

HOPKINS: Oh, yes, that started under Mr. Roosevelt.

LAWRENCE GELFAND (University of Iowa): I would like to ask how public opinion polls were taken into account in the various decision-making processes. Several people have mentioned that Mr. Truman made decisions with respect to what was right for the country, what was in the national interest. But did members of the White House staff, or perhaps members of the departments, take into serious account the various and frequent public opinion polls that were often published in the press? Moreover, for the various programs and policies, how was public opinion generated in favor of certain proposed policies during the Truman era?

JAMES: Of course, a political scientist might interject that the public opinion polling was pretty faulty at that time, witness the predictions of who would win the 1948 election . . .

GELFAND: A recent book by Michael Leigh entitled *Mobilizing*

The White House Staff: Early Period

Consent deals with the period from 1937 to 1947; various allegations are made in that book with respect to the use of public opinion polls. I was curious as to how those present here saw this dimension.

NASH: I am quite sure that if anyone of us had said to Mr. Truman that he ought to shape his course of action because the opinion polls were leaning in a certain direction, he would have been very irritated. However, in two policy areas I was part of an exercise that made a different use of opinion polls and other sources of analysis of public opinion: first in the early stages of developing the Truman policy in the Middle East and then very early in the administration, when there was a heavy filibuster over the FEPC issue. In both cases I made an analysis of the available information in the formal public opinion polls—I had been part of the polling operation in the Office of War Information earlier and had some interest in polling and a slight knowledge of the state of the art as it then existed—and in the correspondence coming in to the tune of thirty thousand to forty thousand letters and telegrams per day.

I am not familiar with the work that you have cited although I intend to have a look at it. I think there is a big difference between the right and wrong use of information polls in this connection. What I was attempting to do (along with Dave Niles and others with whom I was working and to whom I was reporting) was to provide some objective information to the president on where he stood with relation to the public's understanding of his policies and programs—whether he was so far ahead of public opinion that he was bound to be in trouble, or whether he might, in some instances, even be behind it. The state of public support and public understanding of his positions and policies was something that we attempted to provide him with, quite independent of what he might be hearing from the departments.

This relates to some extent to what we were talking about earlier with respect to the cabinet. I do not think it is a matter of interference with the State Department for one of the president's staff to provide him with the best current information on what the American people are saying or thinking about a State Department policy being formulated and about which there are undoubtedly legitimate differences of opinion.

LOCKE: I was not aware that public opinion polls had any influence on the president. They might have given him some new information once in a while, but, as has been said here many times, the president did what he thought was best for the country. His reactions were extraordinarily representative of the reactions of the country as a whole. And this was one of his very great fundamental strengths, in my opinion.

Discussion

Roger W. Tubby: I do not recall the use of public opinion polls; they may have been used and I just never came in contact with them. But remember: President Truman was an extraordinarily good politician, and any president who is a good politician will be ahead of the polls. He ordinarily sensed what was right and sensed what the people wanted before any polls were taken. I think this is perhaps most dramatically illustrated by his reaction to public opinion when he fired General MacArthur. I remember the morning after the announcement, we had bushel baskets of telegrams that had come to the White House from all over the country, and they were overwhelmingly damning the president for daring to fire this great general. I went into the morning staff meeting with a handful of these telegrams and held them up without even saying what was in them. He said, "Roger, see that fireplace over there? Go put them in that fireplace and set a match to them." And so I literally did. I came back to my chair, and he asked, "Now, what's next on your agenda?" But before that, he said, "The American people will come to understand that what I did had to be done." And I believe that is what eventually happened.

Robert L. Dennison: I would like to add a footnote to what Don Dawson said about the qualifications of presidential appointees. At one staff meeting, late in the session, somebody brought up the name of a gentleman who was about to be appointed to some federal position, and that was about all there was to it. As we got up to leave, another member of the staff said, "Well, so-and-so is a knucklehead, and whoever heard of him, and who is for him anyway?"
Connelly spoke up and said, "The president."
The other fellow said, "Gee, he's in good shape, isn't he?"

Tannenwald: Just a couple of observations that I think may have some bearing on the question of the role of John Steelman and also on the question of access to the president. As far as the role of John Steelman was concerned—whether it be semichief of staff, chief of staff, coordinator, or what—I can assure you that during the period when Governor Harriman was special assistant for foreign affairs, it did not extend to the field of foreign affairs. That was the governor's bailiwick; obviously he worked with everybody else on the staff, but that field was not coordinated by anybody.
Secondly, we did have a great deal of contact with Charlie Murphy, and although Charlie might not have been chief of staff, it was always a good idea to talk to him before you went to see the president because, if you did not talk to him beforehand, you would surely have to talk to him afterwards. Thirdly, as far as access to the president is concerned,

there was absolutely no doubt that if you had to see the president, you could.

I was a young whippersnapper in those days, and there were two occasions in 1951 when Governor Harriman was in Europe. First, I had a fight with the Pentagon about delivering tanks to Europe instead of sending them down to the tank fields in Texas. I had to take the issue to the president, and I did not have the slightest problem getting to see him or getting that issue settled. The second issue involved a fight with the director of the Bureau of the Budget over the level of aid for the foreign aid program. Mr. Lawton and I had to go to the president, and I had no trouble at all getting an appointment. When the issue was big and you had to see him, you were able to, no matter who you were.

GIRARD T. BRYANT (Kansas City, Missouri): I would like to ask Mr. Nash about the integration of the armed services. This was an issue which General Eisenhower avoided when he was chief of staff of the army, and yet President Truman made a positive decision in this respect.

NASH: Following the report of the President's Committee on Civil Rights, there was a substantial question about implementation. Oscar Ewing spoke to Clark Clifford and asked for a general meeting between the 1948 convention and election time. At this meeting he pointed out that there was certain specific language in the Democratic party platform with respect to integrating the armed forces that lay within the power of the executive, and he thought that something ought to be done and done quickly. We had a number of proposals in the works that were rather difficult to put into effect, and it was concluded that a ways-and-means committee, the Committee on Equal Treatment and Opportunity in the Armed Forces, should be created. The necessary staff work was promptly done, and an Executive Order was put out setting up this committee.

Many good things came out of the committee, but what really brought about a very rapid change was the Korean War. There were large numbers of blacks in the garrison troops in Japan who had to be thrown into Korea very fast. Circumstances and fate had a lot to do with what happened thereafter: units and individuals had to be put into combat so fast that it was impossible to unscramble them, and that was one of the ways in which policy really materialized. This is why I have never been too clear in my own mind about the difference between policy and operations.

FRANK MITCHELL (University of Southern California): During the spring of '46 and later, James Forrestal advocated the idea of a cabinet secretariat with responsibility for a planned agenda and with an executive officer who would see to it that there would be some proper disposition of cabinet actions. I wonder what the reaction might have been from the White House staff members—just how did they view the idea of a cabinet secretariat?

SNYDER: I might just say that that concept never developed. Therefore, it never became an issue, and never got to the point where the staff had to be for or against it.

MURPHY: I would agree with what Secretary Synder said. I do not know that I ever heard of it at that time. If you asked me what I think of it now, I would say that I think that the Truman White House staff and the Executive Office were organized just about right. The changes since then have, on the whole, not been on the plus side. The staff now, of course, is a great deal larger. From time to time they have had a cabinet secretariat, but mainly I have a feeling that a lot of people have spent a lot of time getting in each other's way.

ROGER W. JONES: The idea of a cabinet secretariat as first advanced by Jim Forrestal was tried out on the Budget Bureau. Elmer Staats will remember this and so will Dick Neustadt. The budget director gave it a very immediate and direct answer which kind of set Forrestal back on his heels. He said, "We are not interested in having you organize the president. The president will organize you."

ROBERT UNDERHILL (Iowa State University): I would like to ask a question about the preparation of messages. Mr. Hopkins has outlined the message preparation for the Economic Report and the State of the Union, but what about the special messages? For example, the Greek-Turkish aid message of 1947? What was the method of input for that kind of a message from those present here, and how was that input effected?

MURPHY: Special messages were prepared in much the same way that the regular messages were. In my time, and so far as I know in other times, it was the responsibilty of the special counsel to see that the staff work went forward. Now the pattern usually was to get policy guidance from the president, of course, and he in turn was getting recommendations and advice from the relevant departments. We always tried to get from the departments a draft of a message as a starting point. I did not work on the special message on aid to Greece and Turkey, but the general pattern of preparation of those messages was the same as for the regular messages.

During the spring of 1948—you remember that was an election

year—the president wanted to point out as clearly as he could the difference between his approach and policies and those of the Eightieth Congress. One of the means he adopted was to send special messages to Congress on issues of concern to him. We did not have an iron-clad rule, but our general operating rule that spring was that we were to have a special message ready to go to Congress every Monday morning.

III

THE WHITE HOUSE STAFF
LATER PERIOD

For the discussion of the White House staff during the later part of the Truman administration, three of the participants drew on material which they had previously prepared and adapted it for use at this conference.

Richard E. Neustadt had written a rather lengthy memorandum as early as February 1953, in which he described the positions that existed on the White House staff at the end of Mr. Truman's presidency and characterized the persons who held these positions. Thus his observations have, in his own apt phrase, "the virtue of immediacy and also of innocence of what would happen under later presidents." Dr. Neustadt, after serving in the Bureau of the Budget, served as special assistant in the White House from 1950 to 1953. He has taught at Cornell and Columbia universities and, since 1965, has been professor of government at Harvard University where, from 1965 to 1975, he also served as associate dean of the John Fitzgerald Kennedy School of Government. His book *Presidential Power* (1960) was widely acclaimed and continues to be considered one of the most influential studies of the presidency. In 1978, Professor Neustadt joined the board of directors of the Truman Library Institute.

Charles S. Murphy has worked in Washington since his graduation from law school in 1934. In 1947 he moved from the Office of the Legislative Counsel of the Senate to the White House where he served first as administrative assistant to the president and, from 1950, as special counsel to the president. He returned to government service during the Kennedy and Johnson administrations when he was undersecretary of agriculture (1961–65) and chairman of the Civil Aeronautics Board (1965–68). He is now in private practice in Washington, D.C., and is president of the Truman Library Institute. His statement for the conference, adapted from an address he delivered at the Truman Library in 1967, stresses Mr. Truman's ability to simplify complex matters, echoes

The White House Staff: Later Period

Mr. Hopkins's observations about the president's orderly way of doing things and his high regard for the office he occupied, and calls attention to his success in the use of staff advisers.

Ken Hechler's contribution vividly illustrates the staff's interaction with one another and with other elements in the government (in this case primarily the Department of State) and also the president's manner of participation in the evolution of a (relatively minor) public statement. Mr. Hechler's memorandum is based on notes prepared in 1952, shortly after the events he describes. Ken Hechler was a special assistant in the White House office from 1949 to 1953. He served as a member of Congress from the Fourth District of West Virginia from 1958 till 1976.

In addition to Messrs. Hechler, Murphy, and Neustadt, the panel for this third discussion session included Adm. Robert L. Dennison, Beth Campbell Short, David H. Stowe, and Roger W. Tubby. Admiral Dennison, a career naval officer, served as naval aide to the president (1948–53) but also discharged a number of functions not normally expected from or associated with a military aide. His prepared statement illuminates both Mr. Truman's methods as president and his perceptions of his role. Admiral Dennison's distinguished naval career culminated with service as commander in chief of the U.S. Atlantic Fleet and a concurrent assignment as supreme Allied commander, Atlantic, for the North Atlantic Treaty Organization (1960–63).

Beth Campbell Short, an experienced newspaper woman, enjoyed both vicarious insight into the White House office while her husband, Joseph Short, was the president's press secretary and direct insight during her service in 1952 and 1953 as correspondence secretary to the president. She later served as press secretary to Sen. A. S. (Mike) Monroney, and since 1966, she has been special assistant to the assistant commissioner of the Social Security Administration.

David H. Stowe, after service in the Bureau of the Budget, was named special assistant to the assistant to the president (Dr. John Steelman) in 1947 and became administrative assistant to the president in 1949. After the end of the Truman administration he engaged in the practice of labor arbitration. Since 1970 he has been a member of the National Mediation Board.

Roger W. Tubby was closely associated with Joseph Short, serving as one of two assistant press secretaries and succeeding to Short's duties after the latter's death in 1952. Mr. Tubby was assistant secretary of state for public affairs in 1961 and 1962 and U.S. ambassador to the European Office of the United Nations and other international agencies in Geneva, Switzerland, from 1962 to 1968. In 1975, he became deputy commissioner of the New York State Department of Parks and Recreation.

RICHARD E. NEUSTADT

During the last twelve to eighteen months of the Truman administration the personalities in the White House office and their relations with one another were relatively stable. This was the last phase of staff development under Harry Truman. This was the staff with which he faced his last session of the Congress and his last political campaign in office. This was the staff that operated after the Soviet atomic bomb, after the Korean outbreak, after "partial" mobilization, after renewed high prices, and after direct controls had lost their shock effect—their emergency flavor—and been assimilated as "normal," familiar features of the governmental landscape.

At the start of 1952, there were twenty-two full-time and three part-time civilian officials in the White House engaged in presidential staff work. There were, in addition, three military aides, one of whom, the naval aide, was—for reasons of personal competence—frequently drawn into staff undertakings akin to those of the civilian officials.

This group of twenty-eight—including the part-time civilians—constituted the president's personal staff. They were the individuals who had some voice in the conduct of public affairs at the presidential level. This group was, of course, only a fraction of the number of individuals on duty in the White House office.

To avoid any possibility of misunderstanding, here is a listing of the groups excluded from this consideration of the president's personal staff:

1. The armed forces personnel handling communications, manning the aides' offices and the medical office, serving as White House chauffeurs, etc.

2. The civilian personnel engaged in purely administrative, clerical, and stenographic duties within the White House office (except for their nominal supervisor, the executive clerk).

3. The Secret Service Detail and the White House Police.

The White House Staff: Later Period

4. The liaison staffs handling government-wide contacts with the public service organizations of the advertising and motion picture industries.*

Apart from these excluded personnel, the presidential staff per se was somewhat smaller in 1952 than during the preceding two years, but that decline was due wholly to the full-scale transfer of Averell Harriman's office from the White House to ODMS [Office of Defense Mobilization and Stabilization] after October 1951.

Aside from the period of Harriman's White House tenure (July 1950–October 1951), the presidential staff in 1952 was somewhat larger than it had been at any time since the first confused months of the Truman administration. This growth of staff occurred almost entirely during President Truman's second term. In the winter of 1947–48—a period of stabilized staff operations much like 1951–52—there were sixteen full-time civilian officials, as compared with twenty-two four years later. The make-up of this full time staff and the pattern of its growth, is shown in Table 1.

TABLE 1

WHITE HOUSE STAFF SIZE

POSITION	JAN. 1948	JAN. 1952
Assistant to the President	1	1
Assistants	3	2
Special Counsel	1	1
Assistants	1	2
Appointments Secretary	1	1
Assistant		1
Press Secretary	1	1
Assistants	1	2
Correspondence Secretary	1	1
Administrative Assistants	3	5
Assistants	2	4
Executive Clerk	1	1
Total Full-time Civilians	16	22

These figures may be compared, roughly, with a total of approximately seventeen (including Byrnes's OWM) on Roosevelt's full-time staff late in 1944 and a total of twenty-three staff appointments announced in the press during the first three weeks of the Eisenhower administration.

Of course, figures of this sort have relatively limited significance.

---

* This little group, transferred from OWI [Office of War Information] to OWMR at the war's end, then attached to OGR [Office of Government Reports] in its short-lived revival, was retrieved by Dr. Steelman from the wreck of OGR in 1947. It existed thereafter as a nominal part of the White House, but without any internal relation to the president's business or to other White House undertakings.

94

Part-time personnel, officials of other agencies, or private citizens may be as much or more a functioning part of a president's "staff" as the full-time officials in the White House office.

Furthermore, the really significant thing is not the number of staff aides, but what they do and how they do it. For the Truman staff, circa 1952, that information is summarized below.

The Assistant to the President (John Steelman)

There are three keys to understanding this post and Steelman's operation in it.

First, the job was the lineal descendant of the OWMR *directorship*. This means that when OWMR was liquidated in December 1946, Steelman, its last director, came into the White House without any loss of status. It means also that inevitably he brought with him a residue of then current OWMR projects and interests, on which he retained "the lead" within the White House for a number of years—for example, housing and education.

Furthermore, the OWMR background meant that in Steelman's new job, as in his old one, he was nominally the president's principal agent in the task of coordinating, adjudicating, and needling—the main domestic operations of the government. The press release announcing Steelman's new appointment stated quite specifically that he would "continue" to assist the president in "coordinating" executive "operations."

Whatever may be thought of OWMR's effectiveness in this role, or indeed of John Steelman's after 1946, the point is that of all the White House staff, he most clearly and most nearly had the "operations" assignment—and the prerogative. Other staff members might be instructed to act on an ad hoc basis or might follow their particular balls of twine into a lot of operational by-ways, but Steelman, alone, had a general mandate.

The second point to bear in mind is that John Steelman's whole prior experience in government had been as an expert mediator, a conciliator, a bringer-together of opposing points of view, concerned less with policy than with agreement and specializing in techniques of settling disputes.

Inevitably, Steelman's approach to his "coordinating" responsibilities on "operations" was deeply influenced by this background. He has often said that coming to the job long after the cabinet was appointed and entrenched, he could not hope, and did not try, to manage cabinet officers or to oversee their affairs. Instead he deliberately sought to be a smoother-outer, a helper with troublesome details, a conciliator, treading warily among the department heads and to-and-fro between them and the president. In the same way, he sought—apparently with the president's assent—to disassociate himself from any labor or political partisanship. Advocacy was not to be his business.

But the choice of roles was not merely a tactical move, in light of entrenched cabinet strength; it seems clearly to reflect, as well, the natural instinct of the skilled mediator.

Third, it should be understood that when Steelman became the assistant to the president, he had already held a White House post for more than a year, as special assistant to the president concerned with labor-relations problems and the settlement of major labor disputes. He had not relinquished this assignment while serving as OWMR director, and when he returned to the White House, his labor-relations duties were simply lumped in with the "coordinating" role carried over from OWMR. But the specific, pressing—and familiar—labor problems naturally took precedence over the vaguer stuff of coordinating "operations."

There has long been a view in many quarters that Roosevelt's White House, and Truman's as well, meddled too much in labor relations. There may have been some justification for this charge in one particular case or another, but as a general proposition it is insupportable. The laws of the land—the Taft-Hartley Act and the Railway Labor Act between them—require presidential intervention at the crisis stage in practically all disputes of national importance. And these legal requirements merely formalize and sanction what is bound to happen anyway. Law or no law, the tradition of presidential involvement goes back to Grover Cleveland.

Nowadays, with big labor, big management, a highly integrated economy, and a Cold War besides, it is quite inevitable that when the stakes are high, all sides will look to the White House, go to the White House, plan their strategy accordingly, and refuse to stop short. Conceivably, the immediate pressure on the White House might be eased if the Labor Department were an "industrial relations" enterprise rather than the labor secretary's being expected to be labor's representative in the cabinet. Under present conditions neither management nor the unions will deal with the secretary of labor when their own bread-and-butter is seriously at stake. They want the president's representative, or better yet, the president himself.

In the Truman White House, John Steelman's office was usually the place they would go. Whatever his title, whatever the formal range of his responsibilities, this was the heart of Steelman's work as assistant to the president.

But Steelman passed to others the detailed staff work on developing policies and courses of action to meet the situations created by the disputes he was mediating or by the eventual terms of settlement. Generally speaking, these tasks devolved more and more on Charles Murphy, the president's counsel, with help from David Stowe and other members of the staff.

In practice, this meant that nobody was actually exercising firm, continuing control of the total staff, and no one staff member was continuously riding herd on the various government agencies involved from time to time. Steelman's mandate from the president certainly left him in position to assert continuing leadership on the policy side, but that was neither his way nor his preoccupation. Murphy, on the other hand, could not hope to assert control over the mediatory operations that Steelman kept in his own hands. Murphy was always mindful of Steelman's titular rights, particularly when it came to bearing down on operating agencies outside the White House.

In practice, Steelman handled a tremendous range of "cats and dogs"—that is, questions, issues, problems (both trivial and great) concerning day-to-day operations and relationships, principally on the domestic side of the executive establishment.

Generally speaking, these things came to him in three ways. First, he was constantly receiving from the president a mass of proposals, pleas, and denunciations about particular federal activities, left off by cabinet officers, congressmen, and the great assortment of private visitors who streamed through the president's office (usually with papers in their hands).

Second, a variety of businessmen, trade union officials, interest-group representatives and members of Congress with some special point of view or ax to grind, frequently called or wrote Steelman urging that the president make so-and-so do this and that about some federal undertaking.

Third, for six years Steelman sat in on cabinet meetings, always there, almost always with his mouth shut. In consequence, he received a great deal of his business from the department heads who were used to seeing him when they got together with the president. "Ask the boss if it is all right for me to do this"; "I want him to know I have done that"; "Some other department is stepping on my toes, does the boss know or care?" All the questions, the beefs, the complications arising out of day-to-day concerns, which were too trivial—or too unjelled—to be taken up directly in hurried sessions with the president, were likely to land on Steelman's desk, whenever or wherever a cabinet officer wanted help or even just to say that he had "checked in."

The heads of independent agencies, whose access to the president was frequently more restricted, made extensive use of Steelman's services in this role. Indeed, the weaker the agency, the more dependent on borrowings of presidential powers and prestige and the greater its use of the Steelman channel. Housing and the RFC [Reconstruction Finance Corporation] were good examples.

Taking all these things together, there was a huge volume of business crossing Steelman's desk or coming in over his telephone. A lot of it was trivial, some of it was very vital, and all of it was spewed up by the great federal machine in daily motion.

Steelman could be, and often was, an effective channel between departments and the president for settling spot problems. He was effective also in the technique of designed evasion, the man who could "study" a problem forever—or lose it completely, if need be. Be it said that much of this "negative" action was undertaken at the president's direct request. Some personalized and personable wastebasket work is bound to be essential to any president.

Steelman handled a very large share of his total work-load personally. Though he had two full-time staff assistants, he never used them as general aides but rather as special-purpose helpers to whom he gave assignments from time to time. Harold Enarson helped out on the labor-relations side, particularly in processing disputes referred from the Federal Mediation and Conciliation Service and the National Mediation Board. Russell Andrews helped with the general stream of visitors and correspondence. The work load of these two men varied greatly, as did their relationship to Steelman's central interests of the moment. They were sometimes in the stream, more often out of it. Neither was in any sense a "deputy."

In addition, until the end of 1951, Steelman had the occasional assistance on a consulting basis of a former staff member, Robert Turner, and the full-time help of Turner's girl Friday, Marjorie Belcher. Miss Belcher occupied herself with winding up Turner's long involvement in certain commodity, materials, and stockpiling questions—an inheritance from OWMR days. Miss Belcher also processed Tariff Commission recommendations under the injury provisions of the Reciprocal Trade Act—documents which came to Steelman for reasons long since forgotten by all concerned.

Generally speaking, in his relations with his own staff, Steelman retained the mediator's instinct. He was his own man and kept his own counsel.

The Special Counsel to the President (Charles Murphy)

In attempting explanations of White House organization, some Truman staff members were fond of saying that while Steelman looked out for "operations," Murphy handled "plans" and "forward programs."

This is a great oversimplification, much too tidy to be accurate, but there is just enough truth in it to make it a convenient point of departure.

Only a hint of Murphy's role is given by a listing of the fixed, well-organized assignments he had acquired or had inherited from his predecessors, Sam Rosenman and Clark Clifford.

Murphy was responsible for the preparation of all the president's speeches, his other major public statements, and all presidential messages to Congress.

Furthermore, Murphy was generally responsible for staff work on the development of the administration's legislative proposals, on the selection of issues and emphases in the president's own legislative program, on the final review of enrolled bills, and on the preparation of Executive Orders. It was to Murphy that the Budget Bureau's legislative clearance operation looked for leadership. It was Murphy who prepared agendas for the president's meetings with congressional leaders and who took their calls on particular headaches about particular bills.

As a natural extension of these jobs it was to Murphy that the president turned during the campaign year of 1952 for such things as the "White House draft" of the Democratic platform; and it was Murphy who captained the writing-and-research team on the Truman campaign train that year.

Thus, the special counsel held the acknowledged staff lead on preparation of all the formal documents which expressed, explained, or defended the president's major policies and programs—foreign and domestic, executive and legislative, governmental and "political" alike. Now if this did not put Murphy "in charge" of policy and program planning, at least it got him deeply and strongly involved in the process. The strength of his position is highlighted by the following observations.

In the first place, messages, speeches, Executive Orders, and the like are not merely vehicles for *expressing* policy, they are devices for getting policy *decided*. They have deadlines attached. And there is nothing like a deadline on the statement of a policy for getting a decision on what that policy shall be.

Thus Murphy had not only the power that goes with choosing the words but also the power that goes with presenting the issues for decision. And as a corollary, he had the responsibility for determining what the issues were, clarifying them, counteracting the premature commitment, counterbalancing the one-sided presentation, flushing out the hidden controversies, and surveying the alternatives.

The preparation of these great "action" documents was rarely an editorial matter. Ordinarily it was a matter of helping the president decide what to say, as well as how to say it. And inevitably, it was also a matter of when—of timing.

Now the strength of Murphy's position lay not only in the fact that these types of staff advice were his to give, but that he had equipped himself to produce results. He had "tooled up," staffed up to carry the load. And while his own organization was not wholly adequate by any means, there was nothing else like it, nothing else to match it, anywhere around the president.

Murphy, as special counsel, operated not just as an individual but as head of a very close-knit team. During the last year, the full-time members of the team were David Lloyd and David Bell, both administrative assistants to the president, and Richard Neustadt, Murphy's own assistant. These three worked as Murphy's general-purpose associates, operating very intimately and very flexibly, working jointly or severally on anything and everything that came along.

Murphy had a second assistant, Donald Hansen, who concentrated on loyalty and security matters and certain other "legal" concerns (which will be discussed later). But Hansen was always available in a pinch for more general assignments. And Lloyd had an assistant, Ken Hechler, who served the whole Murphy group as a lightning-fast researcher, fact-finder, and compiler of background information, particularly in the field of "political" research.

Besides these men, several other members of the White House staff worked for Murphy on an informal, ad hoc basis. Most of the assistants to the other presidential appointees drifted in and out of Murphy's circle, depending on the projects at hand and the needs of the moment. In appraising this staff as a source of strength to Murphy, mere numbers were, of course, a factor. But two other aspects need to be considered.

First, the group around Murphy were the "idea" boys, the bright young men of Truman's White House, responsible, indefatigable, in earnest about the great causes both foreign and domestic that are identified with Truman's name. Naturally, these men were a center of attraction for their counterparts in the agencies, on the Hill, in the Democratic National Committee, and in the Washington headquarters of interest groups espousing Fair Deal programs. There was thus a real network of close, informal relationships between Murphy's group and bright, able, imaginative staff men all over Washington.

Second, Murphy's associates were, by and large, not simply idea men, but reasonably experienced bureaucrats with considerable understanding of the bureaucratic power structure—that is, of the way things are done and how and by whom. Generally speaking, these men had "been around," they knew how to "operate," their acquaintance was wide, their finger-tips sensitized.

President Truman's speeches, messages, and the like were written not by writers, but by lawyers and economists and public administration specialists who had picked up skills along the way as generalists in government. This did not bring the highest literary quality to Truman's public papers, but it certainly meant a sensitive awareness of their potential as vehicles for making or influencing policy.

It meant, too, that Murphy's men had some ability to operate "underground" at the subcabinet level and below, all through the government—obtaining information, exchanging views, sometimes even coordinating a bit of policy, or influencing an administrative action, without the fuss or formality—or futility—that often must attend dealings with and among department heads. Of course, when the shoe was on the other foot, when dealings at the top were necessary to minimize entrenched attitudes and bickering and lethargy among the bureaucrats, Murphy's group was usually free to ignore the second-stringers and go directly to the department heads. Thus, in a relative sense, their experiences gave them the best of both worlds—both bureaucratic contacts and White House status.

These factors all added to the strength of Murphy's position in the policy arena. But there were also some basic limitations in his situation. First, while Murphy had his hands on several of the key "action" processes around which policy was made, there were some others more or less outside the range of his recognized assignments. One of these was the budget process, the determination of the sums to be requested for existing and projected activities. On the budget message, as such, and on new substantive legislation to be proposed thereby, Murphy's claim was certainly well staked out, though he had to share the terrain with the budget director. But on the dollars-and-cents allowances in the budget document itself—the stuff of which policy is so often made, or unmade —there was no mandate or machinery that brought the special counsel regularly into the general dialogue between the budget director and the president.

Similarly, on the issues raised by the course of the military campaign in Korea and by major political developments in the Cold War around the world, the special counsel had no recognized hunting license, no established part to play, unless the president needed to say something or to recommend legislation or to issue an Executive Order.

The absence of a mandate which regularly involved him in these processes did not mean that Murphy or his staff never got into budget decisions or foreign and military policy. From time to time, they got in very deeply. But Murphy's technique was always to move under the cover, however tenuous, of some recognized mandate that he did possess. He always sought a "handle," an excuse, to rationalize his appearance in someone else's bailiwick. And his associates, perforce, followed his cue.

It is hard to say how much Murphy's technique—the constant use of cover, the tendency to await some semblance of a "mandate"—was an inherent limitation in the counsel's job and how much was an outgrowth of Murphy's own temperament and training as focused on the job. To some degree the limitation was, of course, inherent. The post of presidential counsel generates no independent leverage. On the White House staff, all glory is reflected, and partial or total eclipse—sometimes momentary, occasionally sustained—can be a common occurrence.

Unquestionably, however, personality had something to do with Murphy's particular response to his particular opportunities. His mind and temperament were essentially judicial. His long service in the Senate counsel's office naturally conditioned him against "fighting the problem." Though Murphy grew greatly in the White House, still there never were the sharp, continuous clashes of personality and ambition that characterized his predecessor's relations with Steelman, Connelly, and certain cabinet officers. The "mandate" technique helped to minimize all that but at the price—perhaps necessary, perhaps not—of circumscribing the counsel's range of interests and the timing of his interventions.

There was another limitation built into Murphy's operation, and that was time. There was never enough time to do a real job—a complete job—on all the things implicit in his regular assignments. Deadlines on presidential documents limited Murphy's scope even as they strengthened his hand. Inevitably, it was the most concrete jobs, the presidential documents due by a certain date, that got top priority, that is, the larger share of staff energy and attention. The less immediate, less tangible projects always had to give way. Murphy and his associates were relatively alert to the productive but intangible stuff of spying out the landscape, thinking ahead, following up, "operating," on the great issues present and to come. These things they carried on as best they could, in snatches, piecemeal, squeezing their forays in between their work on the endless series of public papers of the president of the United States.

The Truman staff was well organized to *develop* legislative programs, but far less well equipped to lead, guide, or share in the campaigning that is essential to translate programs into law. On the administrative side, the Truman White House rarely failed to state a better policy than it could implement in actions by the governmental agencies.

The contrasts, of course, were not unique to the Truman regime. To some degree these will be found in any administration. The White House staff, however organized, cannot make up for all the weaknesses of party discipline and leadership in Congress; nor can the staff preempt the role of agency direction, from cabinet officers through bureau chiefs and their subordinates.

Moreover, the staff can never be expected to allocate its time to best hypothetical advantage, regardless of the personal preoccupations of the president—those being, after all, the *raison d'étre* of the staff itself. If in Truman's time "disproportionate" staff energy went into speeches and the like, then it is also true that these were among the things that the president, personally, *had* to do, and none but his own staff were handy to help him. In a real sense, the White House staff's main purpose was to concentrate on just those things no one else in the executive had been set up to do. And these unique assignments inevitably impeded the interesting business of looking over the shoulders of other agencies and staffs to see how they were performing.

But granting that no president and no White House staff can ever do a perfect job of follow-through on legislative or administrative action, it also should be said that within the particular context and limitations of the Truman presidency and the Truman staff, neither Murphy nor his associates conceived that they were accomplishing as much as might have been possible, had they been able to cope with their time problems. They never overcame those difficulties, but they knew better than to blame them all on history or the dynamics of American government.

The time problem that faced Murphy and his aides in coping with their regular assignments was tremendously complicated by the spate of crucial ad hoc jobs that came their way. Over the years, it became more and more usual for Murphy to end up as the cleaner-upper of nasty operational crises.

In 1951, for example, it was Murphy who finally worked out a settlement of the RFC controversy between the Fulbright-Douglas subcommittee and the president; Murphy who initially picked up the pieces of the Treasury–Federal Reserve controversy—though these agencies finally came to terms entirely on their own. It was Murphy who did the chief work and worrying on how to put the Wage Stabilization Board together again; Murphy who tried time after time, with proposal after proposal, to obtain definitive action to meet and overcome the issue of corruption and the situations behind it.

The common characteristic of all these problems, and the many others Murphy took on, boils down to this: hard questions and choices of policy were involved in a critical operating situation which had reached such proportions publicly that the substantive issues could be neither evaded nor decided on a purely ad hoc basis. When a matter reached that stage, it usually got into the special counsel's hands, whether by assignment from the president or by tacit consensus among Murphy's colleagues or sometimes by nothing save the workings of his own conscience.

In all these ways and for all these reasons, the special counsel's role in Truman's White House was mainly as a general-purpose policy adviser, a "counsel" in the broadest sense.

The Appointments Secretary (Matthew Connelly)

To understand Connelly's role in the Truman White House it is necessary to consider both the character of his job and the nature of his long association with the president. Together, those things produced for Connelly a formidable position within the staff.

The appointments secretary had his desk just outside the usual visitors' entrance to the president's office, astride the channels of communication. He was the direct personal contact with people who wanted to see and talk to the president. Within limits, he had very considerable discretion in deciding who got to see the president and who did not. While cabinet officers, members of Congress, the White House staff, heads of major private organizations, and the like had a right to entrée which was virtually automatic, as a practical matter, Connelly had a good deal of latitude in deciding when and in what sequence they should go in.

And this power to influence the timing of appointments for the "great" meant more than mere discretion to deny the portals outright to the hoi polloi.

The president's phone was in Connelly's hands in the same sense and to about the same extent as was his door. Incoming calls from the "great" went through directly, except when the president was engaged in conference or with callers. Then Connelly decided whether to interrupt or postpone. Calls from the "near-great" and the lesser-known usually went to Connelly first, for his decision and disposal.

Not only did the appointments secretary handle visits and calls to the president, he also made up the list of presidential engagements: where the president would go and whom he would address, as well as whom he would see. Here, too, as a practical matter, Connelly had considerable discretion—not that he would have presumed to accept or reject a serious invitation without checking, but because in all except the most significant cases, it was he who checked with the president, and thus he who was on hand to give Mr. Truman advice.

There were certain practical limitations, of course, in Connelly's exercise of all these functions. There were ways to reach the president other than through his office door or by phone. Old friends, staff members, cabinet officers, and the like could find opportunities to negotiate arrangements for themselves or others directly with the president. The president himself could, and often did, initiate phone calls and appointments. And there are four doors into the president's office; only the president controls them all. Then too, for the initiate, there was the after-hours call to the chief usher of the White House, the neutral civil servant who relayed messages and got instructions from the president on handling unscheduled phone calls or extending invitations to the residence itself. But granting these limitations, the nature of his official duties gave Connelly a role of great strategic importance, far beyond the mere mechanics of administrative detail.

In the first place, Connelly's physical location gave him an unmatched opportunity to know what was on the president's mind, to gauge his mood, to gain his ear at any time of day. During the course of an average day, the nature of Connelly's job and the location of his desk brought him into much more frequent contact with the president than was the case with any other government official.

In the second place, it was Connelly's business to dispose of the president's time—and there is no more precious commodity in the country. The man who has that to give—or appears to have it—will be sought after, courted, favored, and confided in by government officials, private interest representatives, and, last but not least, the whole party hierarchy—national, state, and local.

Taking these things together, any appointments secretary is bound to have an influence on the course of events. Jonathan Daniels has described the way F.D.R.'s military aide and secretary, General Watson, helped shape the decision to dump Henry Wallace by making sure a steady stream of Wallace's opponents got in to see the president all through the spring of 1944.

In Connelly's case, the opportunities afforded by the job itself were reinforced by his particular prior relations with the president. Alone of the civilian staff, Connelly was a holdover from Truman's Senate days when he had been chief investigator for the Truman Committee, sometime secretary to the senator, and personal jack-of-all-trades in the 1944 vice-presidential campaign. The appointments secretary must always have close, informal, intimate relations with the president; so must a senatorial handyman with his senator. But the nuances are different in these two situations; and the roles, responsibilities, and attributes of office are different. Yet here there was a carryover. Here, at least in some degree, they were combined.

On policy at the highest level—on the grand strategy of the administration, so to speak—Connelly's direct influence was negligible, and his indirect influence was sporadic and secondary. He occasionally advised on the time and content of messages and speeches, but in the later years, at least, he was rarely needed. Nor was he encouraged to take part in the stream of great issues flowing to the president for decisions from Budget, State, Defense. He had little to do with the elaboration of the Fair Deal or with the development of Cold War policy.

But at what might be called the tactical level—the level of day-to-day decisions in the normal grind of domestic government and party operations, including congressional contacts—Connelly's role was often crucial, indirect perhaps, sometimes hard to trace, yet not infrequently decisive.

In the last years he had one and sometimes two assistants helping him with contacts on and requests from Capitol Hill. They kept a low profile there and so did he, facilitating relations and pressing programs.

The Press Secretary (Joseph Short; Roger Tubby)

Characteristically, this office always faced in two directions; outwards towards the correspondents as news source, nursemaid, channel, lead, and buffer; inwards toward the president and other staff as counsel, guide, or fall guy for the press and public impact of every sort of presidential action. Frustrations were inevitable in each of these roles, and a great deal of tension and strain was involved in attempting both at once. Three factors were outstanding among the elements of strain.

First, the three national press associations, the major East Coast newspapers, and two of the radio-TV networks had full-time correspondents on the White House beat, inhabiting the White House press room and accompanying the president wherever he went, in Washington or out. This meant that there was always a nucleus of ten to twenty correspondents on hand all the time, with nothing to do but cover the president.

Relatively few of these full-time correspondents were in the first rank of responsible Washington reporters. Some of them were definitely second-string. The permanent group was thus a pretty heterogeneous lot —not equally competent, not all reliable by any means—but ever-present, always on the press secretary's hands, alternately starving for and overwhelmed by White House news. They were quarrelsome, querulous, bored with themselves, often dissatisfied, and always there.

They were as much a part of the president's entourage as the Secret Service. Yet their employers had not put them there to protect the president. And out of their ambivalent relationship to the staff and to the president came perpetual harassment for the press secretary, who was at once the nursemaid, friend, and protector of this press corps as well as guardian of the presidential gates against their "depredations."

President Truman en route to a press conference with his press secretaries, Roger W. Tubby (*l*) and Irving Perlmeter (*r*), November 20, 1952.

107

The White House Staff: Later Period

Second, the pattern of White House press coverage—and of press corps relations with the staff—was greatly affected by the tempo of wire-service reporting. The wire-service reporter is not called upon for commentary or interpretation. He is expected to produce spot news, sharp and fast, for instantaneous transmission to all parts of the world in time to make the very next edition—and, if possible, to headline it. Speed, compression, sensation: these spell good reporting in the wire-service lexicon.

But for the president and his press secretary these qualities spell trouble and not for them alone. The bear-baiting atmosphere of so many press conferences, which were inevitably geared to wire-service tempo, was hard not only on the president but on his press staff; it was equally rough for many members of the press corps itself. Indeed, the worry and frustration of successive press secretaries was matched by the frustration of the abler, more discerning and discreet reporters.

For the White House staff's defense against the ravages of wire-service tempo, both in press conferences and out, was a protective stiffening, a recoil, an arms'-length attitude toward all (or almost all) the correspondents in the permanent press corps. Naturally, everybody suffered—as much from this reaction as from the difficulties which prompted it.

Many first-rate reporters for great dailies or weeklies—men and women able to reflect and to interpret at more length and leisure than the wire-service staffs—were increasingly cut off from the flow of informal confidential interchange, the background briefings that were essential if they were to do the best possible job not only for their papers but for the president. This they resented and resisted in their turn.

Yet for none was the strain so great as for the press secretary, caught in the midst of this swirl of frustrations, hampered by them constantly, never able to get clear, but only more entangled at each new turn.

The third source of strain for the presidential press officer had an internal not an external origin. The distribution of duties, the channels of authority around the White House for matters of substance—and even of phrasing—left the press secretary in a late-comer's advisory role on almost every phase of the newsmaking process, except for purely technical details. Other people wrote the speeches; others decided whom to recommend for federal offices; others arranged the presidential calendar, deciding whom he would see and where and when.

There was nothing in the rules of the game to prevent a press secretary with a strong enough personality from making his advisorship count—but, unlike his colleagues on the staff, he could not concentrate on any one identifiable area. More pertinently, the nursing of the press filled far too many hours for him to spare much time serving as his colleagues' arbiter, even assuming they would have let him get away with it.

In moments of crisis, where activities had to be improvised around the table, Joseph Short—the strongest personality of all Truman's press aides—often intervened, often decisively. But many presidential actions were brewed more calmly, and the way prepared, the decision taken, the phrase made, by those who specialized in such things. Meanwhile the press secretary, busy with the endless detail of his office, turned to a quick review of the course proposed or the speech prepared only at the end of the process.

Each of Truman's press secretaries struck a different balance in working out his personal role amidst these contradictory pulls and pressures. Temperament and experience had considerable effect on the result in every case. Joe Short, for example, himself a much respected former White House correspondent, was a taut, tense, "ulcer-type." His became a top-level voice on general policy within the inner circle; he was sharp-minded, persistent, and passionately loyal. But the qualities that helped him to be effective there contributed to the disaffection of his former colleagues in the press corps. They saw him as impatient, overly protective, and lacking in appreciation of their special need for background information to guide their interpretations. Short closed off, as nearly as might be, all avenues to the staff save through the press office. But having done so, he then tended—as reporters were fond of complaining—to act less like a press-relations expert than like a confidential policy adviser (which, of course, he did become), more concerned with minimizing the momentary harm the press could do than with maximizing the "breaks" that it might give in response to the right timing and conditioning.

But be it said for Short, it can at least be argued that, during the last two years of Truman's term, there was no other realistic choice.

Correspondence Secretary (William Hassett; Beth Short)
President Truman once wrote, "The Correspondence Secretary takes care of Special Day and Special Week Proclamations, wedding anniversaries, etc. He heads off eager beavers who know how to save the world. He sends messages of greeting to all sorts of meetings and organizations. He must be a genius at work handling, intellectually honest and absolutely loyal. . . ." Mr. Truman might have added that this secretary prepared and supervised the use of form acknowledgments to routine letters from the public, composed special acknowledgments to public inquiries or commentaries of any special interest, and otherwise kept an eye on the handling of mail from private persons.

Unlike the president's assistant, the counsel, or the other secretaries, the correspondence secretary was rarely perceptibly involved in either policy or operations. Indeed, even routine "greetings" to organizations of major political importance—the CIO, say, or the American Legion—were normally subcontracted as a matter of course and actually written, for the most part, by one or another of Murphy's aides.

Unquestionably, these correspondence duties were vital to the presidential operation. They had to be done and done well. But it was largely by accidents of history and personalities that throughout the Truman administration, these duties rated one of the five top White House staff posts. Substantively, the correspondence job as carried on in Truman's time was of a considerably less critical nature than the work performed by Steelman, Murphy, and the other two secretaries.

The Administrative Assistants to the President

Of the five assistantships that were filled during most of Truman's last year in office, two were in the nature of merit promotions for members of Murphy's staff, David Bell and David Lloyd, who continued their work with little essential change. Both served as general purpose writers. In addition, they made excursions into and followed after a variety of policy issues, depending somewhat on their backgrounds and predilections.

For example, once Bell, a Harvard-trained economist who had come out of the Budget Bureau, had gotten into a number of natural resource problems relating especially to western development and electric power, he retained the "lead" in that area for several years. For four years running he was the White House staff man most concerned with general budget policy, especially on overriding problems of defense, and with the actual drafting of the budget message. Along with Turner, he served both Murphy and Steelman as personal eyes and ears on a variety of economic policy issues.

Lloyd, a lawyer, had been in government since the New Deal days with a break for service as the legislative counsel of Americans for Democratic Action. Like Bell, he was tagged with the lead on a number of ad hoc assignments which, once given, remained his for years. Low income housing was one of them. Certain foreign policy issues, like immigration and aid to refugees, were others. In addition, Lloyd became the staff man chiefly concerned on a continuing basis with the great constitutional controversies over presidential powers, especially in the field of foreign policy, that gained prominence in Truman's second term.

A third assistantship was also in the nature of a merit promotion for Steelman's first assistant, David Stowe. Stowe always remained to some extent in Steelman's orbit without much of an established mission of his own; sometimes he aided Steelman, sometimes Murphy. He was rarely in business wholly for himself, but acted as a troubleshooter, fixer, even hatchet-man sometimes, on a shifting set of spot assignments.

For example, Stowe actually managed the WRSB [War Reconversion and Stabilization Board] during the period in which Steelman served as its acting chairman. In 1952, Stowe performed the same service during the months Steelman served as acting chief of ODM [Office of Defense Mobilization]. Because of his long Budget Bureau background handling manpower problems during World War II, Stowe got heavily involved in a variety of similar questions during the post-Korean mobilization. For a time he also did a good deal of work on international air-route cases and on a number of issues growing out of the reports of the presidential commissions on migratory labor and on resources policy. Finally, as a carryover from NSRB days, Stowe became the White House man on civil defense matters and on physical security arrangements for the president and his entourage.

In addition to these three administrative assistants, there were two others on entirely different kinds of assignments, each with fixed responsibilities and separate orbits all their own.

One of these, David Niles, handled problems, contacts, and relations with minority groups, performing for Truman in the same individualized and personalized way he had for F.D.R. While Niles formally left the White House staff late in 1951, his long-time assistant, Philleo Nash, carried on until the end, and Niles remained in pretty constant touch, on an informal "consulting" basis.

Another administrative assistant was Donald Dawson, the "personnel man" of the staff. Dawson held the title of liaison officer for personnel management and as such handled the stream of contacts with the Civil Service Commission and the Budget Bureau on a great variety of matters affecting the career service and the generality of federal employees. But he was also responsible, under Connelly's surveillance, for developing and processing candidates for appointive office, handling the staff work on patronage matters, high and low. In addition, he had a rather vaguely defined responsibility for overseeing internal White House personnel matters and space questions as well—the nearest thing to a regular contact point for the executive clerk, the senior White House careerist.

All of Dawson's major duties involved personnel, but that was about all they had in common. And this curious combination of essentially unrelated—though mechanically allied—functions plagued Dawson from first to last. He and his assistant, Martin Friedman, were forever becoming entangled in the very different requirements of their three distinct personnel assignments. It was sometimes claimed that they tried to handle patronage matters like professional civil servants and technical civil service matters like professional politicians. And this charge, while wide of the mark, does serve to illustrate the apples-and-oranges nature of their basket of assignments.

Consultant to the President (Sidney Souers)

Admiral Souers, a wartime naval intelligence officer, a Midwestern businessman, and a good friend of President Truman's, had been the first secretary of the National Security Council. He had given the council's staff its stamp as a nonpartisan, neutral, careerist "secretariat."

When James Lay succeeded to the secretaryship, Souers remained on hand several days a week as a consultant to the president. In this capacity he served as a sort of informal father-confessor and guardian for Lay, an elder-statesman kind of personal adviser to the president, and an informal link between them, confidant to both.

In other words, Souers served as a sort of super-secretary of the NSC, not a personal substitution for the secretariat's neutrality, but part of it himself. He did not function as the presidential alter ego on the NSC, or even as the NSC staff channel back to his White House colleagues. Instead, he was a quiet participant in the direct relationship between the president and Lay, close-mouthed with his White House colleagues, concerned neither to represent their interest to Lay, nor Lay's to them.

The gap between the White House staff, as a politically oriented, totally presidential entity, and the neutral secretariat of NSC was never bridged in Truman's time on any systematic basis. Murphy, Bell, and others of this group were successful, on a relatively few occasions, but never intensively or for long. This had very serious consequences for the evolution of the NSC and for its utility as part of the presidential staff machinery. But for one reason or another, the missing link was never forged in Truman's time and it remained for his successor to make the first attempt in the role then carved out for Robert Cutler.

The Military Aides

Only one of the military aides was drawn into policy matters during Truman's later years. Contrary to the popular supposition, this was not General [Harry] Vaughan, the army aide, but rather Admiral Dennison, the naval aide. Dennison's involvement was principally a matter of personal competence, an exceptional, noninstitutional affair.

The naval aide, it is true, had one special advantage over his colleagues. As heir to Admiral Leahy's wartime map room, it was to his office that the copies of top-secret cables from our representatives abroad came. Thus, the naval aide joined with Lay and Souers in the morning intelligence briefings for the president and in many ad hoc conferences on matters of great urgency in the military and diplomatic fields.

But Dennison's special role involved much more than these sorties into the fringes of foreign policy. On certain other matters, especially in the field of maritime policy and shipping operations, Dennison gradually became the man with the White House lead. Starting as a consulting expert to the other staff, he ended up with the responsibility for staff work in his own right. On long-range shipping legislation, subsidy policy, and the like, the naval aide negotiated directly with the Budget Bureau, the maritime agencies, members of the cabinet, and even certain congressmen—just like any member of the president's civilian staff, bird-dogging a special assignment.

The Executive Clerk (William J. Hopkins)

Traditionally, this is the post of the senior, nonpolitical, civil service careerist in the White House office, the supervisor of office services and custodian of official documents requiring a presidential signature.

On the side of office services, the influence of the executive clerk was always circumscribed to the extent that the interests of presidential appointees became involved. On space matters and most internal personnel questions—including personal services in the White House budget—the clerk's functions were purely ministerial. Moreover, in the case of traditionally autonomous administrative units—the White House files, the switchboard, and the transportation office—Hopkins's "supervision" was a nebulous and delicate affair.

On the documents side, the executive clerk maintained control on the most informal, least obtrusive basis possible. Only once in Truman's time was a signature document lost irretrievably. This record was a miracle of art over science. Somehow the endless stream of papers flowed, and the orders, commissions, letters, and enrolled bills got to the president, were signed, and sent on their way. But the control system, such as it was, remained to the end nothing more than a vest-pocket affair, a matter of memory, handwritten notations, and general good will.

As for the documents not requiring signature—the reports, memoranda, "think" pieces flowing in from staff agencies and cabinet members —if they came by mail or messenger the clerk received them and got them to the president. But from then on it all depended. The president parceled them out or buried them or mislaid them, as he chose. Hopkins watched and listened. Usually he had a good idea of what had happened, but he was not infallible; and there was never any inclusive written record covering disposal of the nonsignature documents transmitted through Hopkins's hands. And, of course, there were still other papers he never saw at any stage and had no notion of, much less any record.

Some General Observations on Working Relations in the White House Office

President Truman was an exceptionally kindly man, a most considerate, even humble human being in all of his relations with subordinates. It is symptomatic that he was worshipped by his household staff and by his Secret Service agents as no president in memory before him.

In the White House office, there was always informality and at least surface friendliness, and generally everyone had a high morale, reflecting the president's own attitudes and personality.

Truman was not only a considerate superior, he had an abhorrence of caterwauling, knife-throwing, or in-fighting among his subordinates. His staff and cabinet learned, perforce, that for their own survival it was essential to keep their quarrels beneath the surface, maintaining at least the appearance of reasonably good relations with one another.

As far as the staff was concerned, it was inevitable under the circumstances that there be tension between the special counsel and the assistant to the president, between the counsel and the appointments secretary. In Clifford's time, this triangle of hostility was marked and continuous, barely kept below the surface. Murphy, by temperament, was less competitive and combative than Clifford. The tension remained, but in a latent form. Yet there were moments during the last years when the White House staff seemed close to dissolution into warring camps, with Murphy—joined by Short, as press secretary—aligned against Connelly, or sometimes Steelman. But war never broke out; disputes were always kept under cover or patched up. Above all, conflicts among these senior staff members remained on an individual-to-individual and issue-by-issue basis. No fixed, continuing alliances were formed on either side. During the later years, the potential splits within the staff never hardened and rarely came to sharp focus.

It is interesting to note that divisions of responsibility within the White House were never as clearly felt or acted on as during the period of sharp tension when Clifford was counsel. In 1947 and 1948, when power within the staff was relatively polarized and jealously guarded, staff operations probably were at their most effective. Tension drew lines clear and sharp, creating a settled framework for daily operations, with junior staff regularly and informally bridging the staked-out gaps between their seniors. Later, during Murphy's time, there were always broad, shifting areas of fuzziness and uncertainty in the respective roles and relationships assumed by Steelman, Murphy, Connelly, and the ad-

ministrative assistants. Less tension bred more diffusion. The ball sometimes became very hard to find, carried on occasion by many—or not at all.

The Careerist Character of the Truman Staff

Almost all the members of the presidential staff had government
work histories far antedating their White House service. Take the "big
three" of the later period for example.

John Steelman had been commissioner of conciliation in the Labor
Department for ten years before the brief venture in private life which
ended with his being called to the White House in 1945. Charles Murphy
had spent thirteen years in the office of the Senate Legislative Counsel
before his appointment early in 1947 as an administrative assistant to the
president. Matt Connelly had worked on Capitol Hill since the mid
thirties, where he held a succession of staff investigator posts for congressional committees, leading to his Truman Committee assignment and
thence to the White House.

The backgrounds of these men have particular significance in helping to explain their respective points of view and work methods as
presidential aides. But there is general significance, too, in the fact that
all of them had come to the White House from the surrounding bureaucracy, from one end of Pennsylvania Avenue or the other.

And what was true of these three was emphatically so with the lesser
staff. Tubby and Perlmeter, the two assistant press secretaries under
Short, came from the press relations offices of State and Internal Revenue,
respectively. Joseph Feeny, Connelly's assistant in the last year (there
had been two the previous year), had spent the seven years before his
1950 White House appointment as a congressional liaison officer for the
navy. Philleo Nash, Niles's assistant, was for several years an OWI race-
relations expert before coming to the White House in 1945.

Thus, the members of Truman's staff came typically from elsewhere
in the government. But that is not the whole story. For the largest single
group of staff aides came not only from the government, but from a
single agency, the Bureau of the Budget.

Run down the list: Stowe and Bell, both administrative assistants to
the president; Neustadt, Murphy's assistant; Harold Enarson and Russell
Andrews, Steelman's aides; Milton Kayle, in Stowe's office; and Ken
Hechler, Lloyd's assistant—all seven of these men, a third of the total
civilian staff, came out of the Bureau of the Budget, most of them without even a break in service.

This influx from the Bureau of the Budget was the natural result of
James Webb's extraordinarily successful effort to make himself and his
bureau a useful underpinning for the president and the White House in

those early, frantically uncertain years of the Truman staff's development. During Webb's years, the Budget Bureau's staff resources were made available to—and used by—the White House more freely and informally than ever before. And later, when the bureau as an organization retreated to a more normal, institutional role, there remained that heavy repository of transferred individuals, ex-budgeteers who had become full-fledged White House staffers.

Staff Access to the President

Six mornings a week it was Truman's custom to meet for half an hour with the senior members of his staff. During the last three or four years of the administration this group included all the presidentially appointed staff—the assistant, the counsel, the secretaries and administrative assistants to the president—along with the three military aides and the executive clerk.

These staff meetings were not primarily high strategy or policy sessions; they were not so much group discussions as a means whereby each participant could receive and report on assignments, in quick time, and hear something of what his colleagues were doing. The president ordinarily went around the circle, handing out papers or making inquiries and affording each staff member an opportunity to raise any matter he chose.

A great deal of routine business was transacted in this fashion. As far as the military aides were concerned, this was their chief opportunity to settle details about such matters as plans for the presidential plane, the yacht, the Little White House at Key West, and so forth. As far as the civilian staff was concerned, these meetings rarely afforded the time or atmosphere for full dress briefings, discussions, and decisions on major matters—and were rarely used for such—but they did provide a guaranteed daily means for transacting day-to-day business requiring the president's attention. And the staff meetings were useful, too, as a means of glueing together in a flexible, informal way the divergent daily interests and activities of the several individuals concerned.

Apart from these regular meetings, the senior civilians had as much access to the president, day or night, as his outside appointments and their sense of discretion allowed. His door was always open in emergencies, at any hour. While Connelly occasionally delayed his colleagues, he never presumed to deny them access for more than a few hours at a time. And though Connelly's own access was always assured, Murphy, Steelman, and Short managed to see the president almost as often as they might have wished and usually with relatively little delay.

In addition to the staff's access to him, the president had access to his staff and made considerable use of it. Unlike F.D.R., Truman was physically able to move about the White House at will. Particularly in the mornings between about 8:30 and 9:30, the president often bobbed into an office to discuss something that had occurred to him overnight or to give a decision on a matter that had earlier been left for him to study. Murphy and Short, particularly, were the objects of these excursions, and they, in turn, were habitual visitors to the president's office during these free moments early in the morning.

CHARLES S. MURPHY

Mr. Truman set out to do the best job he could; I suspect that his ambition was to be a good president rather than a great president. I believe his experience demonstrates that if one does a good enough job of being a good president, he becomes, in fact, a great president. I suspect it is also true that one who strives too hard and too consciously for greatness might end up being not even a good president.

Mr. Truman's approach to the presidency involved many elements that one might usefully bring to any job. By his very example, he was a great teacher. Many of the lessons he taught are transferable not only to other occupants of the Oval Office, but to the whole spectrum of human affairs.

I wish to speak first of President Truman's gift for simplification. Not only could he simplify complex matters, he could also keep simple matters simple. Both are important. I mention this gift for simplification first not because it is necessarily of first importance, but because of its pertinence to my purpose here. I wish to deal as clearly—and, therefore, as simply—as I can—with some rather complex matters, as well as with some other critical matters so simple they are frequently overlooked in discussing the awesome office of the presidency. Unfortunately, my talent for simplification is not nearly as great as President Truman's.

Some forty-odd years ago—just after the repeal of Prohibition—a witness for the California wine industry was appearing before the Senate Finance Committee in support of an amendment to liberalize the labeling of wine. He complained about the federal Alcohol Administration's restrictive interpretation of the existing law, saying, "They have reduced the amplitude of the purview thereof to an inconsequential latitude." Well, if President Truman had been making the same point, he certainly would not have said it that way, and everyone would have understood what he meant.

He said that his idea of a speech was "a direct statement of the facts without trimmings and without oratory."

To express one's self in language that is simple and also precise requires, first of all, precise thinking. This is excellent mental discipline; and if it is practiced hard enough over the years, it can get to be a way of life. I believe this was the case for President Truman. I do not know the extent to which it is a natural talent or an acquired skill, but I do believe he felt he had mastered an idea only when he could express it in simple terms. And I must say that on more than one occasion when we were wrestling with an idea together, I didn't understand it either until he put it in simple terms.

When speaking of the American presidency, it may be asking too much to say "keep it simple," but serious efforts in that direction are likely to produce good results.

I will not dwell at length on how hard Mr. Truman worked at his job as president; this is not an unusual trait among American presidents. I will simply record that for seven years and nine months he spent virtually every waking moment working at being president.

It is hard to convey the intensity that this continuous effort requires. The most nearly comparable effort which occurs to me, and one that is widely shared, is "cramming" for and taking examinations. If you think of stretching those few days of intensive study into a continuous period of almost eight years, you begin to get the idea. Fortunately, the human mind and body are sufficiently adaptable to sustain this kind of continuous effort provided one has the will.

Mr. Truman was an orderly president. He was not a fanatic about this kind of thing, but he was neat in his dress, neat in his personal habits, and he had a regular daily schedule which he followed closely unless there was some particular reason for departing from it. And when he did rearrange his schedule, it was usually to accommodate others.

Some may think that it is relatively unimportant for the president to follow a regular schedule, but they are wrong. The president must accomplish an enormous amount of work and he must have people to help him. To have an opportunity to do their part, they need to be able to plan their own schedules and to keep them. Thus, it makes a great deal of difference in Washington if the president has his lunch regularly at the normal luncheon hour.

President Truman understood very well the importance of regulating his own schedule to fit the needs of his staff for timely guidance and directions. For example, "speech conferences" with the staff were set more often at times of my suggestion than of his. If his schedule was so tight that they could not be fitted in during the day, he would come back to the Cabinet Room in the evening—and he would come cheerfully. It is a unique experience to be telling the president of the United States he has come back to the office for a meeting after dinner—and, of course, I never put it in just that way.

Speaking of the staff, when I think of President Truman I often think of an advertisement that was current some years ago: "Tough but, oh, so gentle." In many ways, President Truman really was as tough as a boot, but with his personal staff he was extremely gentle. In fact, he was more lenient at times than he should have been, and that got him into trouble more than once. On the other hand, the staff returned his kindness with an extraordinary amount of hard work, voluntary overtime, and wholehearted, single-minded devotion.

The ways in which he showed consideration for his staff were countless, and Mrs. Truman joined him in this. I am sure that on her part, this was a natural manifestation of the nobility and generosity of her nature. I am sure, too, that this was the real motivating factor for him. But I also suspect he was quite conscious of the dividends this approach brought him in terms of extra effort from his staff.

There are different kinds of inspirational leadership. This particular kind might be the goal for almost anyone in a position of leadership. I commend Mr. Truman's style to executives everywhere as a possible means of getting more work, better work, and happier work from their employees. But remember that one prerequisite for its success is that the man at the top has to work harder than anyone else.

From start to finish, Mr. Truman regarded the office of president of the United States with enormous respect and his tenure there as a trust of the highest order. He was not sanctimonious; at the same time, however, he was completely incapable of doing anything as president that he thought was wrong. The problems of the presidency are so complicated and unprecedented that—for all of Mr. Truman's wisdom and talent for simplification—it was frequently difficult to tell what action was right and what was wrong in a particular situation; but what he thought was right was what he did.

He used to say to me, "Murph, I can't do that. It wouldn't be right." He didn't say, "I won't"; he said, "I can't." That was the only reason he gave and the only reason he needed. If I pressed him about some of these things, as I did on occasion, he would get more formal and call me "Murphy."

Much has been said about President Truman's courage, but I do not know how much credit he is entitled to on this score. I have frequently heard that the highest form of courage is to be brave even when you are afraid. As far as I was able to tell, however, President Truman was never afraid of anything. So that leaves me with the philosophical question of how courageous a man can be if fear is absent from his make-up.

President Truman never stopped studying, never stopped learning. As long as he was in the White House, he made a conscious and deliberate effort to learn how to be a better president. He was almost sixty-one years old when he came to the presidency, almost sixty-nine when he left it. But few men at any age have such an intensive, productive, and successful learning experience.

He learned by choice, not just as a by-product of experience. Although he was by far the wisest and most knowledgeable man among the group that worked with and for him, he always kept trying to learn something from the rest of us. He made it extremely easy for his staff to tell him what they really thought—whether it was yes, no, or maybe. Harry Truman was not surrounded by yes-men. We all knew who was boss, and we accepted his decisions and followed his orders. But we were encouraged to be both honest and candid in expressing our views.

I have heard, with some amusement, discussions of an alleged battle between liberals and conservatives for President Truman's mind. I would note first that he had a mind of his own and made it up for himself. And on most of the issues that usually distinguish liberals from conservatives in our political idiom, he was a liberal before he came to the White House and remained one all the time he was there. His liberalism was based on practical knowledge from earlier experiences and on his study of history; they were views he held with deep conviction.

He was not what you would call a professing liberal. Indeed, he seemed to have some distaste for persons who flaunted their liberalism. But on the issues, there was never any real doubt in my mind about where he stood and was going to continue to stand. Within his official family he always had a few conservatives whose views on social and economic issues differed sharply from his own. I asked him why he did this. His answer essentially paraphrased his words in *Mr. President:*

> I like to have people understand each other, and that is why I have every shade of public opinion in my Cabinet. . . .
> I have got a cross section of the thought and economics of the whole population of the United States in the Cabinet, from left to right. And this makes for valuable discussions, and the only way you can get ideas. And I let everybody have his say before I come to a conclusion and decide on a final course of action.

I have heard it said that President Truman was not aware of the battle for his mind that was going on around him. It would be closer to the truth, I think, to say that he was drawing up the battle plans for both sides.

The White House Staff: Later Period

President Truman did not take the liberal position on every economic question. For example, he had an unshakeable belief in the virtues of a balanced budget. He carried this belief with him when he left the White House. In 1963, President Kennedy recommended a tax cut at a time when he did not expect it to result in a balanced budget. President Truman, in New York City at the time, was asked about this on his morning walk by a newspaperman; the former president replied that he did not think taxes should be cut until the budget was balanced. Understandably, the comment bothered President Kennedy, who sent me to talk to President Truman about it. I did so. Finally President Truman said that although he was extremely sorry to have caused any trouble for President Kennedy, he could not retract what he had said because that was what he believed. But he said he would try to keep quiet on the subject thereafter. I reported this to President Kennedy, and so far as I know, that ended the matter.

I spoke earlier about President Truman's orderliness. This was manifest also in his continuing and substantial moves to improve the organization of the presidential office—the institutional aids to the presidency. The need for this was brought home to him very sharply by his own sudden succession to the presidency and the lack of preparation for that transition. I believe that Mr. Truman had seen President Roosevelt privately only three times, each very briefly, since his inauguration as vice-president and that no provision had been made to keep him informed of matters in the executive branch. This was far less troublesome in the domestic field than in defense and foreign affairs because Mr. Truman's experience in the Senate had given him an intimate knowledge of domestic issues and problems.

In defense matters and in foreign affairs, the new president felt his lack of current information very keenly. He did several things about this. First, he resolved to try to see that those who might succeed to the presidency thereafter would be fully and currently briefed on defense and foreign affairs. He arranged such briefings for the man in line to succeed him in the event of death or disability; and during the 1948 and 1952 campaigns, he also arranged such briefings for the Republican candidates. This was Mr. Truman's idea. Next, when he first came to the White House, he set about studying day and night until he had caught up on the information that was available. And soon he set about improving the machinery for gathering and evaluating information.

He put it this way in *Mr. President:*

> One of the basic things I did was to set up a Central Intelligence Agency. Admirals Leahy and Souers, and the State, Defense, Treasury and Commerce Departments all helped me to set it up. . . .

Charles S. Murphy

Strange as it may seem, the President up to that time was not completely informed as to what was taking place in the world. Messages that came to the different departments of the executive branch often were not relayed to him because some official did not think it was necessary to inform the President. The President did not see many useful cables and telegrams that came from different American representatives abroad. . . .

I decided to put an end to this state of affairs. . . .

The Central Intelligence Agency now co-ordinates all the information that is available to the State Department, the Department of Defense, and the individual offices of the Army, Navy and Air Force, the Department of Commerce, and the Treasury. In this way I am able to get a concentrated survey of everything that takes place. If I need any elaboration I ask for it. I get a report from the Central Intelligence Agency every morning. In cases of emergency I get special reports. I get special reports on the situation in Korea throughout the day. I get a special report every day from the Secretary of State covering the entire diplomatic field. And once a week the director of the Central Intelligency Agency comes to see me and makes a personal report.

Next we should note the creation of the National Security Council as a major presidential staff agency to provide continuing analysis and policy advice on defense, foreign policy, and security matters. The NSC became an extremely valuable aid to the president.

As I look back to consider who was President Truman's principal White House staff man for defense and foreign policy, I conclude that he himself was. It also occurs to me, somewhat ruefully, that perhaps this is why his presidency is so much more highly regarded in terms of foreign policy than in some other respects.

Intelligence reports were brought in each morning by the staff of the National Security Council and the president's naval aide, who spent about thirty minutes going over them with the president. Once each week, the director of the CIA joined these meetings for a more extensive review. No other staff members were present.

The president met periodically with the Joint Chiefs of Staff. Usually, no one else attended these meetings.

He met frequently with the secretaries of state and defense, both together and separately. It was usually in these meetings that policy questions in the fields of defense and foreign policy were raised and settled. These cabinet officers usually got "the word" firsthand from the president himself.

No part of the civilian White House staff had a major and continuing responsibility for staff work in the defense and foreign policy fields such as apparently exists today. The National Security Council and its staff perhaps performed much of this function. Otherwise, the White House staff was generally assigned to work on matters in these fields on an ad hoc basis. For example, one of my early assignments in 1947 was to work with Gen. Lauris Norstad and Adm. Forrest Sherman in preparing the "unification" bill which created the Department of Defense [initially, the National Military Establishment], the National Security Council, and the National Security Resources Board. Later that same year, I was assigned to work on drawing up the program of interim aid for Europe that preceded the Marshall Plan.

The special counsel to the president received more assignments in the foreign policy and security fields than other members of the White House staff because of his regular responsibility for the staff work on presidential speeches and messages to Congress. The president, of course, made speeches and sent messages on most of his major policies and actions. It follows that those who worked on the speeches and messages got a crack at almost everything. Frequently, the work went on at two levels—president to cabinet members, White House staff to departmental staff. This system worked pretty well, but sometimes with amusing side effects.

I remember once we had labored long, through many drafts and many conferences, on an important message to Congress and finally met for the final "freezing session" with the president and cabinet members. General Marshall, who must have been secretary of state at the time and who had not participated in the earlier drafting sessions at the White House, pulled a document from his pocket and from time to time during the discussion would ask about including in the message some language he would read from this document. After several of these interventions, Clark Clifford, who was then special counsel, said, "General, may I ask, what is that document from which you are reading?" General Marshall replied, with some emphasis, "It's a copy of the draft I sent to you as my recommendation as to what the message should say." I'm afraid he thought his views had not been given "due process."

When I became special counsel, I got into the foreign policy and defense problems more deeply than before—largely by the speech-message route. In fact, my initiation in 1950 was quite vigorous, with NSC-68 and Korea. This was a strenuous period that involved a basic redirection of our defense posture. A number of messages were sent to Congress reporting on the situation in Korea and asking for additional legislation and appropriations. Toward the end of the year, the president sent a special message requesting massive new appropriations for defense. The need was urgent as well as great. At the staff level, we were struggling mightily; our efforts reflected the decisions we had been handed, but there were some critical gaps in these decisions. One was the exact amount of money to be requested. We could not get an estimate from the Department of Defense, and time was running out.

I was thoroughly persuaded by then that whatever we asked for would not be enough. So I filled in the blank space in the draft with the highest number I had heard anyone mention and sent it to General Marshall for clearance. His response was to send a message to the president saying that he would like to know who was secretary of defense— Was it he or was it someone on the White House staff? But I got my number!

In the domestic field, President Truman delegated or assigned a great many responsibilities to members of his White House staff on a continuing basis. While it is true that a line cannot be drawn separating the assignments of all his staff members between domestic and foreign affairs (the press secretary, for example, obviously dealt with both), I do tend to think of the organization of the staff predominantly in terms of domestic affairs.

The Truman staff operated as staff rather than as line officers. Cabinet members and agency heads had direct access to the president as a matter of right and were not subject to orders from the White House staff. The president insisted on dealing personally with the director of

UPI

President Truman looks on as Charles S. Murphy is sworn in as special counsel by Tom C. Clark, associate justice of the Supreme Court, February 1, 1950.

the Bureau of the Budget and the Council of Economic Advisers and other Executive Office unit heads, although these personal dealings were supplemented by much joint work at the staff level.

I believe that President Truman had his staff organized just about right in terms of achieving a balance between definite, continuing responsibilities and the flexibility to meet special problems, having enough institutionalization but not too much, distributing responsibility among staff members so that they could operate effectively but were not unduly tempted to build their own empires, and keeping the number of staff members who reported directly to him both manageable and diverse. Incidentally, President Truman was quite an ego deflator in a gentle way, and a couple of his staff were even more effective, in a way that was not gentle at all.

During the Truman administration there were also major changes in the parts of the president's staff that are within the Executive Office but outside the White House office. Notably, these include the establishment of the Council of Economic Advisers in 1946 and the National Security Council and the National Security Resources Board in 1947. The NSRB later was superseded by the Office of Defense Mobilization to meet the exigencies of the Korean War.

Overall, I believe that President Truman did so much to strengthen the institutional aids to the presidency that the changes can properly be regarded as a "quiet revolution" of major proportions. Most of the reforms he instituted appear to have endured, though there have been subsequent changes, of course. I am not prepared to say whether all these changes are improvements or not; I believe that some of them are.

Much has been said—and rightly so—about President Truman's great decisions. Nothing can account for the correctness of so many momentous decisions except his own ultimate wisdom and judgment. Nevertheless, he did have a technique for mobilizing brains, as well as facts, to help him reach decisions and to help him plan for the future—a talent worthy of more attention than it has received. I can do little more here than list some examples, but I hope this can be the subject of more extensive study.

Before President Truman decided to drop the atomic bomb, he appointed a very distinguished civilian committee to study and advise him on the moral and political issues as well as the military ones.

The critical decision in favor of civilian control of nuclear energy was reached with the advice of a distinguished committee that studied the questions in great depth.

The ultimate commitment to the Marshall Plan was preceded by studies of three special committees as well as very extensive study within various government departments and agencies.

The decision to resist aggression in Korea was reached over the course of two days and nights of intensive discussions with the government's top civilian and military leaders, drawing upon all the knowledge, skills, and judgment they possessed.

The order to relieve General MacArthur of his command was issued only after the president had discussed the matter for days with the secretary of state, the secretary of defense, the Joint Chiefs of Staff, and his special assistant for foreign affairs and had received their unanimous advice that the action was necessary.

Another group of examples of President Truman's technique of organizing brains is represented by the commissions he appointed to study and make recommendations on important national problems and policies. These commissions included:

1. National Commission on Higher Education
2. Advisory Commission on Universal Training
3. President's Committee on Civil Rights
4. President's Committee on Equality of Treatment and Opportunity in the Armed Forces
5. Commission on Migratory Labor
6. Advisory Committee on Management
7. President's Scientific Research Board
8. International Development Advisory Board
9. President's Communications Policy Board
10. President's Airport Commission
11. President's Commission on Immigration and Naturalization
12. President's Materials Policy Commission
13. Water Resources Policy Commission
14. President's Commission on Health Needs of the Nation

Although this list is not complete, it is impressive. I have long felt that the range of President Truman's studies and policy statements covered every topic of significance to the American government at least once. All of us could profit from a review of the reports of the study committees and commissions he appointed. His mobilization of this kind of talent is clearly the work of a man who had his eyes on the future as well as the present.

KEN HECHLER

[NOTE: These notes made in 1952 reflect staff work on a nonmajor address, involving primarily the Department of State. Other related material in the Truman Library and Department of State files has not been examined.]

On January 11, 1952, Frederick C. Oechsner, acting special assistant to the assistant secretary of state for public affairs, sent a memorandum to Assistant Press Secretary Roger Tubby, outlining a program for President Truman's participation in ceremonies marking the tenth anniversary of the Voice of America, which was to be celebrated on February 22, 1952 (Washington's Birthday). The original idea was for President Truman to deliver a five-minute address on or near the U.S. Coast Guard vessel *Courier*, which was equipped to transmit and rebroadcast the Voice of America signals with tremendous power. The program was scheduled for between 2 and 4 P.M. on February 22 and was to include remarks by the secretaries of state and treasury, the commandant of the Coast Guard, and several members of Congress. It was hoped that Senators Lodge, Benton, and Mundt would participate.

On several occasions early in February, there was some brief mention of the State Department request. Since February 22 was a holiday and the president planned to be cruising on the *Williamsburg* at that time, he requested that the Voice of America program be shifted to Sunday afternoon, February 24, at 3 P.M. This would enable the president to complete his cruise uninterrupted, step off the *Williamsburg*, and take part in the *Courier* ceremonies at the Navy Yard without much lost motion. The Department of State wanted members of Congress from the Appropriations, Foreign Affairs, and Foreign Relations committees there because of their role in funding the Voice of America. In discussions at the White House staff meetings, the occasion was described as an opportunity for psychological warfare, rather than simply as a way to

128

commemorate the achievements of the Voice of America on its tenth anniversary.

Primary responsibility for drafting the president's remarks was given to David Lloyd. On February 8, Lloyd handed me Oechsner's memorandum, along with a first draft by the State Department which Lloyd labeled as "rather rambling and tepid." To get started on a discussion of a new theme, Lloyd called a meeting for Monday, February 11, attended by Joseph Phillips and Ben Crosby of the Office of Public Affairs at the Department of State; Walworth Barbour, acting director of the Office of Eastern European Affairs at State; Marshall Shulman, Secretary Acheson's special assistant and top speech writer; and myself. Roger Tubby was to have been there, but he was ill that day.

At the meeting, Barbour and Phillips warned that many Western European countries were actually afraid of this type of propagandistic operation; and Barbour and Phillips felt it was dangerous to give the Western Europeans strong evidence that we were inciting the Soviet Union. We generally agreed that the best approach would be for the president to emphasize that this ship was on a mission of peace rather than to signal the start of a large-scale, aggressive or provocative program.

On Saturday, February 15, Ben Crosby called me to say that because of strikes, lack of spare parts, etc., the captain of the Coast Guard ship was not sure he could get the *Courier* to Washington in time for the February 24 ceremonies. Understandably, Crosby was very agitated. I told him that it was the State Department's responsibility to get the vessel to Washington since they had committed the president to a definite speaking date. The State Department then turned to the assistant press secretary, Irv Perlmeter, for help in getting the White House to intervene. Perlmeter told me that the State Department ought to fly the ship down to Washington piece by piece if necessary once they had committed the president to the date of February 24.

But the problem remained and was bucked back to the White House again. So at a White House staff meeting discussion, the president agreed to postpone the speaking date until March 4. Now, with the date firmly set, getting a good draft together became a must. On Thursday morning, February 27, I telephoned Joe Phillips at the State Department and said it was imperative that we have the State Department's current ideas by that afternoon. At a meeting that morning in Charles Murphy's office with Dave Bell and myself, I remarked that the State Department was concerned that the president's remarks might be "too provocative." Dave Bell exploded: "What can a little ship do? It has no guns. It just has a radio. There's nothing provocative about that, for crying out loud!"

The White House Staff: Later Period

Late Thursday afternoon, State sent over their draft, along with two other drafts which Phillips said they had rejected but sent along "because we might want to see them." Lloyd looked them over and then suggested we concentrate on broadcasting a message of peace and friendship directly to the peoples of the Soviet Union and China. Lloyd pointed out that we had helped both nations when they were invaded and suggested I look into the 1951 congressional resolution of friendship for the peoples of the Soviet Union, which had been transmitted to President Shvernik. I promised to produce a new draft by the next morning.

I read the congressional resolution, but found little inspiration except in the technique of piercing the Iron Curtain to get directly to the Russian people. Then I read the State Department draft and picked out those portions that seemed appropriate. But the central theme was missing. In desperation, I picked up the two "rejected" State Department drafts. Buried in one draft was a brilliant phrase, thrown in by a chap named Holder of the Eastern European Affairs desk, to the effect that the ship carried not weapons of destruction but a cargo of truth. I decided to salvage this concept and feature it, and the "cargo of truth" phrase not only stayed in every subsequent draft but also was selected as the title of the address.

The draft started with a brief description of the mission of the ship and led into the "cargo of truth." Then I worked in the idea that many peoples had contributed to the construction of the ship. There followed a simple message to the peoples behind the Iron Curtain. Then to personalize the president's message came this sentence: "I say to you with all my heart that we yearn for peace, and we want to work with you to secure peace." (This latter thought survived.) I wasted some time going through John Masefield's poems, including one called "Truth," which included a phrase about man having "but an hour of breath to build a ship of Truth in which his soul may sail," but it turned out to be a bit macabre for this purpose.

Dave Lloyd took the draft and polished it. He observed that "this was not a Christmas speech" as he struck out the last four words of the expressed aim: "to bring peace on earth, good will toward men." I protested that this was a natural phrase, but Dave took it out. (It did not reappear, incidentally, until the president in delivering the speech looked up from his manuscript when he read "peace on earth" and ad-libbed "and good will to all men.")

Some phone calls came in from the State Department, imploring us to emphasize that the ship was only one part of our whole "campaign of truth" and not to give the impression this was everything. Lloyd worked this in during the day on Friday (February 29). Jim Loeb (recently added to Charles Murphy's staff) looked at my draft and made a few useful suggestions. One was that we use the *Courier*'s name and indicate that it was carrying a message. Jim also suggested that I strike out the section that indicated that listeners were assembled peacefully to hear the message, as though at corner grocery stores. After some discussion, Lloyd rewrote the ending so it would sound less like we were working closely together with the peoples of the Soviet Union and China.

Just before lunch on Friday, February 29, Lloyd and I spent about an hour and a half tightening up the draft, pepping it up a little, and honing it down to three legal-sized pages. Then we sent copies over to Charlie Murphy and to State. State had two comments: first, that the ship was broadcasting in a manner designed to increase the volume; and second, to say that we should have faith that all peoples will "once again" walk in the sunlight of peace and justice was not historically accurate, inasmuch as some people had not always lived in peace and justice.

Murphy's reaction was that the three-page draft was too thin and could use more affirmative substance. He rewrote the middle section, adding some stirring phrases about the meaning of truth and its relation to peace. He also added a paragraph denouncing the wickedness of the Communist doctrine.

Just after lunch on Saturday, March 1, Murphy, Bell, Loeb, and I assembled in Murphy's office to review the redraft. Lloyd attacked the paragraph about the wickedness of communism, contending we were directing a message to these people and should not denounce them as wicked before we extended the olive branch of friendship. After some argument about the relation of this thought to the domestic political situation, the phrases were eventually dropped.

We had one sentence that read: "Our arguments, no matter how meritorious, are not going to influence people who never hear them." Dave Bell said, "My Aunt Minnie would have to stop and think when you got to the word *meritorious*," and he suggested replacing it with *good.* Jim Loeb fought hard on this, saying that an argument could be a good one, without necessarily being a right one, so he suggested *valid* as an adjective. Whereupon, Bell commented: "Oh, Jim, you're splitting hairs." Loeb responded: "Isn't that what we're supposed to be doing here?" After some laughter, the adjective *good* remained.

In commenting on the sentence, "We must use vigorous, hard-hitting methods," Murphy said that "methods" sounded too much like government gobbledegook. Suddenly he asked, "What was that thing Phil Spitalny and his all-girl orchestra used to open their program with?" Bell laughed and sang out, "We must be vigilant, we must be diligent, American Patrol!"

The White House Staff: Later Period

In my first draft, I had the phrase: "As president of the United States, I say with all my heart that we yearn for peace. . . ." Dave Bell contended that *yearn* always made him think of someone sitting off in a corner and sobbing for something he couldn't get. But for reasons I couldn't quite comprehend, the word *yearn* stayed.

About 2:30 P.M. on Saturday, March 1, the revised draft was sent to the White House staff room for retyping. Murphy asked me to clear it with the State Department so we could have it ready for a freezing session with the president at noon Monday. This was a pretty tough assignment, since everybody had gone home over the weekend.

The speech was retyped by 4 P.M. I roused Marshall Shulman at home. He protested he had had a total of four hours of sleep in the past three days preparing Dean Acheson's television speech of the night before reviewing the Lisbon conference. We agreed that it would be difficult to get clearance at that hour and decided to have a crash clearance session early Monday morning. By 10 A.M. Monday, however, there were agonized wails from the State Department. They were bitterly upset by the omission of the paragraph that the *Courier* was only one small part of the Voice of America and the "campaign of truth." They strongly insisted that this paragraph be reinserted and that there also must be included something on the exchange-of-persons program.

Lloyd harrumphed: "I'll put in the libraries and information centers, but unless and until the State Department gets a better phrase for 'exchange of persons,' I refuse to have the president endorse something that sounds so much like white slave traffic." At 1 P.M., Monday, March 3, the speech was again retyped. Murphy then asked for a final review of the draft with Lloyd and me prior to the scheduled 4 P.M. freezing session. The changes were generally minor, like the last-minute protest by the State Department objecting to the statement that Russian and Chinese rulers were attacking us, in light of the fact there was no physical attack. I suggested *assailing* instead of *attacking*, which was accepted all around.

We got the eight copies of the finally retyped *Courier* speech just about at 4 P.M., and I brought them to the Cabinet Room. There Murphy, Bell, George Elsey, and Marshall Shulman were hard at work on the mutual security message to Congress, which was due to be sent to Capitol Hill within forty-eight hours. Drafts, books, papers, and notes were splattered all over the Cabinet Room; and in the midst of the confusion the president came in. He immediately said to George Elsey, "Well, having you here is just like old times." Elsey and Shulman swept up their papers and adjourned to work on the mutual security message elsewhere.

Then Press Secretary Joe Short came in. Bell and Murphy sat to the president's right; Short, Lloyd, and I sat to his left.

Fingering the *Courier* draft, the president commented: "Well, this certainly has the virtue of brevity. That's more than you can say for the one I have to give on Thursday on mutual security. I worked on that one last night, and the Madam says it's a darned good speech—and she's my best critic. I'm going to work on the Tuesday speech this evening. By the way, can you get me a final of the Thursday speech by Tuesday because I want to have at least two days to work it over before delivering it?"

Murphy and Bell pursed their lips into a silent whistle. They had counted on finishing the message to Congress first and then going to work on the March 6 fireside chat on mutual security; now they knew they had to drop their work on the message and go to work on the fireside chat instead.

Someone asked the president how his eighty-nine-year-old mother-in-law, Mrs. Wallace, was getting along. The president said: "Well, she feels OK in the mornings, but not so good in the afternoons. I thought I ought to summon her sons, and they all came in. She appreciates the thought, but you know the old lady called them all in this morning and said: 'Boys, I want you to know that I love you even more for coming here this way. But I'm old enough to go, and you have big jobs to take care of back home. When I go, I'll know you've been here, so that's all that matters—you can go home now.'"

Then the president picked up the *Courier* draft and started reading it aloud, pausing after each page for comments. After the first page, Bell pointed out that there were an unusually large number of *s* sounds in the first two paragraphs: speaking, ship, special, ship, special, mission, precious, etc. The president laughed good-naturedly and responded: "That *s* sound doesn't bother me near as much since the dentist fixed my teeth. I don't whistle on 'em nearly as much as I used to, Dave."

Joe Short said, "Can't somebody get me a better and clearer page 3 so the girls in the Staff Room won't go blind retyping this?" I made a hurried search and discovered to my horror that the carbons were all faulty on page 3. The president quipped, "Page 3 has pernicious anemia."

Joe Short asked that a colon be inserted at one point, and the president recalled that "Charley Ross was the greatest guardian of the colon and the semi-colon in days gone by." I suggested that the word *particularly* be changed to *especially* since it was easier to pronounce, and the president said, "I'm 225 percent in favor of that change."

The president commented that the sentence about libraries, motion pictures, newspapers, and magazines was very dull. Lloyd pointed out how strongly the State Department had fought to leave it in. The president made a kindly, but somewhat derogatory remark about the ability of some people in the State Department to take a very simple and declarative statement and stretch it out into something of extreme complexity.

When we reached page 4, Bell wondered aloud how many people would understand the word *assailing*. Joe Short quickly defended *assailing*, stating it was a good old headline word which all newspapermen and readers would comprehend. There was a rather spirited discussion of the word, with attempts to find a substitute. I then made a rather weak pun: "Since it's a ship, isn't it OK to have it assailing?" There was deep silence; then with his deep Mississippi drawl, Joe Short expressed throaty disgust: "Oh, God, no!" But the president laughed enough to keep the word *assailing*, and that's the way he delivered it.

When he had finished reading and commenting, the president said: "Well, that's a very fine statement. I'm going to work on it some more tonight."

It was drizzling on the morning of March 4. I went aboard the *Courier* and up to the top deck, where there were seats for about two hundred people. The audience was enthusiastic. The president delivered his address in clear and measured tones. He had his heart in it, and the entire address was inspiringly delivered. The audience reaction was warm, positive, and enthusiastic. There was a genuine ring of conviction in the president's delivery. The chilled crowd gave him a rousing reception.

Within an hour of my return to the White House, I received three telephone calls—from Ben Crosby, Joe Phillips, and Doug Knox of the State Department. They all offered congratulations and said that the Department of State was highly pleased with the entire ceremony and in particular with the president's address.

I telephoned Bob Thompson, chief of publications at the State Department, and asked him for printed copies of the speech. Thompson did a quick and beautiful job on the printing, and we had the 1,500 copies by 9 A.M. March 5—less than twenty-four hours after the president delivered the speech. I called Charley VanDevender, director of publicity at the Democratic National Committee, and India Edwards, chairman of the Women's Division, and forwarded them copies when they were printed. I told Executive Clerk Bill Hopkins he could have five hundred copies for inclusion in the president's correspondence.

I asked Park Armstrong, special assistant to the secretary of state in charge of intelligence, to run a special survey abroad to gauge the reaction in foreign countries, and the results were enthusiastic and positive. Dave Lloyd said the president was highly pleased with the speech and had commented to him favorably on several occasions since its delivery. The newspaper and editorial reaction was very favorable, and they were still writing and editorializing about it on March 9—five days after the speech.

I called Frank Kelly of Senate majority leader Ernest McFarland's office and arranged to have him place the text of the speech, along with an editorial from the *New York Times*, in the *Congressional Record*. The *New York Times* editorial of March 5, 1952, read in part:

> Going over the heads of their Governments, President Truman yesterday broadcast directly to the peoples of Soviet Russia and Red China a message of peace, hope and friendship.
>
> He told the Soviet peoples and the Chinese that, contrary to the flood of lies and calumnies unloosed against us by Communist propaganda, we remain their friends. He recalled to them that only a decade ago we went to their aid to liberate them from the most savage invasions in history. Finally, he assured them that it is only the aggressive policies of their own rulers that compel us to arm in self-defense, and that if these rulers would abandon their senseless policy of hate and terror and follow the principles of peace there are no differences between us and their countries that cannot be settled by peaceful means.
>
> Mr. Truman spoke from the new radio ship Courier, which has been equipped for "Operation Vagabond" to carry the campaign of truth waged by the United States through the Voice of America closer to peoples behind the Iron Curtain. But in thus dedicating this new instrument of the campaign he also inaugurated a whole new phase of the campaign. For his broadcast was one of the most direct appeals made by an American President to the peoples of other countries over the heads of their hostile rulers since President Wilson's days.

ROBERT L. DENNISON

Questions have been raised about the structure of President Truman's staff and particularly whether he had a chief of staff. The answer to this is no. The president, through his regular morning staff meetings, eliminated the need for a chief of staff.

The titles of various staff members described in broad terms their primary duties—press secretary, appointments secretary, correspondence secretary, and so on. Many other tasks were assigned to members of the staff on an ad hoc basis. However remote, these usually had some relation to the member's primary responsibility. I will give some examples.

I was assigned the task of acting as a coordinator of federal maritime affairs, working principally with government claims of overpayment of construction subsidies to several of our largest shipping lines. Many departments of the government are involved in federal maritime matters —principally Justice, Commerce, Labor, State, and Defense. The president gave me the job probably because ships and defense matters were involved.

In another area, I recall the time when Louis Johnson closed a naval hospital at Long Beach. This caused a widespread adverse public reaction because this hospital was involved in treating paraplegic veterans. I was given the job of chairing a committee, which included Dr. Howard Rusk and Dr. Howard Abramson, to get matters straightened out. Our efforts led to certain changes within the medical division of the Veterans Administration and indeed in the VA itself.

Here the basic difficulty arose through closing a *naval* hospital, so the president again assigned the clean-up task to me.

I am sure other staff members had the same experience with ad hoc assignments. In my case they occupied a great deal more time than the protocol and liaison duties of a naval aide. I could not have begun to handle these assigned duties without the wholehearted, highly professional assistance and advice I received from the Bureau of the Budget.

Jim Webb, Elmer Staats, and Roger Jones were some of those I remember best. Of course the members of the president's staff helped each other; to me, working with such a group was tremendously rewarding.

While it is true that the president had no chief of staff, either designated or "acting," the commander in chief did have a chief of staff. Fleet Admiral William D. Leahy was chief of staff to the commander in chief under Roosevelt and subsequently under Truman. Because of his position and relative seniority, he was presiding officer at the meetings of the Joint Chiefs of Staff.

Under the National Security Act of 1947 the Joint Chiefs organization was given statutory recognition; and when the position of chairman was established, General of the Army Omar Bradley became the first chairman.

Before Admiral Leahy left the White House, President Truman called us to meet with him. He told Admiral Leahy that he wanted arrangements made so that all the information that Admiral Leahy had been receiving from the Joint Chiefs of Staff, the State Department, the Atomic Energy Commission, and so forth should be sent to me so that I could carry on with the briefings as Admiral Leahy had previously done. Again, although this task was outside the normal duties of a naval aide, the assignment was a logical one.

I feel I should attempt to explain certain attitudes and characteristics of the president as I saw them. My explanations may help resolve or clarify some seeming inconsistencies or conflicting views in the record.

The general impression created by the president was that he was simple, honest, forceful, and direct. All these adjectives apply except for "simple." He was the most complex man I have ever known and the most interesting. It was only after about two years of association that I felt I had his full confidence. Still, no matter what his worries or concerns were, he always appeared patient and willing to listen to other people's problems.

He also had a strong sense of custodial responsibility for the office of the presidency and was ready to protect all the powers of this office.

President Truman saw himself in three distinct and separate roles—first as president of all the people, second as commander in chief of the armed forces, and third as the leader of the Democratic party. He always knew in his words or actions which of these roles he was portraying. The one possible exception was his 1948 nonpolitical transcontinental railroad trip, which had strong overtones of domestic politics.

He sometimes carried this separation to extremes. For example, in various inscriptions to me, he consistently refers to himself as "Your Commander in Chief" or "Your former Commander in Chief."

The White House Staff: Later Period

On several occasions I heard the president mention an incident he had witnessed in World War I involving the reprimand of an officer by his senior before the officer's own troops. This disgusted and dismayed the president; and he pointed out to me that when the president reprimanded someone, it came from the court of last resort and the poor victim had no place to go.

Only once did I hear the president reprimand anyone. On this occasion I was briefing the president in his office when a staff member came in to report something to him. The president was incensed and spoke up in strong terms. The staff member immediately left and the president turned to me and said, "Bob, it hurt me to do that but it had to be done." I am sure he was right.

I have been with the president on occasions when he had what appeared to me to be a perfectly normal and amiable conversation with a caller. After the caller left, he would say to me, in effect, "I certainly set him straight," or, "I let him have it." The president's remarks seemed to me to have no conceivable relation to the conversation I had just heard. He may have been commenting on what he wished he had said or perhaps his words were too subtle for me to understand.

James Byrnes, then secretary of state, made a trip to Moscow in December 1945. On his return he stopped in New York City and made a strong policy statement before consulting with the president. Dean Acheson told me that Byrnes had told him that when he, Byrnes, later reported to the president they had a normal, friendly talk, no scoldings, no strong words. On the other hand, the president told Acheson that he had told Byrnes in no uncertain terms what he thought of his behavior.

One footnote on the president's distaste for reprimands. During a chat with the president I mentioned my admiration for Justice Holmes and noted that most of his minority opinions had, through the years, become the majority opinions on the Court. The president said he had no use for Holmes; his reason was that Holmes had bullied and humiliated young, inexperienced attorneys appearing before the Court.

There may be a general impression that the president made many "off-the-cuff" decisions; relieving General MacArthur is often given as one example. In this case, however, the president followed his standard procedure.

I once asked the president what his decision-making process was. He explained to me that his procedure involved four steps.

First, get all the facts you can, remembering that you seldom will have *all* the facts. If you do, the decision will be almost automatic.

Second, consult your trusted advisers but remember that the secretary of state is going to see the problem in the light of national policy considerations and the secretary of defense from the standpoint of national defense, etc. This may explain why some advisers left the president's office thinking each had sold his point of view as the solution to the problem, while the president had accepted it only as one factor in reaching his final decision.

Third, after gathering the facts and consulting with advisers, go off by yourself, evaluate your advice, and make your decision. (Up to this point there seems to be nothing unusual in the president's procedure. The method is almost standard. However, the president explained to me that the final point was the most important.)

Fourth, having made the decision, *never look back*. Go on to the next one.

Considering the many difficult, vital decisions that President Truman made, it seems evident that he was able to follow his own decision-making procedure.

I will end with a few brief remarks on the president's views concerning the cabinet and National Security Council.

There were some, James Forrestal for one, who believed that the cabinet should follow the British example with a cabinet secretariat, a formal agenda, prepared position papers, etc. I attended only a few cabinet meetings. They seemed to me to be rather dreary affairs with little being accomplished. I gathered from what the president told me that this was the way he wanted it. He didn't want anything resembling an executive committee. He felt he could meet with individual cabinet members any time he felt it was necessary and that that should suffice.

The National Security Council came into being during President Truman's administration. I gathered from things he told me that he felt it was rather unnecessary He explained to me that he could control the council by controlling the agenda for its meetings; and furthermore, when he chaired the meetings, he could control the trend and results of discussions. I have seen him do this and it was a great performance.

Working for and with the president (commander in chief) and with my colleagues was one of the most interesting and valuable experiences of my life. I learned more from President Truman than from any other man I ever knew, and I am forever grateful.

DISCUSSION

C. A. NEWLAND (chair): It might be helpful to review the White House staff as it looked toward the end of the Truman administration— its makeup, its recruitment, who the people were, what their functions were.

RICHARD E. NEUSTADT: As I recall, after Governor Harriman and his little staff moved into an Executive Office role and out of the White House per se, the number of full-time people who had something to do with policy was about twenty-two. Then there was Sidney Souers who was a consultant two or three days a week—I forget which—and several more people in such a status. Of the three military aides, Admiral Dennison was certainly in the policy business and not merely a specialized military functionary.

If I recall correctly, the press office had a press secretary and two, maybe three, assistants. Dr. Steelman had a couple of assistants, and one of the administrative assistants, David Stowe, worked with him.

Charlie Murphy had Dave Bell and Dave Lloyd, who had become administrative assistants, working with him, and I think he had two other assistants (of whom I was one). Then on all foreign policy messages and speeches Dean Acheson's personal assistant, Marshall Shulman, was ordinarily associated, so you could call that another hat or something. That makes four or five people around Murphy.

Don Dawson's was a two-man office as I remember. I think one ought to include Bill Hopkins who, though a careerist, performed functions that are now performed by layers of special assistants. Jimmy Lay should certainly be counted as a member of the staff. (Although he was performing a secretarial function, his entire staff was counted as being in the Executive Office as I recall.) Philleo Nash was there from first to last; I can't remember whether you had assistants or not—certainly not many?

Discussion

PHILLEO NASH: I was a vacant assistant to a vacancy at that point.

NEUSTADT: By contemporary standards it was a very small staff, but by 1952 it was a larger staff than Mr. Roosevelt's had been, though only by a very moderate amount.

NEWLAND: Let us look at that staff. Were there some factors about this staff that may not be in the records?

KEN HECHLER: It was a very informal staff even though everybody knew precisely what their lines of authority generally were. It was a happy staff and the morale was tremendously high. The reason for this was the personal interest that the president took in each individual, in his family and his personal life, as well as the opportunity, for example, to go down to Key West, Florida, for a work-play period every year. This has not yet been mentioned. It gave the morale of the White House staff a very important lift every year; the president and staff would go down at about Thanksgiving time and stay until nearly Christmas. The staff had an opportunity there to work closely together, as well as to play volleyball, fish, swim, and talk in relaxed circumstances with the president and his family. But in addition to that, on the job there were many factors that enabled us to work together more closely.

The White House mess, I think, was a contributing factor because in addition to the morning staff meeting, at noontime most of us would eat together and trade ideas back and forth as to what we were doing and what problems we were confronting.

One of the earliest things that happened to me when I joined the White House staff late in 1949, was that the president invited us all over to Blair House. He said he was "baching it" that night, that the "Boss" was in Missouri. We had a little staff dinner together and I was just on cloud nine: Here you are, and here is the president of the United States, playing the piano, in the shadow of the portraits of Monroe and Jefferson and Jackson, making you feel that you are part of a momentous time in history. Of all the jobs I have ever had, I have never seen higher morale nor more hard working people nor a group that got more fun out of its work.

DAVID H. STOWE: One of the things that impressed me was the change after the '48 election. The many things we said about the value of the staff really came into full focus during the second four years. The learning period had been accomplished; now Mr. Truman moved out into *his* program and *his* administration, and that infused a lot of vigor into the staff, through the staff meetings. We were watching things unfold as he would talk to us.

The White House Staff: Later Period

I do not want to pass up the opportunity to say that, as important as the staff meeting was, there was one individual who probably played, next to President Truman, the greatest role in coordinating the operation of the staff, and that was Bill Hopkins. Because Bill knew where *everything* was, he, in his own quiet way, was able to coordinate even those things that did not quite get coordinated in the staff meeting.

There was another interesting change in that a substantial number of new faces now appeared. There were six people who came over from the Bureau of the Budget: Dave Bell, Harold Enarson, Russ Andrews, Dick Neustadt, Milton Kayle, and Ken Hechler. So, added to a number of us who were career types, this marked the formation of a staff with government experience, people who knew the operation of the government and were able to coordinate.

Key West, Florida, gathering of the White House staff, November 26, 1951. *Left to right:* Roger W. Tubby, John R. Steelman, Kenneth W. Hechler, Dallas E. Halverstadt, Richard E. Neustadt, Gen. Harry H. Vaughn, Donald S. Dawson, Milton P. Kayle, President Truman, Russell P. Andrews, David Noyes.

Discussion

There was a period of time, certainly during the war under F.D.R., when the Bureau of the Budget became almost the center of the government's domestic operations. After President Truman came in, and particularly when James Webb became director of the budget, the Budget Bureau and the Treasury Department came to work closely together. The cooperation between Jim Webb and Secretary Snyder and their staffs in the entire budget operation became, perhaps of necessity, quite different than it had been during the Roosevelt period. Without knowing, I have the feeling that this was one of the coordinating movements that President Truman, in his own inimitable way, was able to accomplish to get the maximum value out of the Treasury and out of the Bureau of the Budget—two operations which inherently have to work in the same area with the same mind.

I see the second four years as a period of professionalism, generated by the leadership of the president and molded by his concept of cooperation and coordination.

NEWLAND: Dave, you mentioned that about a third of those twenty-two staff people came over from BOB. They came into a situation where there were others, like Matt Connelly and so on. What was the relationship between the people who came from BOB and those who had had long personal service with the president—some even while he was in the Senate.

Paul Begley, AFC

White House staff volleyball game (Margaret Truman setting up the ball), Key West, Florida, November 25, 1951.

The White House Staff: Later Period

STOWE: I can only answer for myself. I think all of us know the great value of Matt Connelly. I always found that the staff members who were there before I arrived and those who came after I did never had a moment's difficulty—the group just seemed to blend. I can't give you any particular device which blended it, but maybe others could.

ROGER TUBBY: I was not going to comment on that just yet, but I do want to point to the feeling of respect and affection and loyalty that we all had. I came to the White House from the State Department, and my associate, Irv Perlmeter, came from the Treasury—when Joe Short was press secretary. There were so many little personal things that meant so much, personal awareness of our individual lives, our family lives, that endeared President Truman to us. And I think he was as interested in those of us on the immediate staff as he was in the guards at the front gate or the other people on the White House staff. He was, I think, really just a great human being.

BETH SHORT: May I speak up on that? One of the things I remember best was the time Joe was being sworn in as press secretary. The ceremony was to be early in the morning, at 8 o'clock, and we did not know about it until the night before. I had three small children (two boys and a girl) to get ready, their suits washed, and so forth. One of the boys had two front teeth out at the time—he was nine—and he said, "I won't go. I'm not going to go see the president of the United States with two front teeth out. The rest of you can go, but I won't go."

We did finally get him into the president's office. Suddenly, after we had all spoken to the president, I looked around and he was not there any more and neither was my nine-year-old son. There were people waiting to greet the president, and Chief Justice Vinson was there to do the honors. Just about that time President Truman and Steve walked out from behind those circular curtains in the Oval Office, and the swearing in began.

On the way home I asked Stephen, "What was going on when you and the president disappeared?" He said, "You know, Mother, now I don't mind having those two front teeth out. The president took me behind the curtain to show me that he had a tooth out, and the only difference is, he is going to have his capped today and I have to wait until mine grows in."

There were so many things to make each individual proud and happy to work for President Truman. He has never gotten enough credit for being the first president to appoint a woman to the top staff.

When I got the call from Matt Connelly asking me if I would take Bill Hassett's job as one of the three top secretaries—this one in charge of correspondence—I said, "Matt, please tell the president that I feel just as Joe does, that when the president of the United States asks you to do a job, you, of course, do it as a patriotic citizen, but if he is asking me to do this as some kind of an honor or a way to help the Short family finances, I am sorry I cannot do it."

Matt said, "Oh, you know better than that, Beth, the president wouldn't . . ."

I said, "Well, you go tell the president that that's what I said."

He called me back after a while, and said, "The president said to ask you where do you think he was when you covered him for the Springfield, Missouri, newspaper back in 1930-something, when he was running for the Senate? How do you suppose it was that the only time he asked you to ride on the *Independence* was when he was going to the Thirty-fifth Division reunion at Springfield? He is a good politician, and he knows that you wrote for the Associated Press and covered Mrs. Roosevelt and the president at various times, and he wants you to know that he wants you to do this job and he wants you to start tomorrow or the next day."

I hardly had a chance to take a breath before Matt added, "The whole top staff is going out for Adlai Stevenson on a whistlestop, and you will be the only one left at the White House, and they are leaving in two days. If you don't come in right away, you'll be the only one left in Washington and you won't even know which door leads where."

NEWLAND: The press office has been referred to by those around the administration as a "homicidal center," a rough operation. It certainly has been that in recent years. Do you care to comment on that, Mr. Tubby?

TUBBY: The pressures were, and are, indeed very great. In fact, three press secretaries, Steve Early, Charlie Ross, and Joe Short, all died —literally—on the job, and Irv Perlmeter, my associate, had a heart attack. But having said this, I would have to note that Jim Hagerty went through eight years afterwards; but maybe the pace was somewhat different under President Truman's successor.

There is an adversary relationship that exists between the president and the press, or between his press secretaries and the press, which is inherent and natural and often quite healthy. With President Truman there was (and this has been referred to earlier by Averell Harriman and others of the cabinet) an openness and a candor in the morning staff meetings which gave all those present a feeling of what the others were up to and what the president was interested in having done. The press secretary's role then was not simply to be a transmission belt from the president to the press, merely passing on whatever it was that should be passed on to the press; the job was a two-way street.

President Truman was very anxious to know, not only through us in the press office but through others on the staff, through the cabinet, and through people on the Hill, what the people out in the country were interested in and what they wanted. For our part, we would brief him not only on what had been in the papers or on the radio—TV was very new in those days—but on what some of our friends in the press corps were saying about things.

One of the things that endeared the president to me especially was his candor. You had a feeling that he would, figuratively, pick up his cards, sort them, and share his hand with you and the others of the staff, consulting with you on how it might best be played. The result was that during our own briefings with the press corps, we were fairly confident of where the president stood, and we also knew that he would back us up, if necessary.

In preparing for the president's own press conferences, the press staff would try to guess what questions might be asked and then offer recommended answers and provide background material in each category for each question and answer.

This we usually did on Mondays, coming up with fifty or sixty possible questions. We then referred them to the various departments and asked for recommended responses.

When these came in, we would go over them, maybe check back, and put the material into a black looseleaf notebook for the president. He would take it with him the night before he was to meet the press and go over it. Then on the following morning we would get together, update that material, and check with the staff on whether we ought to recommend some changes.

This system, I think, worked very well; I did pass it on to Jim Hagerty and I think it was used by Eisenhower. I do not know whether it has been used since. But I think that in this way, we avoided the kind of things that came up in the U-2 case or with the Bay of Pigs—when the press staff, both in the White House and in the State Department, were not informed as to what was really going on.

NEWLAND: You noted that, after delivering the briefing material to the president, you met the next morning. Can you elaborate on that?

TUBBY: Yes, usually about half an hour before the press conference itself, the regular staff would meet with the president and go over the recommended responses, and various members would make their own comments.

Discussion

In those days, because the White House was being renovated, we held press conferences over in the old State-War-Navy Building next door, in the old Treaty Room. The president was respected and liked by most of the correspondents, but he was neither respected nor liked by most of their publishers. The Democratic party, of course, has always faced a rather hostile press, but the president went into his press conferences as if to battle. I think he relished the challenge. There were times when he would be pressed, and I remember one which was rather embarrassing for me. The president said that he had delivered an ultimatum to Stalin in connection with the Russian troops stationed in Azerbaijan in northwest Iran. I had not heard of the ultimatum having been delivered, and so I got up and whispered to the president, "Are you sure it was an ultimatum?"

He turned to me and then said to the press corps, "Why, Roger is questioning whether it was an ultimatum, but I sent an ultimatum, I sent a very strong message to Stalin."

Of course, there was Merriman Smith of the UP with his "Thank you, Mr. President," and the mad dash was on for the phones.

Going down on the elevator I said, "Boss, are you sure it was an ultimatum? That is a pretty strong word—I mean, you do something or else."

"Why," he said, "well, you check it out, and if I am not right you set the record right."

So when I got back I checked very carefully with State and Defense and he *had* sent a strong message, but not what was normally thought of as an ultimatum. I then put out a statement to indicate the nature of what he had sent.

There were always good relations between the president and Charlie Ross and Joe Short and the rest of us who worked on press. We found over and over again that what the president always wanted to know was whether something was the right thing to do. Even if on occasion we would say, "If you do this, Mr. President, you are bound to get a pretty strong adverse reaction," his reply always was, "It is right, isn't it?" And this was certainly the case with the firing of General MacArthur.

I remember going into the Oval Office with the ticker tape from the Associated Press when MacArthur had sent the message to Joe Martin in which he said, in effect, that he felt that Chiang's troops should be unleashed and that we ought to go to the Yalu and beyond. When I took this in to the president, he was reading General Bradley's book about the landings in Normandy. I gave it to him, he glanced at it, put it down, and turned back to the Bradley book. I said, "Mr. President, I think this man is not only insubordinate, but he is insolent. He ought to be fired."

The White House Staff: Later Period

I was very junior to be giving any opinion about such a matter, but he picked up the ticker and read it again and said, "By God, Roger, I think you are right."

Of course, he would probably have fired MacArthur shortly anyway. But, just to conclude the story, when that action was taken, Joe Short called the press in at about 1:00 A.M. to give them the news. I got through doing some background briefing at about 3:00 in the morning, and then I decided that rather than go home to Rockville and then turn around and come right back, I would sack out on one of the couches right there in the office. The president was up at about 6 o'clock, as usual. I went into the gym to try to clear the cobwebs out of my brain; and as I was punching a heavy bag I heard a familiar chuckle behind me, and Mr. Truman said, "Belt him a couple for me, Roger."

By the time of the staff meeting there were bushel baskets of telegrams, overwhelmingly against the president. I remember picking up a bunch of those telegrams and just holding them up, not saying what was in them, and the president said, "See that fireplace over there, Roger? Go put them in there and set a match to them. The American people will come to understand that what I did had to be done. Now, what's next on the agenda?"

He had made his decision, and he would not fret and fuss over it. He felt he was right, and that was it.

NEWLAND: While we are on this topic of press relations, are there other aspects of it that others would like to bring up?

NASH: It seems to me that somebody ought to lay low that allegation that President Truman spoke from the hip and that he spoke without adequate preparation. Because he spoke emphatically and aggressively and briefly, there were assertions that he was not thinking on his feet. In the areas that I dealt with this was never true at any time. But he certainly could slip one off when he wanted to.

TUBBY: He read the [background] materials very carefully. If he was dissatisfied with a response recommended by one of the departments, he would insist that the secretary or somebody else topside in the department give him a better response.

HECHLER: I am sure we are going to get into the speech-making process a little later, but it should be noted that the press secretary was always in on the final freezing session of a speech, when the president would read it over, and occasionally the press secretary would also make comments as to both phraseology and substance.

Discussion

WILLIAM J. HOPKINS: I might mention also that in the material the president signed (such as legislation, Executive Orders, proclamations, messages to Congress), it was always the practice to make sure that the press office knew about it. That protected the president and gave the press office and the president control of these documents until it was time to have them announced or moved forward.

SHORT: I remember when Joe decided that he needed two assistants instead of one, right after the president had appointed him. Joe was the first press secretary who had ever moved across the hall from the press room, where he had covered the White House off and on for twenty years either for the AP or the *Baltimore Sun*. Joe felt that he simply could not know everything that went on. He wanted someone who was an expert on domestic affairs and someone who was an expert on foreign affairs, so that when the reporters who covered the White House heard an announcement from the president about Indonesia or the United Steel Workers, they would have someone in the press office to whom they could come for background information. That really was his purpose in hiring Roger Tubby, because of his experience at the State Department, and Irv Perlmeter, because he had been in the Treasury and with the AP and was very well informed.

NEWLAND: We may want to return to some aspects of the press and press relations, but let us now turn to the rather closely related item of speeches—the background research for them, their role in the decision-making process, etc.

HECHLER: The primary leadership in the speechwriting area, of course, was with the special counsel, Clark Clifford and later Charlie Murphy. The major assistants in that area were Dave Bell, Dave Lloyd, Dick Neustadt, and. . .

NEUSTADT: George Elsey, for a short period.

HECHLER: Yes, particularly in the earlier period before he joined Governor Harriman in the Mutual Security Agency. I can just talk about this from a worm's-eye view; others here can comment further. The thing that impressed me most about the speech-writing operation was the fact that the president himself was so thirsty for facts. In an age when we talk about substance and style, his emphasis came down heavily on substance, both in the initial instructions given in the staff meetings and in the tremendous amount of background research on facts and figures—the area where I had responsibility.

I was just making a list of some of the studies which I put together, many of which formed the bases for possible speech themes. I recall, for example, early in 1950 when the Republicans were attacking the Fair Deal as socialism, the president thought it would be a good idea to make a collection of "scare words" or "calamity howlers" that had been spread by various critics of every piece of legislation back to the Sherman Antitrust Act of 1890 and the Interstate Commerce Act of 1887. This resulted in a rather large compilation that took me six weeks to put together; it formed the basis of some of the quotations that were used to ridicule that particular opposition argument.

Don Dawson has mentioned bipartisan appointments. Once when the president was making an address on bipartisanship, he asked that I put together a history of bipartisan foreign policy with particular reference to what his part had been in it. This resulted in a rather fat document which was eventually taken over by Senator [John] Sparkman and published as a Senate document. But the factual, substantive base came from this study the president had asked for. This also helped form the factual basis for some speeches.

Then, after Sen. Joseph McCarthy started ranting, the president asked one day to have someone compile a history of witch-hunting and hysteria. This again was a rather extensive study, starting with the Alien and Sedition Acts and going down through the anti-Masonic movement, the Ku Klux Klan, and post–World War I hysteria. The president used this as the basis of many informal speeches that were done off-the-cuff.

All of us know what a tremendous respect for history President Truman had. Just before General MacArthur was relieved, I got a hurry-up call at about 6 o'clock in the evening: By very early the next morning I was to produce a document on the relations between General McClellan and President Lincoln. I did not have any idea what it was for, but as I began to develop this—and kept the Library of Congress open all night while I was looking—I began to see the tremendous similarity between one Mc and the other Mac and the manner in which they looked at their presidents and commanders in chief. This just served to illustrate the instinct for the jugular and the consciousness of history which President Truman had. His knowledge of history enabled him to put his finger on the essence instead of just viewing history as a stream of dates and events.

Unlike the messages to Congress and the major speeches, the whistle-stop speeches on the road were much shorter, much less detailed, and were developed in the form of outlines rather than complete texts. This enabled the president to use them as a springboard when he got on the rear platform, something he did with tremendous facility and great good humor. For instance, there was the time when he said that things had

Discussion

gotten so rough in the farm country that the grasshoppers were eating the handles off the pitchforks. Now that was not anything the staff could ever have supplied; it was a vintage Trumanism.

NEUSTADT: On major speeches and messages, a draft—either originating in the White House or coming from a department as a draft—would, after a certain amount of exchange and polishing, become the subject of work around the table. At first only Charlie Murphy's associates would be involved, along with other people in or near the White House who had something special to contribute. Marshall Shulman, for example, Dean Acheson's special assistant, joined whenever we were treating foreign affairs. But if the situation was important, as the round-table procedure continued it would begin to involve senior officials and the president.

I can remember a number of major messages to Congress in the later period with the president coming in and out of our sessions, looking over a penultimate draft, with Averell Harriman there, or with Averell coming in and out and Ted Tannenwald spelling him. I remember situations in which Dean Acheson, who had a very good sense of timing, would come in, take off his coat, sit down, and join the roundtable till the end. This progressive roundtable system served at least two purposes. It focused on policy details in which principals were able informally to exchange views and make recommendations and in which everybody got a chance to gauge the president's feelings, mood, and attitudes toward the subject at hand. For the junior staff it was the substitute for staff meetings, and this was one of the reasons I wanted to bring it up. There could have been only a very few people on the White House staff who either did not see the president daily, in morning staff meetings, or did not see him two or three times a week in one of these roundtable sessions. This is important because it is so *unlike* the pattern of subsequent administrations.

Collective drafting, with its policy dimensions and its interchange characteristics, was enormously time consuming, but it could be done—for both major legislative matters and major speeches and addresses—by a staff as small as Charlie Murphy's because there was a long tradition of using the Executive Office agencies as backup staff: the Bureau of the Budget, especially its Legislative Reference Division and some key examiners; the Council of Economic Advisers, particularly during Leon Keyserling's period after the first chairman's inhibitions about use of the staff had disappeared; and Averell Harriman's group during the time he was special assistant and when he changed formal hats. It was possible for those of us who nominally were in the White House to get help and support of all sorts from people in those agencies. And it was also possible for them to get immediate access to reliable information about the president's views, so the exchange was mutually profitable. A good deal of the secret of the small size of the Truman staff relates to the efficacy with which the Bureau of the Budget, the Council of Economic Advisers, and so forth were able to backstop White House staffers.

This arrangement was reintroduced during Kennedy's administration, partly by the fortunate accident that Elmer Staats was deputy director of the budget and David Bell was budget director and partly because Ted Sorenson, the new special counsel, was thoroughly brainwashed before the twentieth of January on the importance of these relations. The system was not really effectually carried out during any of the more recent administrations, and this accounts in good part for the great increase in the numbers of people formally called the White House staff.

CHARLES S. MURPHY: I would like to say just one more word about speechwriting, and it is perhaps something of a personal comment. I never had any particular talent for writing speeches, and whenever possible I got the work done by other people; only as a last resort would I do some of it myself.

I do wish to mention two speeches for which the only assistance the president got came from me. One was when Princess Elizabeth came over and presented an overmantel to the White House, and the president had to have something to say in response. And the other one was—you know the Memorial Bridge that goes across the Potomac River to the Lincoln Memorial—there are great big gold-colored horses at the end of the bridge, gifts of the Italian government; and this was another opportunity I had to assist the president.

THEODORE TANNENWALD: I think the record ought to show at this point that Charlie Murphy's willingness to write was, in fact, the key to how the committee system for writing speeches worked, because in the final analysis that's what happened on many occasions.

NEWLAND: Let's move to another series of problems that may illustrate how the staff functioned: intelligence activities. I would like to call on Admiral Dennison to get us started on that. How were intelligence briefings handled regularly—while at the White House, perhaps when on the *Missouri,* or on the train, etc. How did the material get organized, and how did you get it to the president?

ROBERT L. DENNISON: Shortly after I had reported for duty at the White House, Admiral Leahy left. But before he did, the president sent for the two of us and asked Admiral Leahy to make arrangements so that all the information he had been getting from various sources—the Joint Chiefs of Staff, the State Department, the Atomic Energy Commission, and the other sources—would continue to come and would come then to me. The president also told me to take over the intelligence briefings that Admiral Leahy had previously conducted.

I want to make it clear that in no way did I become an adviser to the president. I could not possibly replace Admiral Leahy in that capacity. Of course, the president would occasionally ask my advice, but I was careful not to volunteer it. My function was to give him the information, having used some judgment and discretion in screening out unessential or irrelevant matter, and to avoid indicating in any way what I thought about the matter unless he asked me.

When General Bradley became chairman of the Joint Chiefs of Staff, he came over to see the president and talk about the handling of information from the Joint Chiefs. The president had sent for me so that the three of us could discuss the matter. General Bradley and I were not acquainted—I had met him but I did not know him—and it may be unfair to say that perhaps he felt that since I was wearing a blue suit, I might be biased toward naval interests. He told the president that he would like to undertake the briefings. The president asked us both to go into the Cabinet Room and write out some kind of agreement; when we brought it back, the president said, "Well, this is fine."

One morning not long after that, the president sent for me and said, "I just read in the newspaper about something that has happened in Korea. Why wasn't I informed?"

I told him that I did not know anything about it either until I read it and then I reminded him of the agreement we had with General Bradley. The president said, "Oh, yes, but I am sure it won't happen again." But of course, it did. General Bradley found that he had so many responsibilities that he just did not have time to get over and adequately brief the president. Furthermore, it was difficult for anybody who was not just outside the door simply to pop in and see the president when there was urgent news. So the president concluded that this arrangement was not working too well and that we should go back to the previous briefing practice. That was fine with General Bradley and fine with me. There were, of course, others briefing the president. Sidney Souers and Jimmy Lay used to brief him; they were there with me many, many times, or I was there with them.

When I first knew him, the president wanted some way to coordinate the presentation of intelligence. Just after the war, I was political and military adviser to Forrestal, and he and Patterson and Byrnes called themselves a committee of three. I attended the meetings with Forrestal,

The White House Staff: Later Period

Howard Peterson was with Patterson, and Doc Mathews was with Byrnes, but we were not to take any notes. Before this system went into effect, where each principal had somebody sitting with him, I would get calls from the State Department or the War Department asking why the navy had not done something that I had never heard of nor had anybody else in the navy. Forrestal would have made some promise and then forgotten to tell anybody.

So we decided, Matthews, Peterson, and I, to agree after the meeting on what the three principals had said; and then we would go back and brief our respective departments on the sense of the meetings and boil it down into something understandable.

These meetings, of course, ceased after the National Security Council was set up.

NEWLAND: Governor Harriman, you earlier referred to your stint as a special assistant to President Truman for foreign affairs, and you observed that there were some who said you were a precursor of Henry Kissinger's. You disagreed. Why?

W. AVERELL HARRIMAN: I will be glad to elaborate. I think you will agree, Admiral Dennison, that the National Security Council really was not very important under Truman. It had been established, with Admiral Souers as secretary, but it never had the deliberative role that it later played when Robert Cutler was in charge under Eisenhower nor did it play a major role in policy decisions.

One of the problems was the conflict between Secretary of State Acheson and Secretary of Defense Johnson. Johnson was attacking Acheson because of his position in the Alger Hiss case, and the president asked me to do what I could to support Dean. I soon found that it was quite impossible to get any cooperation as long as Louis Johnson was in the Defense Department. After the Inchon landing he was asked to resign, and General Marshall took his place. It was almost necessary to have a man of General Marshall's standing to enlist the support of the people during the Korean War.

I tried my best to bring the cabinet together prior to their reaching decisions. I had a very small staff, headed by Theodore Tannenwald. We had very capable men. I had a representative on each one of the departmental committees that had anything to do with national security, war production, or international problems. I tried to get to know what the president wanted to have happen, and I used these men, who were well briefed, to try to get the staff-level interdepartmental committees to make these recommendations. I think we were quite successful in many cases in getting the interdepartmental committees to make the

Discussion

recommendations the president wanted. That was a useful function, and it meant that the president did not have to intercede between cabinet members. It never occurred to me to do what Kissinger did—to get between the president and the members of the cabinet. I tried to make it possible for meetings between the president and the secretary, whoever he might be, to be as fruitful as possible, and to put the president in a position to deal with the problems that came before them. I think in that effort we were reasonably successful.

George Elsey was in my group, Lincoln Gordon, General Roberts for defense matters, Charlie Collingwood for public relations, and Sam Berger in intelligence and labor matters. Each was an extraordinarily effective individual, and in an interdepartmental meeting, each one knew more about his subject than almost anyone present.

TANNENWALD: I would like to make two points that are important in terms of understanding how this working arrangement operated. The first point is a philosophical one: it worked well precisely because Governor Harriman recognized that Dean Acheson as secretary of state had a relationship with the president (and the secretary of defense in the same way). The governor did not try to interpose himself between the cabinet members and the president. This philosophy was imparted to the governor's staff, so that when we went to these interdepartmental meetings, we pushed the departments to do what they were supposed to do and did not take over for them.

The second was a highly personalized element that I do not think can be overlooked. This system worked, particularly after Secretary Johnson left the scene, because Mr. Harriman was—and had been for many years—very close to Acheson, who was the secretary of state, and also enjoyed very good relations with General Marshall. Beyond that, Mr. Harriman had almost the same kind of close relations with the deputy secretary of defense, Mr. Lovett, that he had with Mr. Acheson. It is the personal link that counts: No matter how you set up these structures, they work only in terms of the human beings who occupy the key positions. During this period, the three men—Lovett, Acheson, and Harriman—were very close to each other, knew how each other's mind worked, and had great respect for each other.

As a footnote, one of the most significant things is that during the period that he was White House special assistant, either Governor Harriman or a representative of his always attended the daily staff meeting held by the secretary of state.

HARRIMAN: I would like to add a word to Admiral Dennison's comments on Admiral Leahy. Admiral Leahy was the chief of staff of the president of the United States in his capacity as the commander in chief of the armed forces. General Marshall recommended that to President Roosevelt—I know because he told me so. General Marshall was impressed by the fact that Churchill had General "Pug" Ismay as his personal chief of staff and he could see the value of that arrangement. But he said to me, "I am an army man; therefore, I have got to recommend a naval officer. Who do you think would be the best?" Together, we went over the list and the obvious person was Leahy. But it should be made quite clear that Leahy was the chief of staff to the president as *commander in chief*, and that continued during the Truman period.

NEWLAND: Admiral Dennison, you noted that President Truman carefully distinguished between his role as commander in chief and his other roles. Could you comment further on that?

DENNISON: President Truman clearly saw himself in distinct and different roles: the president of all the people; the commander in chief of the armed forces; the leader of the Democratic party. The amazing thing to me was his ability in his actions and decisions to distinguish very sharply between these three roles. I never saw an occasion when he took an action or made a decision where I could not identify the role in which he saw himself. Even in minor things: I have a number of inscriptions—he signed himself "Your Commander in Chief" when he was speaking to me as a military person and his aide (or former aide), but without that title on other occasions and in other contexts.

TANNENWALD: I would like to recite a true story, which some of you have heard me tell and others have participated in; it ties in with the MacArthur episode, with the speech-writing system, and with the comment Admiral Dennison just made about the roles that the president played. During the preparation of what turned out to be the 1:00 A.M. press release on the firing of General MacArthur, I tried unsuccessfully to persuade Charlie Murphy and the others that the statement should contain a reference to the fact that the president was doing this on the unanimous consent of his principal military and civilian advisers. We met in the Cabinet Room at 10 o'clock that night to go through the statement with the president (under the system that has already been described); just as Mr. Truman was about to hand the statement to Joe Short to be released, he followed his practice of asking whether there were any other comments. The rule of the house was that, even if you were the lowest man on the totem pole, you still were entitled to speak up, and so I took advantage of the opportunity and made my point. I will never forget how he looked at me and said, "Son, not tonight.

Discussion

Tonight I am taking this decision on my own responsibility as president of the United States, and I want nobody to think I am sharing it with anybody else. This [consent of the advisers] will come out in forty-eight or seventy-two hours, but tonight it is my decision, and mine alone." The episode taught me what I already knew, but it brought it home more clearly: This man knew what it meant to be president of the United States.

NEWLAND: To move to another topic which some have suggested might help us understand President Truman's administration better, let us look at his consciousness of history and his consciousness of administration, particularly with respect to the transition to the Eisenhower administration.

HECHLER: Very briefly, on the morning after the 1952 Jefferson-Jackson Day dinner in Washington when President Truman announced that he was not going to run again, during a session in the Cabinet Room on some other matter, the president remarked on the terrible lack of preparation or briefings he had had when he took over from President Roosevelt in April 1945. Mr. Truman expressed his absolute determination that this would not happen again, regardless of who was elected president in 1952. So as early as March 1952, there was the determination that whoever was president, whether a Democrat or a Republican, there must be a smooth transition which was thoroughly planned. This, of course, grew out of President Truman's deep consciousness of history.

TUBBY: In the field of press relations, Jim Hagerty came in and H.S.T. told us all to be very detailed in describing how we prepared for press conferences, how we handled the press briefings other than the president's own. And this we did. I think in these briefings with the Eisenhower staff all of us contributed wholeheartedly, without any reservations at all, and I think this was a very good system.

JOHN W. SNYDER: One point ought to be brought up: even before the campaign had actually started, President Truman invited Eisenhower to come over to the White House for a general discussion, but the general, for his own reasons, declined.

ROGER W. JONES: Actually the concept of a smooth transition antedated the 1952 election by four years. Even though at least some of us in the Bureau of the Budget did not believe—and certainly the president did not believe—that there was going to be another president in January 1949, he gave us very explicit instructions to find out what it was that Dewey was talking about and what kind of positions the Republican party might take. This was a fairly casual kind of an operation, but he did start worrying about the transition as far back as 1948 and then formalized it in 1952.

ELMER B. STAATS: President Truman was fully aware of the conversations that were taking place between the Bureau of the Budget and Dewey's people in 1948. He had sanctioned the procedure and urged that we cooperate. Then in 1952, the day after the election, Fred Lawton and I went to see President Truman and told him how important we thought it was to have someone work with us in developing the new budget. He called President-elect Eisenhower immediately, and eight days later Joe Dodge was on the scene. Our instructions from President Truman were to give Dodge every bit of information bearing on the budget and to treat him just as if he were part of the present administration.

JONES: And Dodge never took advantage of this. He took no action that could possibly be considered a violation of the confidence that had been placed in him.

STAATS: This procedure played a tremendous part also in the stability of the Bureau of the Budget personnel, I might add. Because of the confidence built up by the virtue of the trust President Truman placed in the incoming budget director, by the time Dodge was ready to take over he was prepared to keep all of the bureau's staff without any change at all.

SNYDER: President Truman set up a committee of Secretary Lovett, Governor Harriman, Secretary Acheson, and myself and then invited President-elect Eisenhower to the White House again. This time he came, and we had a session around the cabinet table and exchanged views of what was likely to happen—what should be checked on—with his prospective appointees for those various offices (Defense, State, Treasury, and so forth). As we walked out, the president said to the four of us, "There is one thing definite, I want you to cooperate to the fullest with these people and see to it that they know the problems that are before each of your departments."

SHORT: In my area, the transition operation was very limited. Because I had so recently learned the job myself, mostly from Bill Hopkins and from Bill Hassett (who was retired but had come down to fill me in), I was really prepared to help whoever was going to handle the Eisenhower correspondence. I was all set to explain how we handled the roughly fifteen thousand letters a week that came to the president. Mr. Truman did not permit the use of an "auto-pen"; he personally signed the letters to personal friends and those papers which he was required by law to sign himself. Otherwise I wrote or approved all letters and signed "Beth C. Short, Secretary to the President." I did try to give our correspondents the feeling that the letters from the White House expressed President Truman's feelings. I studied his style and tried to write as he did, concisely and clearly. I thought all this was important and I was prepared to explain it.

One day three people came into the office—Roger Steffan, who was the incoming administration's transition specialist, Sherman Adams, and Arthur Vandenberg, Jr., who was the only one I knew. I spoke to him, he introduced me to the other two, and Sherman Adams said, "Mrs. Short, can you tell me where that door goes, right there by your desk?"

I was in Bill Hassett's old office which was about the nicest one in the White House, next to the president's. And I said, "I don't know, Mr. Adams, I have never used it."

He said, "Is it locked?"

And I said, "I don't know, I have never tried it."

"Do you mind if I try it?" He walked back and tried the door. It was open on my side, and then there was a little passage and another door which was locked. He said, "That's all I need, Mrs. Short, thank you very much." And that was all.

NASH: I gave a briefing and *nobody* came. I followed instructions to the letter. I had a briefing book and a status book, and I waited and waited and waited. Afterwards I found out that when they looked at the organization chart, Sherman Adams saw our operation and said, "What do they do?" Somebody told them, and he said, "Oh, political, we don't need that. We are going to treat everybody alike."

SHORT: I have a story that is secondhand; John Steelman told this to a friend of mine and maybe some of the rest of you have heard of it and can corroborate it. When they [the Eisenhower transition team] came to see Steelman, they asked him what his people did; he said, "Well, you know, they would study up on this subject and then go in and tell the president about it. The president tells us that he wants us to know about these matters, and I have somebody work on it, and they tell him." According to my informant, Sherman Adams looked at John Steelman and said, "You don't mean you let all those people go in to see the president on all those little things?"

Steelman said, "Yes, we do."

Sherman Adams is supposed to have said, "But there aren't more than four or five times a year when you need to bother the president."

The White House Staff: Later Period

SNYDER: At the Treasury, we set up a suite of offices for George Humphrey, who was to come in as secretary. I called him up and asked him to come and see me and the offices we had set up. He immediately filled them with his prospective appointees; we worked with them for two months very assiduously, going over all the pressing matters—financial and economic problems, taxes, and all that sort of thing. We had really no trouble in the Treasury transition. We even went down and counted the gold to be sure that it was all down there.

HARRIMAN: The same was true in our transition in Mutual Security to Mr. Stassen.

TANNENWALD: We spent hours with Mr. Stassen.

HARRIMAN: He had all our people come in and see him, and the reward was that everybody got fired.

TANNENWALD: I stayed for three months.

HARRIMAN: If you were not fired, you were the only one.

CHARLES F. BRANNAN: I do not think this will add a great deal to history, but Secretary Benson decided that he did not want to come to the Department of Agriculture to be briefed. But the press kept pushing him, so finally he did come with a retinue of reporters and photographers behind him. He came into my office and, as I recall, asked three questions. The first one was what was my secretary's salary; the second was how much salary did Mr. [Wesley] McCune [Brannan's executive assistant] get; and the third one was did I think it was proper for him to take his kids to church in the official automobile? The press kept insisting that we have a picture taken together but he refused and left.

HOPKINS: This matter of the outgoing administration expecting the new people to come in and see them to find out how things are done—I think in each administration that has been expected, but it never happens. You sit there and wait for the phone to ring, and it never does. The incoming administration is coming off a winning election; they feel they know the answers and that they can do it better than the people who have been there. That is traditional, and it is not unique to President Truman's changeover.

Of course, when he came in under the unfortunate circumstances of President Roosevelt's death, it was a case of "the king is dead, long live the king." In a matter of twenty-four hours, all the desks were wiped clean and everything was boxed up in huge wooden cases that had been borrowed from the Treasury Department—the kind in which paper

Discussion

money is received—and shipped off either to the Hyde Park Library or temporarily to the National Archives. Within forty-eight hours we were working with the new administration and the papers of the outgoing group were gone.

There is some question of whether the old concept of the outgoing president having possession of his papers is a great drawback to the incoming group. I have never felt that it was, because most of these documents originate in one of the departments and agencies, and the case file can be rebuilt. That was the situation when President Truman came in. There were some instances in which we had to go to the Roosevelt Library at Hyde Park or the National Archives to get papers, but very few. It was not any great problem.

In 1952 President Truman wanted to make sure that there was a proper changeover, but even at that he was very supportive of his staff. He named Dr. Steelman, as I recall, to be the liaison with the incoming group. Roger Steffan had been chosen as sort of a housekeeper for the new administration and arrived as a representative of Governor Adams several weeks before the changeover. He was moving around the office making inquiries and giving advice and even orders which, in a few instances, got back to President Truman.

One day the president happened to meet Mr. Steffan out at the doorkeeper's desk and walked up to him and said, "I hear you have been pushing some of my people around. I don't like it," and walked off.

Things changed a little bit after that; it was a little smoother so far as we were concerned.

HECHLER: I think one of the points, aside from the papers, is that President Roosevelt never fully briefed Vice-president Truman on the problems of the presidency. And this is what President Truman determined should not happen to his successor, be he a Republican or a Democrat.

NEWLAND: Would anyone care to comment on the relationship between President Truman and President Hoover and on the importance of the Hoover Commission's report?

SNYDER: Shortly after the war was declared over, President Truman sent an agent to take a careful look at the conditions in Europe, particularly the food conditions. That was Mr. [Will] Clayton. He made a most thorough and valuable survey and came back saying that something would have to be done and done quickly.

Several of us who had known Mr. Hoover recommended that Mr. Truman invite him in and talk to him about it. He did, and ex-President

The White House Staff: Later Period

Hoover came in to see him. They established an almost immediate rapport, and President Truman invited him to go over and serve as food administrator, a job similar to what he did after World War I.

HOPKINS: That was the first time President Hoover had been back in the White House since he left on March 4, 1933.

SNYDER: Mr. Hoover told me later that that added ten years to his life; it made him feel like he had a place of importance again.

STAATS: We heard President Truman say many times what great respect he had for Hoover's work as war food administrator. He also felt that Hoover was a victim of circumstances in the Great Depression, and he had some feeling that a lot of things that happened were not Hoover's fault at all. The payoff of all of this was that during the time these various reorganization plans were before Congress, whenever we ran into trouble on the Republican side of the aisle, Mr. Hoover was there to organize the effort to get the votes. Without that kind of relationship much of what was accomplished would not have happened.

STOWE: There were two later occasions which brought this very forcefully to my mind. One was when many of us were trying to raise some money for the Truman Library—the president was really doing all the work, we just sort of went along. But we were having some problems in California, and at a session we had at the Waldorf in New York, somebody suggested that it might help if we could persuade President Hoover to become the honorary chairman in California.

A few minutes later the president got up, walked out, and was gone for some ten or fifteen minutes. When he came back he had a little grin on his face. Somebody asked him where he had been and he said, "Well, I have been downstairs to see President Hoover, and he is going to serve as chairman of my committee out in California."

The second time was during the 1960 Kennedy campaign when President Truman and I spent many evenings alone for some six or seven weeks as we traveled around the country in everything from a little four-seater plane to a big jet. I remember on at least two occasions that he recalled with great warmth his feelings for President Hoover, his indebtedness to him for the work he did after the war, and most importantly, the work he did on the Hoover Commission and the support he gave to the many Truman reorganization plans that were passed by the Congress.

JONES: Let me add one small vignette on the other side. One day in May after President Eisenhower was inaugurated, President Hoover did us the great honor of coming down to the White House mess and

162

sitting at the big table for lunch. There were six of us at the table, I will mention no names except my own, but two disparaging remarks were made about President Truman. President Hoover pushed back his chair and said, "That's enough!" That ended that conversation right then and there.

HARRIMAN: We have not emphasized enough that President Truman was one of the best read men in American history, and particularly on the presidency, and that he had an enormous respect for the presidency. Part of the reason why he did this for Mr. Hoover was because Hoover had been president of the United States. Mr. Truman was repaid by being treated abominably by President Eisenhower, which I need not go into at this time.

MURPHY: I probably ought to say something about President Hoover. In 1948 President Hoover was still a natural target for people who took a narrow, partisan political view of things. The campaign was important to some of us, and as we worked on speeches for President Truman, we repeatedly put in things about President Hoover that were not altogether complimentary. They were not mean and vicious, but they were not complimentary. President Truman regularly took them out. Only once did I get one in that stuck.

In North Carolina, where I grew up during the depression, people whose automobiles broke down and would no longer run would put shafts on the front of them and hitch mules to them. People called them "Hoovercarts." I started talking about "Hoovercarts" in the 1948 campaign, and everybody said they had never heard of them. President Truman was going to make a speech at the North Carolina State Fair that fall, and I put in a reference to "Hoovercarts"; he used it, and I must say, it just went over great.

NEWLAND: Could I come back to the issue we were on at the beginning of this discussion: What was the working pace in the White House during this period? You were talking about daily staff meetings at around 9 or 9:30, six days a week—what were the hours? I can remember another administration when the hours were early morning til late at night, seven days a week—what was it like under Mr. Truman?

DENNISON: I told the president once that he was the most difficult man I had ever worked for or ever could imagine working for. He asked "What do you mean?" I said, "I have been with you when I know you have had tremendous concerns and worries on your mind. But you never show it. We are not perfect, I know damn well I am not, but you never change your attitude, you are always cheerful and understanding, patient, kind, and it is really difficult to work for you because I know I am not that good."

He just said, "Don't worry about it. If you do anything wrong, I will let you know."

NEUSTADT: I am sure everybody worked hard, and the hours were long. For the staff that revolved around Charlie Murphy there was a certain periodicity about it: When we were involved with a message or speech, or getting ready for one, or cleaning up after one, it was just continuous—you barely got home to sleep. Then there would be a breather of, maybe, a day or two, which did not coincide with weekends. I do not know whether any others of the staff managed more regularity. It does not seem to me that we had very much, and you could tell the results in terms of the families—wives and small children suffered. But I do not think that is peculiar; it is the general situation around the White House.

MURPHY: I agree with most of what Dick said, but I do not remember the breathers.

NEUSTADT: Charlie was the head of the unit, so he got no breathers. The rest of us—because of Charlie—sometimes had it easier.

TANNENWALD: As one of those who had to divide his time, I got no breathers. If you had a regular job in one of the other agencies, you frequently were coopted to work on speeches or messages, but the other job still had to get done.

MURPHY: We had a limousine and along about 11 or 12 o'clock at night, we would load everybody in the car and the driver would start taking us home. When we passed each fellow's house, we would wake him up and let him out, and then we all got back in the morning.

But we did have a lot of fun. You could hear Dick Neustadt laughing across the hall, and then the rest of us laughed too.

TUBBY: I think it was a lot of fun, even with an early riser for a boss. Sometimes, when I first started out there, he occasionally would call up at 6:00 or 6:15 A.M. and say, "Roger, what's this story in the *New York Times*, what is this all about, where did this come from?" When I first started out I would be a bit groggy, but then my wife and I changed the location of the phone so that she would answer first and nudge me with her elbow and get me kind of alert.

Of course, on the press side, we would often get calls all through the night from correspondents whose papers were going to bed in Shanghai or Tokyo or other far-away places. But I think all of us agreed

Discussion

that he was such a marvelous guy to work for, and it was such a marvelous atmosphere to be in, that we did not mind it at all. But, like Dick, I think it was tough on the wives and children.

HOPKINS: President Truman was so orderly in his habits that it made everything much easier than in other administrations.

HECHLER: It was a beautiful, wonderful experience, working hard along with highly competent people. You really had a sense of history about it, too, at the end of every day, working for a great president of the United States.

IV

THE EXECUTIVE OFFICE AGENCIES

When the President's Committee on Administrative Management proclaimed in 1937 that "our president needs help," it recommended that all staff functions normally associated with top-level management be grouped in one organizational structure to be known as the Executive Office of the President. At first congressional opposition sharply curtailed this plan, but World War II made necessary a number of administrative arrangements which were placed under the broad umbrella of the Executive Office concept. During President Truman's administration, Congress created two major units to serve the president in a staff capacity, the Council of Economic Advisers and the National Security Council. In addition, of course, the Bureau of the Budget continued in its important role within the Executive Office, and as emergency agencies were created during the Korean War, they were placed in the Executive Office.

In the fourth session of the conference, the focus of attention was the Executive Office and its several units. The view from the Bureau of the Budget was represented by Elmer B. Staats and Roger W. Jones, both men with long and distinguished careers in public service.

Since 1966 Elmer Staats has served as the comptroller general of the United States. Prior to that, except for four years (1954–58) spent as executive officer of the Operations Coordinating Board of the National Security Council, he had been in the Bureau of the Budget since 1939, where his duties included service as chief of the War Agencies Section (1943–47), assistant director for legislative reference (1947–49), executive assistant director (1949–50) and deputy director (1950–54, 1958–66).

Roger W. Jones was Staats's deputy and, later, successor in the Legislative Reference Division of the Bureau of the Budget. He served as chairman of the U.S. Civil Service Commission (1959–61) and deputy undersecretary of state for administration (1961–62) before returning to BOB as special assistant to the director. From 1968 to 1971 he was assistant director of the Office of Management and Budget and continued as a consultant to OMB until 1975. His prepared statement addresses itself primarily to the roles of the president and of the BOB in the legislative process.

Leon H. Keyserling, one of the three initial appointees to the Council of Economic Advisers and the council's chairman from 1949 to 1953, provides a panoramic view of the council's role and functioning during the Truman administration, including an assessment of President Truman's way of using the council. Since 1953, Mr. Keyserling has been a consulting economist and attorney. He is also the founder and president of the Conference on Economic Progress.

Walter S. Salant, after serving as an economist with several government agencies, joined the staff of the newly formed Council of Economic Advisers in 1946. He remained in this position until 1952, when he became a special consultant to the North Atlantic Treaty Organization (NATO). From 1954 to 1976, he was a senior fellow of the Brookings Institution. Mr. Salant supplies two episodes which illustrate some of the problems of the White House organization under President Truman.

Theodore Tannenwald, in the framework of a broader discussion, also provides an episode illustrative of Mr. Truman's way of doing things. He also discusses the speech-writing procedure, the creation of the Mutual Security Administration, and the presidential transition in 1952–53. Mr. Tannenwald served as counsel to Averell Harriman, special assistant to the president, (1950–51) and as assistant director of the Mutual Security Administration (1951–53). He was appointed a judge of the United States Tax Court in 1965 and reappointed to a full fifteen-year term in 1974.

The functioning of the National Security Council in relation to the president as described by James E. Lay, Jr., who served first as assistant executive secretary of the NSC (1947–50) and then as its executive secretary (1950–61). Thereafter, Mr. Lay was deputy assistant to the director of the Central Intelligence Agency (1961–64) and executive secretary of the Central Intelligence Board (1962–71).

ELMER B. STAATS

President Truman had very little formal administrative machinery other than the Budget Bureau at the time he came into office. He had the residue of the Office of War Mobilization which former Justice Byrnes previously headed; by this time it was headed by Judge Vinson, and subsequently was run by Dr. John Steelman, who previously had been concerned primarily with labor matters. So the president had two principal arms—one, the Budget Bureau, and the other, the Office of the War Mobilization and Reconversion. Very shortly after he became president, OWMR was terminated, partly to symbolize the emphasis upon a peacetime economy.

Obviously, the Bureau of the Budget was not the proper agency to carry on programs and policies of a highly political character. Dr. Steelman became the assistant to the president. The Budget Bureau was asked to draw up a statement of the functions of the new assistant to the president, and in visiting with Dr. Steelman about the draft which we had prepared, we had labeled it "special assistant to the president." He made the point very strongly that he thought this concept inadequate. I asked him what he had in mind; he said he thought that there had to be developed something closer to a chief of staff or chief assistant. He changed the draft to "*the* assistant to the president" and subsequently obtained President Truman's approval for that change. It turned out to be really quite a significant change. One of the reasons is that it formed the basis for Dr. Steelman's view that this title gave him a charter as the chief of the White House staff (though it is clear that he never really functioned as such). Furthermore, it was important because this title was carried over after the Truman administration into the Eisenhower administration, and as *the* assistant, Sherman Adams clearly became the chief of staff.

At the end of the Truman administration the president had in the Executive Office the Bureau of the Budget, the Council of Economic

The Executive Office Agencies

Advisers, the National Security Council, and the National Security Resources Board. But there was another significant development which I think should be discussed with respect to the presidential staff, and that is the Korean War. Beginning in June 1950, the outbreak of the Korean War, one of the things that became clear very quickly was the fact that the president still did not have the machinery in his own office that could coordinate the mobilization effort we were making—particularly since we did not know with any certainty whether that effort would have to be accelerated. No one could be sure if controls would have to be developed in such a way as to enable us to move quickly on to much more elaborate and comprehensive controls. It became obvious that the National Security Resources Board, a multi-headed, cumbersome agency, was not adequate for this purpose. At the time, Stuart Symington (formerly secretary of the air force and later a senator from Missouri, who had been head of the Reconstruction Finance Corporation) was chairman of the Resources Planning Board. He argued strongly that the National Security Resources Board could perform this function. He took this issue to the president several times, including one very warm discussion in a cabinet meeting, but the president's decision was to establish under his wartime powers a new agency headed by Charles Wilson, who had been the chief executive of General Electric. Wilson subsequently appointed Gen. Lucius Clay as his deputy, bringing him back from Germany for this purpose. The machinery developed under Wilson became the center of coordination and planning in the Executive Office for the Korean War period. This staff agency subsequently was merged into an Office of Civil and Defense Mobilization during the Eisenhower period, representing a combination of the residue of the NSRB and the Office of Defense Mobilization (which had been headed by Wilson); the civil defense function was added later in 1958.

Aside from the question of what formal machinery was established during the Korean period, the thing that impressed me most about the staff work under President Truman was the fact that it operated so informally. The leadership centered around the special counsel to the president, Clark Clifford, a fact which was most significant. I suppose the issue of whether the assistant to the president became chief of staff, or whether the special counsel to the president was chief of staff was never faced directly. The two offices functioned in different areas, and in fact, there was no particular need to resolve this point. Clark Clifford tended to exert more and more influence, it seemed to me, partly because he was the one the president looked to either to write his speeches or to organize the speech-writing. Clifford handled a great deal of the legislative liaison work with the Congress. He reviewed draft legislation which had to be seen by the president and looked over enrolled bills as they came to the president for action. After being reviewed by the Bureau of the Budget, the bills came through his office on the way to the president. After Clifford left, he was succeeded by Charles Murphy who had been his assistant and who tended to follow pretty much the same work pattern.

President Truman's staff meetings brought his staff around the president's table. He recognized that his staff had grown and saw the need for some discussion of the activities of each principal staff member to review the status of his work, and so on.

Perhaps it would be of some interest to note that during this period, growing out of the National Security Act of 1947, Adm. Sidney Souers was appointed as the executive secretary of the National Security Council. The president had known Admiral Souers for a good many years. Souers's job was pretty clearly outlined by the statute; as a practical matter, of course, the title of executive secretary meant whatever the president wanted it to mean. In fact, President Truman used Admiral Souers primarily as his liaison with the intelligence community. He used to refer to Souers as his intelligence man and, frequently, as his "cloak-and-dagger" man. President Truman never saw the National Security Council as a major deliberative body. In dealing with various problems, he preferred to operate much more informally; unlike President Eisenhower, he was not used to sitting down with a deliberating body and systematically going around the table for debate and statements of position.

Toward the end of President Truman's administration disagreement developed over the level of our foreign aid effort, particularly for the budget year 1953–54. This was the budget President Truman had to prepare but which would be carried out by the next administration. There was disagreement not only over the question of need—the level of effort—but also over the kind of foreign policy posture President Truman should leave in this very controversial area. One suggestion was that this matter be brought before the National Security Council for action. After the matter had been reviewed in the Bureau of the Budget, President Truman ended up by having a meeting in the cabinet room. Present were Averell Harriman, director for mutual security; Dean Acheson, the secretary of state; Robert Lovett, the secretary of defense; the three secretaries of the armed services; the Joint Chiefs of Staff, the director of the Bureau of the Budget, with some of his staff; and various representatives of the White House staff. On this particular occasion, the president went out of his way to go around the table asking for the views of all those present. I had never seen him do this before, but in this particular case he made a very special point of asking every principal there what his view was and approximately what level of foreign aid effort he would recommend. This, of course, was after the substantive issue had been laid out on the table, along with the pros and cons and differences in the program at different funding levels. President Truman made his decision before he left the room. This was the first time I had seen him take this kind of action in such a formal way.

ROGER W. JONES

It is doubtful whether any student of the presidency has been able to digest the mass of presidential literature which has appeared in recent years in publications of all kinds. A thoughtful sampling of articles which have appeared in the professional journals suggests that the authors, almost unconsciously, use the administration of President Harry Truman as a kind of high-water mark, or measuring stick, of initiative in the legislative process over the last forty years. Comparisons or contrasts with the Truman administration are particularly evident when the president's constitutional role in the legislative process is a major part of the discussion.

In analyzing the reason for this focus, five realities about the Truman administration provide an answer. First, President Truman had the most exhaustive knowledge of the presidency of any president, with the possible exception of Woodrow Wilson. Second, Mr. Truman had a great sense of order in assigning lines of responsibility for the legislative programs advanced during his administration. Third, he chose to give legislative programs a central and concentrated attention which was both new and unique. Fourth, he used the institutional machinery of the federal government to the fullest in carrying out his constitutional duties with respect to legislation, separating the politics of program and policy from the politics of partisan commitment and position. And finally, he resisted most effectively invasions by Congress of the president's constitutional role.

It is difficult to be certain about the exact timing of the various steps which President Truman took or approved in establishing the policies and mechanisms adopted to advance the goals of his administration through legislation. It is less difficult to identify what those policies and mechanisms turned out to be. Some critics have argued that this kind of precision in identification is possible only with hindsight and that the legislative processes of the Truman administration came into being, if not

173

accidentally, at least without much direct presidential involvement. No person who participated directly in the handling of legislation during the Truman administration can accept that argument, however. The president was very much involved.

His September 1945 message to Congress was, to a large extent, the baseline for the Fair Deal. It was also a charge of all executive agencies to accept his substantial catalogue of the nation's needs, even though he frankly admitted to Harold Smith (who continued as budget director until June 1946) that some of his goals probably would not be reached. There was not enough of a consensus among the Democratic members of Congress to give him genuine hope for favorable action. Certainly, the election of a Republican Congress in 1946 did not improve the chances.

With the election of the Eightieth Congress a number of things

ACME Photo

President Truman signs the $3.75 billion British loan bill, July 15, 1946. *Left to right:* Treasury Secretary John W. Snyder, Chief Justice Fred M. Vinson, Secretary of State James F. Byrnes, Sen. Alben W. Barkley, and British Ambassador Lord Inverchapel.

happened. President Truman decided to have the Bureau of the Budget conduct on his behalf an institutionalized process of liaison with all the committees in both Houses, with their Republican chairmen, and with both the majority and minority staffs of the committees. He felt that it was important—particularly when Congress was controlled by the opposition—for the committees to have information available about the relationship of pending legislation to the president's program without, in the majority of cases, directly involving either him or the White House staff. Accordingly, the director of the Bureau of the Budget appointed a career civil servant as the legislative liaison officer to head up this institutionalized process. With the president's approval, the director also instituted a more thorough process within the Budget Bureau to coordinate and clear agency reports to Congress on pending legislation. These institutional arrangements were designed to supplement, but in no way to replace, the clear, effective, and timely enunciation of plans which the president provided through his regular meetings with the Democratic leadership.

The practice of annually preparing the president's comprehensive legislative program was also adopted. This legislative agenda was presented in the State of the Union, Budget, and special messages; and it was nurtured by the special assignment of lead responsibility to a department or agency and by expanded central clearance through the Bureau of the Budget's agency reports and testimony on program items.

Truman's budget directors—successively, James Webb, Frank Pace, and Frederick Lawton—provided through the bureau's career staff four kinds of assistance. First, the bureau took charge of collecting legislative proposals throughout the executive branch. Second, the bureau made initial recommendations, separating the proposals into items that ought to be considered as part of the president's program; items that could be included in departmental legislative programs; and items the staff believed to be unnecessary, untimely, or inconsistent with the president's program. Third, the bureau developed preliminary cost estimates for items that might be included in the president's legislative program and prepared analyses of the fiscal and programmatic implications of the major items. Fourth, working with various agencies and the White House staff, the bureau developed projections about the time needed to prepare transmittal messages and legislative drafts and about committee schedules which might affect the timing and consideration of legislation.

The interlocking elements of this machinery were not, it is true, all preplanned. There was a natural process of evolution. The system soon became more pertinent and useful for domestic issues than it did for defense matters and international affairs. Although the Department of

Defense (and its service departments), the State Department, and the other agencies with responsibilities of an international nature prepared legislative programs, by and large, these were handled differently and at the higher political and policy levels. The reason for focusing attention on the domestic legislative program was, in large part, the result of escalating agency demands to resume activities curtailed or abandoned during World War II and to initiate new programs in response to the public's postwar needs and desires. Furthermore, the president's interest and concern about developing a rational and greatly expanded domestic program necessitated the coordination of proposals to avoid duplication and budgetary competition. It was, therefore, natural for the White House staff to work directly with the Budget Bureau staff and to use the bureau as an institutional agent of the president.

This machinery might not have developed as it did were it not for the election of the Eightieth Congress. But after President Truman's reelection in 1948, the institutional processes which had begun more than two years earlier certainly took on a more positive and definitive existence. For the first time in executive branch history, the president set forth his entire legislative program, along with estimates of the cost, in a specific section of the annual budget. The wisdom of this procedure was challenged by a number of the president's political advisers, largely on the grounds that the Republican opposition would claim credit for a budget reduction whenever pieces of new legislation were not enacted. President Truman, however, did not accept this argument. He maintained that both Congress and the American people were entitled to full information about his legislative goals and their associated costs. The record of the way in which he handled press questions either at the annual budget "seminar" or in his regular press conferences proves conclusively how carefully he personally had fitted the elements of his legislative program together and how energetic and persuasive an advocate of that program he was prepared to be.

In addition President Truman further institutionalized the existing system for preparing and submitting agency reports and views, together with the Budget Bureau's analysis, on all enrolled bills. Facsimile copies of enrolled enactments were circulated by the Budget Bureau not only to agencies directly affected, but to all agencies with a pertinent interest in the particular bill. The schedule for presenting agency reports and the Budget Bureau's analysis and recommendation was made tighter so that the White House staff and the president had several days' leeway to conduct any further examination or analysis before Mr. Truman approved or vetoed a bill. The president also greatly increased the Budget Bureau's staff participation in preparing veto messages, signing statements, and the memoranda of disapproval issued on bills he pocket-vetoed.

Until Mr. Truman became president, the approval or veto of private relief bills had depended largely on the recommendation of the agency chiefly affected. It had become quite customary for agencies to recommend a veto on many kinds of private relief bills on the grounds that they were discriminatory and thus would interfere with a uniform application of the general law. President Truman took a different view. In essence, his position was that in a constitutional sense any private relief bill represented either a petition to Congress for the redress of a grievance or an expression by Congress that there was some justification for an exception to the existing law. He gave close attention to the issues involved and adopted the view that equity demanded consideration of each private enactment on its own merits as well as an assessment of its effect on the general law.

Thus, President Truman approved many private relief bills to reverse the rigid and horizontal application of a general law that created hardships which he considered unjustifiable—for example, mandatory exclusion under the immigration laws of persons convicted of minor offenses ("crimes involving moral turpitude") or of persons with a history of certain diseases. Similarly, President Truman did not believe that it was equitable in every instance to enforce the statute of limitations.

A second manifestation of President Truman's interest in private legislation was the full support he gave to the successful effort to persuade Congress to consolidate individual private relief enactments dealing with the same subject into omnibus bills whenever possible. Here again the institutional approach of an agency staff working with the committee staff proved beneficial.

President Truman's knowledge of the presidency, his tremendous respect for the office, and his determination that its constitutional powers be in no way impaired, led him to regard his legislative duties most seriously. He examined every aspect of presidential responsibility for legislative initiative and judged it in light of the constitutional provision that "the executive power shall be vested in a president of the United States." The federal agencies and their staffs, both political appointees and career civil servants, soon recognized that the uncompromising clarity of his position required the highest degree of their institutional vigilance in conducting legislative activities. Perhaps the best example is to be found in the agencies' change of attitude during the Truman administration toward what in government parlance had come to be known as the "legislative veto."

For some years there had been a growing tendency by Congress to enact laws delegating broad power but also providing that either the president or the agency charged with carrying out the law had to come to an agreement with a congressional committee (or subcommittee) on just how the law was to be administered. President Truman believed that such provisions were unconstitutional and directly challenged the executive authority of the president. This attitude played a very important part within the agencies in increasing the feeling that the officers discharged their duties as an extension of the president: No executive agency was to acquiesce in sharing administrative responsibilities with the legislative branch.

Although in later administrations some compromises on the use of the legislative veto gained acceptance on the grounds of political necessity, the fact remains that President Truman's stand (which had been taken occasionally by previous presidents) has had an enduring effect upon the legislative process. Certainly in the years since the Truman administration, the position which he took with such forcefulness has been a major safeguard against any erosion of executive power. Within the agencies he inspired respect and a better understanding of the real meaning of the constitutional provisions concerning executive power and responsibility for legislation by institutionalizing the procedures for handling legislation. He opened the door to a new kind of participation in the legislative process by officers of the career service. His faith and trust helped make them see the larger picture and transcend narrow allegiances to agency programs and the constituencies of those programs. He expected the bureaucracy to provide maximum assistance both to him and to the office of the president.

And, with the Bureau of the Budget in the van, the bureaucracy responded and thus contributed to Mr. Truman's effective conduct of the presidency.

LEON H. KEYSERLING

A president's first task with respect to primary advisers is to select them. The principles which Truman applied in 1946 in choosing the three original members of the Council of Economic Advisers were far better than those used by all subsequent presidents. (The qualifications and "fit" of the members chosen is a separate issue, which I shall discuss below.) With exceptions too rare to be noted, all subsequent presidents have selected the members of the CEA from among distinguished professors of economics at universities; in practical terms they have looked to the chairman to pick the other two members; and at times they have permitted an outgoing chairman virtually to designate his successor. This has been wrong in theory and has produced unfortunate results. The structure of economic thought and of research, writing, and teaching at universities should create no presumption that professors engaged in these activities are uniquely—or even particularly—well equipped to serve on the CEA and deal with matters involving an integrated overview of the whole economy and an integrated grasp of national economic policies. This erroneous presumption has meant excessive "inbreeding" within the CEA and excessive reliance upon one school of economics at any given time. It has made the other two members of CEA so indebted to the chairman, or so similar in background and thought, that the president really gets the benefit of only one person's advice instead of three. It could be argued that one adviser rather than three is preferable, although I do not share that view. But it does a disservice to the president and is disingenuous to create the impression in Congress and with the public of three advisers when there is really only one—plus two staff members, albeit of higher rank than the regular staff. The process has also had the highly undesirable result of abbreviating tenure among CEA members, who have come in for a while, burnished their reputations thereby, and then returned to the university from whence they came or gone on to something else.

The Executive Office Agencies

President Truman, in contrast, made the selection of the original CEA members a presidential choice in fact as well as in form and also obtained advisers of various backgrounds, independent of one another. He chose a "professional economist" in Edwin G. Nourse, a former president of the American Economic Association and head of the School of Economics at the Brookings Institution. The president chose John Clark, who had experience in politics as a member of a state legislature and as a delegate to a national convention and who had acquired one of the larger American fortunes and served as vice-president of Standard Oil of Indiana. In 1929 (before the stock market crash) Clark had sold his stock holdings and moved to Johns Hopkins University where he earned a Ph.D. in economics and served thereafter as dean of the graduate school of business. And the president chose me. I had completed at Columbia University all of the requirements for a Ph.D. in economics except writing a thesis, a project I had abandoned when I entered the New Deal in March 1933. I had been an instructor in economics at Columbia just before then, and I was a lawyer as well as an economist. When I was appointed to the CEA, I had had more than thirteen years of federal government experience both on Capitol Hill and in the executive branch, had conducted the studies and written the bills for some of the New Deal's most important economic and social legislation, and had had top-level administrative experience as deputy administrator and acting administrator of [the Public Housing Authority] one of the larger federal agencies.

The next question is whether President Truman selected three members for the original CEA (and other members later on) who could combine their useful independence and differences in background with a recognition that their utility in giving advice to the president depended upon reasonable harmony, instead of the bickering and breakdown that had confronted, for example, the early TVA [Tennessee Valley Authority]. Here again, Truman made sound selections. As conceded generally —even in Nourse's book, *Economics in the Public Service* (written after he left public service in distemper and before he had regained his equilibrium)—the three original members of the CEA under Truman achieved a remarkable degree of harmony on economic matters as such. (The sole exception was on the noneconomic issue of testifying before the Congress, which will be discussed below.) For the period from 1946 to 1953 as a whole, there were six Annual CEA Reports to the president (five of them published), ten Annual and Semi-Annual CEA Reports transmitted to the Congress with the Economic Reports of the President (only beginning in July 1948 were there separate CEA Reports, which reduced the president's Economic Reports to very brief documents), more than twenty-five unpublished CEA Quarterly Reports to the president, and a considerable number of unpublished CEA reports to the president on special subjects, often undertaken at his request. In only two or three relatively unimportant instances was the CEA divided in these reports, the most significant being a difference of about $2 billion in the acceptable size of the defense budget when Louis Johnson was secretary of defense.

The benefits which President Truman derived from the degree of harmony within the CEA on matters of basic policy and approach were not achieved by presidential fiat or prescription, but rather by his judicious original selection. Although the president picked CEA members of various backgrounds and independent minds, he recognized that he was picking men to serve his administration in jobs of cabinet-level importance and that they therefore had to be closer in their own thinking to the policies of a Democratic administration than to those of a Republican administration. This was true of Nourse, Clark, and myself. Nourse called himself an "independent" in politics; Clark and I had been conspicuously identified with the Democratic party. But on economic views and approaches, the three of us were very close, although our views were not identical. I had long been identified as a Keynesian, with a strong belief that the government's policies could be used variably to promote economic stability and growth. But unlike many later CEA Keynesians who took this position but did great damage to economic policy by placing too exclusive a reliance upon it, I had always pointed out that the behavior of investments, profits, prices, and wages in the private economy had an even larger quantitative influence. Thus, I had always insisted on an integrated analysis of the needs and potentials of the economy as a whole, accompanied by goals for achievement, and urged the use of public policy not only directly but also to influence without controlling (except to a degree in time of war) the decision-making processes within the private sector.

Nourse was also of the Keynesian viewpoint and, like me, was distrustful of it only in the sense that some claimed too much for it. And he, perhaps even more than I, directed attention to the need for delicate adjustments in the private sector. Accordingly, we were both committed to a combination of vigorous and definitive national policies and national efforts through education—or what some call the jawbone method—to influence the private sector.

Clark was less precise and less articulate in his general views, but as a liberal in economic and political philosophy, he had no difficulty in serving within the Truman administration framework. In those rare instances of economic policy where Nourse and I disagreed, Clark was very likely to come down on my side (as he did on the question of relations between the CEA and Congress); and he joined with me in being much more interested than Nourse in monetary policy and in low interest rates.

As I have suggested, the only serious difficulty and discord within the Truman CEA involved the issue of whether the CEA should testify before the Congress on occasion, particularly before the Joint Economic Committee when it held hearings on the Economic Reports of the President. From the outset, Nourse insisted that CEA should not, alleging that to do so would force him either to disagree publicly at times with the president or to defend presidential policies which he deemed unsound. Clark and I felt strongly to the contrary. We pointed out to Nourse repeatedly that to enjoy being chairman of CEA but avoid tasks which he temperamentally regarded as onerous was like trying to have one's cake and eat it too. We felt that men of integrity were obliged to support the president for whom they worked when the differences between the president and themselves were slight and to resign when they were sufficiently great and that the chairman of CEA was indistinguishable in this matter from a cabinet secretary, the budget director, or the head (or heads) of the military establishment. Under the law the Economic Reports were prepared and sent to Congress with the assistance of the CEA, which created the normal expectation that the reports would be explained to Congress by the CEA. The Economic Reports had to have some executive branch "trustee" when they got up on the Hill; and it was patently inadequate and slightly ridiculous when, due to the unwillingness of the CEA chairman to appear before Congress, Averell Harriman and Charles Brannan and Paul Porter, in turn, had to explain and defend the overall economic policy of the president. Finally, we argued that regardless of the substantive merits, it was usual and proper for a procedural matter regarding the functions of CEA to be determined by majority vote and not by the chairman acting unilaterally.

But despite the strong views we held, Clark and I never pressed this issue with the president nor put it before the public; instead, we acquiesced in the Nourse position until mid 1948. Despite this, Nourse advertised our internal difference in the media, thus creating the public impression that Clark and I were too "political" while he remained "objective." This charge was damaging to the CEA for a spell, but in fact, the charge arose only because of my defense of presidential policies in which I believed. Nobody, at any time, charged me with recommending to the president for "political" reasons any policy in which I did not believe; nor did President Truman ever exert the slightest "political" pressure on me.

Nourse's own position, however, on the issue of testifying before Congress may well be suspect (and I mention this only because it bears on my evaluation of President Truman's behavior in this matter). Nourse made speeches all around the country in part defending and in part attacking President Truman's policies—and, incidentally, thus negating his alleged reason for not wanting to appear in the one forum in which it was really necessary. The plain fact is that Nourse did not want to be closely affiliated in the public eye with President Truman's policies. This was not because of any substantial disagreement with them, but rather because of his desire to remain CEA chairman. The Republican congressional victory in 1946 had led him to expect the election of a Republican president in 1948. Shortly before the 1948 election, Nourse wrote to Senator Taft (chairman of the Joint Economic Committee in the Republican Congress), sounding the senator out as to his—Nourse's—chances of holding on to the job come 1949. The reelection of President Truman was a severe disappointment to Nourse (I remember the look on his face the morning after and the candid remarks of his secretary); his resignation in the summer of 1949 was due in large measure to the Truman victory. Thus, Nourse really behaved more "politically," in a narrow personal sense, than either Clark or I. This friction within the early CEA might have destroyed another agency or impaired its main work; not so in the case of the Truman CEA, for the reasons I have already stated.

The friction over congressional testimony affords one of the very few instances of which I am aware when President Truman fell short in a matter of administration or "command." The question of CEA members appearing before Congress was not an economics issue at all (where the CEA members' differences were to be respected by the president); it was an issue of the orderly and proper functioning of a vital government agency. My conviction is that President Truman, at the outset of a problem of which he was fully cognizant, should have told Nourse promptly in early 1947 what the president's concepts about the role of the CEA were—and should have made clear what they were. Instead, the president remained silent until mid 1948, when he quietly passed the word that those CEA members who wished to testify on the Hill could do so, but that Nourse need not.

Consequently, Clark and I appeared before the Senate Banking and Currency Committee in mid 1948 during its hearings on inflation. He and I first appeared before the Joint Economic Committee in early 1949, as did the three CEA members (after Nourse's resignation) each year until the end of the Truman administration. With the advent of the Eisenhower administration, the new CEA chairman, Arthur Burns, finessed the matter of congressional testimony in a peculiar way: he agreed to appear before the JEC, but only off the record. Every CEA chairman since Burns has defended the president's program vigorously and openly before the JEC, through the media, and all around the U.S. Because I had blazed the trail, no one called them "political" for doing so; and but for Nourse, no one would have done so in my case, for it represented an accepted course.

I have never been sure that President Truman was correct, even on the grounds of political strategy, in his tender temporizing with Nourse for almost three years. The president privately referred to Nourse, not too admiringly, as "the old gentleman" but seemed to overestimate his public prestige. If the president had told Nourse, early in 1947, what the CEA should do on the Hill, I do not think it would have produced a resignation at that time. And even if it had, the negligible public stir would have been no greater than when the inevitable resignation occurred in mid 1949. It has always seemed to me hard to understand why with Nourse, President Truman departed so evidently from his habitual decisiveness in doing what he thought was right, regardless of projections about public reaction.

Over the years, President Truman found increasing use for the CEA, both in its direct relationship to him and in its relations to others, in and out of the administration. This was reflected in the amount of authority and encouragement that he gave the council. Nourse's claim in *Economics in the Public Service* that Truman had only perfunctory interest in the work of the CEA and held it or the chairman at arm's length is entirely without justification; Nourse simply did not comprehend the nature of the presidency. The CEA met regularly with the president at least six times a year as a matter of course during the Nourse years, and the chairman and the president met even more frequently. Near the beginning, the three members were also invited on occasion to attend cabinet meetings to brief that group on the economic situation. After I became CEA chairman, my reasonably frequent requests to visit alone with the president were always welcomed. Whenever I phoned Matt Connelly for this purpose, I always got a date set immediately, and it was never too far off.

The council or the chairman always sat around the table with the president and members of the White House staff to go over the drafts of the Economic Report line by line as it neared its final stage; and during the Truman administration (unlike succeeding ones) there were two Economic Reports rather than one sent to the Congress each year. In addition, as earlier stated, the CEA submitted four Quarterly Reports to the president and from time to time was requested to furnish reports on special subjects.

Leon H. Keyserling

Beyond these contacts between the president and the CEA which might be characterized as "normal," I was often asked to prepare or work on drafts (or portions of drafts) of presidential speeches and/or messages, sometimes asked to write a talk for him on economic subjects, and in many instances asked to join the president and the White House staff to go over these line by line.

There was still another kind of opportunity for me to be in direct contact with President Truman. From time to time when I became chairman of the CEA, or at least from the time of the advent of the Korean War, I was invited to all or most meetings of the cabinet and even of the National Security Council. I did not attend these meetings as an onlooker, sitting against the wall, available to answer questions that might be posed, but rather as a full participating member, sitting at the cabinet table (where the NSC also met) and being accorded by President Truman exactly the same treatment as the others during the course of the discussions. This was a strong indication of President Truman's appreciation of the importance of the CEA—and/or perhaps of his regard for me. To the best of my knowledge, no subsequent chairman of the CEA has been fully accorded this status.

The utility to the president of the CEA and/or its chairman depends also upon the opportunities accorded by the president that enable the advisory body or individual to maintain contacts with others in the government, to influence them, and to benefit by their specialized knowledge and experience. In these respects, President Truman's conduct was excellent. The continuous working relations of the CEA with other agencies and individuals were indispensable to the CEA's work; these relations were known to President Truman, and without his personal action at times, especially in the formative period, they would not have been so full nor useful. At the cabinet level, I maintained cordial relationships with those secretaries concerned substantially with economic policies. In the early stages, drafts of the Economic Reports and the council's Annual and Semi-Annual Reports (which were published and submitted to Congress) were sent to the appropriate cabinet officers for their comments. The CEA was not instructed nor obliged to accept these comments, but I can recall no important instances when initial differences of emphasis or opinion were not ironed out before the president accepted the documents and they were submitted to Congress. I maintained a similar relationship, much less definite and regularized, with Chairman [Thomas B.] McCabe of the Federal Reserve Board.

I am not going to discuss separately the relationship between the CEA and the Bureau of the Budget except to state that it always operated on practically the same basis as with the cabinet departments.

Beyond this, the initial stages of formulating the federal budget for each fiscal year benefited by the CEA's appraisal of the economic outlook and its policy implications. I must admit, however, that there has always been an unfortunate tendency—and especially so recently in both the executive branch and the Congress—to deal with the budget excessively as an entity in itself. In fact, the budget is only one instrument, to be sure the most important, of national economic policy; and it has long been my view that the "Budget in Brief" should be an integral part of the Economic Report. All too frequently, the Economic Report has been a rationale for the budget, instead of the budget being derived from the Economic Report.

These top-level contacts were facilitated by the formal and practically year-round relationships which I initiated between members of the CEA staff, the staffs of various departments, and some others. These links were especially fruitful because they followed about the same organizational pattern as that of the CEA staff.* By common consent of all CEA members, even when I was vice-chairman, I was predominantly responsible for the organization of the CEA staff and for the direction of its studies and work programs; I gave these tasks constant and intense attention. In some agencies large and small, these tasks are entrusted to a ranking staff member rather than to the agency head (or heads). I am convinced that this is a very bad practice; it may happen because agency heads are sometimes selected for reasons other than their competence and/or because they devote relatively too much time to external public relations.

The CEA's contacts with members of the White House staff did not—and could not have been expected to—add as much to the "economics" of CEA work as did the contacts with others, detailed above. But the White House staff contacts did add greatly to the council's influence with President Truman, both directly and through his staff's confidence in the CEA. The continuing contacts of the White House staff were both with members of the CEA and with its staff, but were never along disorderly lines; and the demarcation between the two lines of contact soon became clear. My own contacts with the White House staff were frequent, ad hoc in timing, and usually impromptu, with the initiation coming from either side.

---

* As of May 1, 1951, the interagency committees working with the council (through a CEA staff member designated by me to serve as chairman of each) were: Current Economic Analysis; General Economic Policy; Fiscal Analysis; Agriculture; Wage-Price Policy; International Economic Policy; and Short-Term Projections. Within the CEA at that time, there were also staff committees on statistics; editing; long-range projections and requirements (including industry structure, business investment, and materials); manpower; and public works development and housing.

Leon H. Keyserling

Despite their obvious propinquity to the president, the White House staff never behaved, at least in my area of work, as a super-layer between me and the president, nor did it ever compete with me. Indeed, the staff never acted as if it and I were peers, nor even as if I were first among equals in advising the president about economic policy; it always acted on the premise that this was predominantly my job and not theirs. Nonetheless, the staff's involvement in my services to the president was essential. And the very reason why the White House staff never overstepped was simply because President Truman, as a good administrator, did not give two people the same job, knew whose job was whose, and supported the person to whom a job was assigned.

If I were to list my contacts with these White House staff people in the order of their influence with the president and the extent of their contacts with him (as I saw it), I would place Clifford first, when he was there, and then Murphy, when he succeeded Clifford. Next were Bell and Elsey and Lloyd and Stowe, whom I set forth alphabetically. It was a rare experience to be associated with these men. Although I cannot estimate quantitatively the extent to which my influence with the president was due to the support I received from these men, who saw him more frequently and whose basic views and sympathies were so similar to mine, clearly the extent of my success in influencing policy was very substantially attributable to these men. But this was a circular process; in turn, my influence on them was not inconsiderable. We respected and liked one another, and we were all selected by President Truman and were devoted to his purposes and to him personally.

My contacts with John Steelman, the assistant to the president, were inconsequential during my years on the CEA, except that he contacted me and had (or claimed to have) considerable influence in the selection of the CEA members. I should mention, however, that Steelman could well have been a thorn in the side of the CEA, primarily because of his "conservative" views and alliances and also because of his aggrandizing tendencies. But the actions of President Truman himself and the great influence with the president of other members of the White House staff, especially Clifford, prevented it from happening. I hold this to be a mark of President Truman's excellent judgment; it had very little to do with organizational or administrative patterns. (By the time Murphy succeeded Clifford, I was less dependent on others to help me with the president.)

When the CEA presented the draft of the first Economic Report to the president in late 1946, it was completely rewritten and mangled in Steelman's office. If this practice had been tolerated, the CEA would have become an adviser to Steelman rather than to the president, and

The Executive Office Agencies

that was neither the intent of the Congress nor sensible on any grounds. But largely on my personal insistence, with strong support from Nourse, all concerned parties sat around the table in the chairman's office and brought the draft back very close to what the CEA had originally intended. This incident was never repeated; Steelman never again intruded. He did persist, however, at least during the Korean War, in preparing and publishing reports at regular intervals on the economic situation and outlook. My own view is that President Truman should have put a stop to this. But he may be excused on the grounds that the Steelman reports never attained the dignity or public acceptance of the CEA work and, therefore, were not really damaging. Still, they were clearly wasteful. If published reports were desirable with this frequency, the president should have asked the CEA to prepare them.

It should also be added that in the sharp policy differences which sometimes arose between the liberal and conservative forces within the Truman entourage, the distinct and valid impression is that Steelman usually lined up on the side of the conservatives—ordinarily including Treasury Secretary John Snyder and Commerce Secretary Charles Sawyer. Such a division is neither unusual nor undesirable; it may be helpful. The fact that President Truman almost always adopted the liberal view is attributable in a large part to the skill and persuasiveness of Clifford, in some part to Truman's increasing respect for and confidence in me, in part to some of the other liberal members of the cabinet and White House staff, but most of all to President Truman himself. After all, he made the decisions.

The manner in which the president's Economic Reports and the CEA's published reports were initially drafted within the CEA should be described. The CEA initially drafted the Economic Report of the President, which until mid 1949, as I have said, was a long and comprehensive single document; thereafter, the president's report was very short, also drafted initially within the CEA, and ultimately transmitted to the Congress with a very comprehensive CEA report. I have already depicted the contacts with President Truman and others in the later stages of preparing these reports. In drafting the CEA report, the various CEA staff committees prepared memoranda in their respective fields and made some attempts to integrate them. But when I was vice-chairman as well as when I was chairman, I always rewrote these considerably, modified some of the interpretations, asked for additional coverage, and worked the entirety into a unified and cohesive draft. In the case of the Economic Report of the President, after it became a brief one, I did the draft myself and then consulted with the staff. Thereafter, for both the president's and the CEA's reports, the three members of the council went over the two drafts with selected members of the staff and made any changes in style and substance we deemed desirable. When this task was completed, we circulated the drafts in the manner I have already explained.

All this was entirely in line with my firm concept of the appropriate division between staff and agency head (or one designated agency member). This setup within the CEA never caused any difficulty between me and other members—indeed, it was much appreciated by Nourse when he was there—partly because it was obviously sound and turned

ACME Telephoto

Leon H. Keyserling, chairman of the Council of Economic Advisers, outlines economic fluctuations during the first six months of the year, July 25, 1950.

out to be workable and partly because neither Nourse, Clark, nor the later CEA members, [Roy] Blough and [Robert] Turner, had any inclination to exercise the role which I performed.

Under Truman the Economic Reports of the President and the published reports of the CEA were much more comprehensive in an important respect than under subsequent administrations. Instead of concentrating almost exclusively on fiscal policies and recommendations related thereto, they treated specialized problems requiring microeconomic programs and policies. A substantial part of the work of the CEA staff, under my direction, looked into problems of current or potential shortages in steel and a number of other basic lines of production. This type of work, which commenced in earnest for a couple of years before the Korean War and was indicated in the 1949 and July 1950 reports, was contained extensively in memoranda within the CEA. With the advent of the Korean War, attention to these specific areas of the economy became much more intensive and, not without the influence of the CEA, was carried forward largely by the Mobilization Agency. Yet, when the January 1953 reports were issued, Prof. Alvin Hansen said that they were the best examples he had seen thus far of planning documents. Our economic situation in recent years would have been much better if similar planning and more comprehension and cohesiveness in the development and application of national economic policies had been carried on.

With the advent of the Korean War, there were a number of other important examples of my contacts with, influence upon, and help from those who advised the president directly. As mobilizer, Charles E. Wilson held regular meetings of his staff, I believe about once a week, to follow up on the mobilization program. Of course, I would not put myself in the position of being a member of Wilson's staff or as being under his direction in any way, but I was invited and did attend these staff meetings. This gave me a good opportunity to know what was going on in this field, to let Mr. Wilson have the benefit of my advice (which he frequently took), and, not infrequently, to differ with him. Some of these differences ultimately came to the attention of the president in one way or another. Indeed, Mr. Wilson and I differed on the issue which ultimately led to his termination by President Truman and replacement by Henry Fowler. Nonetheless, my relations with Mr. Wilson were always friendly and continued for many years after we both had left public office. I also maintained similar useful and cordial contacts with Eric Johnson, Michael DiSalle, and Alan Valentine when they were involved in the Korean War.

Second, during the Korean War there was an advisory committee to Mr. Wilson (or to the president, but that met with Mr. Wilson—although

President Truman attended on some occasions), composed of representatives of industry, labor, and the general public. It was appointed, I believe, by the president. At the instance of the president and with his encouragement, I briefed this group from time to time on the economic aspects of the war effort.

Third, there were frequent meetings during the Korean War of a working group that dealt primarily with National Security Council problems and documents; most of the people at these meetings were high-level staff members rather than their principals. But I deemed these meetings to be of sufficient importance for me always to attend them in person. This was valuable to me, and I believe that it was valuable to the president. In any event, he thought so.

There was also a session that was in some ways more important than any of the contacts I have described (other than the meetings with President Truman himself). From late 1946 or early 1947 to about the time President Truman announced he would not run for another term, a small group met on Monday nights for dinner and discussion at the residence of Jack [Oscar R.] Ewing. This group regularly included Ewing, Clifford, Murphy, Undersecretary (and then Secretary) of Agriculture Brannan, Assistant Secretary of Labor David Morse, Assistant Secretary of the Interior C. Girard Davidson, and J. Donald Kingsley and John Thurston, who were assistants to Ewing. A few others, such as Howard McGrath when he was chairman of the Democratic National Committee, attended very irregularly.

The task of this group, with the knowledge and approval of President Truman, was to develop policies and programs that the president might adopt in the national interest—with due consideration for achieving better results in the 1948 presidential elections than the Democratic party had managed in 1946. Although all the president's top-level advisers, including me, played a part, it was Clifford who primarily reported to President Truman the positions formulated by this group. Clifford's role within the White House and his consummate skill, tact, and powers of persuasion with the president were unquestioned. I do think that in matters of substance rather than tactics, perhaps due to my longer and wider range of experience with domestic policies and programs and my more intensive study of them, I made as large a contribution as any other person to the deliberations and decisions of the Ewing group—and in that sense to what ultimately affected the actions of the president. The proper apportionment of credit between contributions of substance and of persuasion I must leave to others in their evaluation of the evolution of the Fair Deal.

In the discussions at these Ewing-group meetings, I sometimes advanced political arguments in support of the substantive positions I espoused; but I never advanced for political reasons a position which I thought undesirable in substance. And while I cannot appraise in every case the extent to which other members of the group were affected by substantive and political arguments, I have already stated my strong belief that in general we were people of like minds: We thought much the same about what was good for the country; we accepted the Democratic philosophy of "watering the economic tree at the bottom"; and we were deeply desirous of doing what was right by helping a president with the same intent.

I turn now to the nub of the whole matter: President Truman's response to the CEA services, as reviewed above, and the effects of his decisions on the economy and the people. In my contacts with President Truman at group meetings, including those of the cabinet, I deemed him to be an excellent and discerning presiding officer, so to speak, rather than a dynamic leader or innovator. He listened well; he elicited the best from the people around him; he maintained a calm and friendly atmosphere; and he stated his own positions clearly. He seemed to play no favorites, although it became obvious over time that without hurting anyone's feelings he valued the opinions of some more than of others. There are, however, natural limits to the productivity of relatively large group meetings, and most of the president's important decisions were made on the basis of discussions with a smaller number of people or with only one person. His decisions were sometimes made in their presence and sometimes when he was alone.

In my meetings with the president alone, or in meetings between him and the CEA as a whole (which usually ran from fifteen to thirty minutes), he exhibited the same qualities and proceeded in much the same fashion as I have just described. His knowledge of the workings of the government, as is well known, was exceptional for a president. A good part of the time, he knew his own position on an issue when it was first brought up and stated it firmly and clearly. Otherwise, he listened attentively to the position expounded by those with him, and then usually stated his views at once. In almost all cases involving my direct contacts with him, he agreed with my position, which of course made me feel good. But I did not regard this as unusual; he had confidence in all or most of his major advisers and acted on the principle that they knew what they were talking about and were highly competent in their specialized fields.

I have just stated some of the reasons why President Truman almost always accepted the basic economic policies which I recommended or joined in recommending. But there were other, and perhaps more fundamental, reasons for this. The president and I were essentially compatible in our economic and social philosophies and in our concept of the role of the federal government. Without being at all an expert in economics, which no president is likely to be, President Truman had unbounded confidence in the unrivaled capabilities of the American economy. He recognized fully the need to call forth the greatest possible use of our bountiful resources through optimum real economic growth. He felt the imperative need to harness our productivity to the service of the people at large. He held fast to the traditional Democratic position that the economic tree should be watered primarily at the bottom, without treating any sector unjustly.

Harry S. Truman was an uncommon common man, and he represented first and foremost the people in all that he did. Perhaps he had read more than most presidents. But he seldom paraded the knowledge thus gained (although his reading of history entered into many of his judgments), and he never intellectualized. And because of the broad mutuality of approaches to economic policy between President Truman and me, I never found it necessary to expound general philosophy or theory to him, and he probably would not have had much interest if I had attempted to do so.

I want to add a few comments beyond what I have already said about the advisers close to Truman. Regarding the White House staff, I have already discussed Clark Clifford rather fully. Charlie Murphy, whom I had first known near the beginning of the New Deal when I worked for Senator Wagner and he was in the Office of the Legislative Counsel on Capitol Hill, was relatively reticent and quiet on the White House staff and sometimes made self-deprecating remarks in an entirely unwarranted fashion. But his heart beat for the common man, especially the farmer, and no one could have had better judgment or been more fundamentally outspoken and candid when the occasion arose. David Lloyd had a thorough grasp of economics, read widely on the subject, and after leaving the White House wrote an excellent book on government spending, *Spend and Survive*, which I reviewed favorably in the *Washington Post*. He also wrote two good novels. He was perhaps the most intellectual member of the White House staff, although of no higher mentality and of considerably less patience and tact than some of the others. David Bell was also a highly trained economist with an excellent mind, who was very precise in his thinking and cross-questioning. George Elsey was very able and endowed with a very fine personality; some people would call him "clean-cut." My contacts with David Stowe were much less frequent, but I had high regard for his abilities in general and for his knowledge of labor relations in particular. I have already said a good deal about Steelman, but in all fairness I should add that he was very hard working, had great ability along some lines, and was, in my opinion, fundamentally honest. I think that his lining up with the conservatives was not mainly ideological—I do not think he had too much ideology—but was rather because he seemed to value the approval of these people. All in all, as I have said, this description of the White House staff, to the degree that it is accurate, speaks worlds about the president who selected them.

Among the cabinet, I was closer to the liberals than to the conservatives, although I was on good terms with all of them. Shortly before Truman appointed me chairman of the CEA, he took me aside in the Cabinet Room and said, "You have won Snyder and Sawyer completely over." I replied, "Mr. President, I had to sell my shirt to do it." And President Truman replied, "Oh, no, you didn't!" My closest cooperation and most enduring friendships with members of the Truman cabinet were with Brannan and Harriman; I was also relatively close to Secretary of the Interior [Oscar L.] Chapman and Secretary of Labor [Maurice J.] Tobin.

There was only a single instance when President Truman's treatment of me may have been less than fully generous, although I cannot pass judgment on this because I do not know all of the facts. When a vacancy at the top occurred, President Truman usually filled it very quickly, especially when there was a second man whose qualities he knew—for example, when he replaced Frank Pace with James E. Webb as director of the budget. But my appointment as CEA chairman was not until about eight months after Nourse resigned. Almost immediately after that resignation, the president said to some of the White House staff people, "Now we can appoint Leon." But it seems that two lines of resistance developed.

First, some of the Establishment economics professors did not like the fact that I did not hold a Ph.D. in economics (I have described my record in that field); and more importantly, they thought that I was too "political" (also discussed above). They came down from Massachusetts and visited with Secretary of Labor Tobin on this subject. He told them that the arguments they cited against my appointment were among the best reasons for it. Second, there may have been some initial opposition among some of the cabinet conservatives; just prior to my appointment as chairman, President Truman told me that I had completely won them over.

These movements and possibly others led John Steelman to contact some economists and ask them whether they would be willing to serve on the CEA, although it is not clear whether he was referring to a membership or to the chairmanship. This, in turn, led in some quarters to the story that President Truman appointed me as chairman only after others had turned the job down. There is no evidence of this, and it is not true. President Truman never offered, nor authorized anyone else to offer, the chairmanship to anyone else.

In addition to what President Truman told the White House staff people as soon as Nourse resigned, at an early stage he assured Jack Ewing that he intended ultimately to name me chairman and asked Ewing to pass the word along to me: "Tell Leon not to worry and to keep his shirt on." Nonetheless, the long delay was embarrassing to me and, in my view, unnecessary. If the president had known me as well when I was vice-chairman as he came to know me during my almost three years as chairman, the appointment delay would not have occurred.

In my considered judgment over the years to date, Harry S. Truman was a great president. He knew where he wanted to go and how to get there. He was not sensational, but he was sound in the best sense of the word. His sympathies and his concern for the lot of the common man were the hallmarks of his entire domestic performance. In the important spots, he put the right people in the right jobs, and he used them about as effectively as possible.

WALTER S. SALANT

I shall confine myself to two small episodes. The first has no great, general significance but may conceivably indicate something about how Truman operated during his first months in office; the other illustrates the distance between the president—and indeed the top White House staff—on the one hand and the working levels of the government on the other.

The first episode concerns the firing of one of the most courageous public officials I have known. William H. Davis was chairman of the War Labor Board during most of World War II and became the economic stabilization director a month before Truman became president. In September 1945, President Truman announced at a press conference that he was reorganizing the Office of War Mobilization and Reconversion and that as a part of that reorganization the Office of Economic Stabilization, then outside of OWMR, would be converted into the Economic Stabilization Administration within OWMR. As I recall the story, a reporter asked the president, "What happens to the chairman [sic] of the OES?" President Truman answered, "Well, he won't have anything to do. John Snyder will take his job." At that moment Davis was attending a meeting in the East Wing of the White House; a reporter dashed over there from the press conference to report this interchange and to get Davis's reaction. He was stunned; he had not been told in advance. The first hint we in his office had of Truman's action came when the office driver, who had driven Davis to the White House meeting in the office car, returned without him. Davis's secretary asked, "Herbert, where's Mr. Davis?" Herbert answered, "He said he wanted to walk. It kinda looked like he had something on his mind."

President Truman apparently fired Davis because of an erroneous report of something Davis had said about wage policy a few days before, and he later apologized to Davis. But the president's decision to fire Davis was impulsive, and his casual announcement to the press before telling Davis himself was brutal. However, both the impulsiveness of the action and the subsequent apology appear to have been characteristic. Underlying the free rein Truman gave to his impulses is the question of whether there was some suspicion or even animus that affected his attitude toward officials with whom he had no prior close personal relations. As Davis's successor, it will be recalled, Mr. Truman appointed U.S. District Court Judge J. Caskie Collet, who had no experience in stabilization matters but whom the president knew from Kansas City.

My second observation relates to the origins of the Point Four Program. As someone who is interested in this bit of history because I had something to do with it (although I do not know how much), I can testify that there are a number of partial accounts. Of the five that I have read, all but two are so different that nobody could recognize that they are about the same program if it were not identified by name, substance, or the occasion of its announcement. According to the Truman memoirs, the idea of the Point Four Program came from Truman himself; he had had it in mind for several years. According to Dean Acheson, "Technical help for developing countries had for some time been a feature of the Good Neighbor policy in the western hemisphere. The idea of expounding it on a worldwide basis originated with Clark Clifford."[1] According to Clifford, however, he, the president, and other members of the White House were looking for some fresh and provocative ideas for the president's inaugural address when Clifford remembered what he called "a State Department memorandum that had crossed my desk a few weeks or a few months earlier which advanced the idea of technical assistance to the less developed countries."[2] Clifford's reference to a "State Department memorandum" certainly suggests that the program had been proposed officially by the department. The memorandum Clifford must have had in mind came from a State Department official and was probably on the department's letterhead. But the writer, Benjamin F. Hardy, Jr., had smuggled it into the White House (through George Elsey) because his proposal that a worldwide technical assistance program be made part of U.S. foreign policy had twice been rejected by the department when Hardy had made it through channels.[3]

So far, then, we have four "originators" or sources of the idea: Truman himself; Clifford; the State Department, officially; and Hardy, personally.

---

[1] *Present at the Creation*, p. 265.

[2] Quoted by Cabell Phillips, *The Truman Presidency*, p. 272, from his interview with Clifford.

[3] See *Whistle Stop* 1, no. 1 (Winter 1973); and Betty Snead, "Origins of the Point IV Program," in *War on Hunger* (Washington, D.C.: Agency for International Development, 1973).

The Executive Office Agencies

Hardy's idea was clearly confined to technical assistance, and this came to be the accepted view of the Point Four Program. The question of whether a program intended to promote economic development should include any substantial amount of capital appears, from the published accounts, to have received little attention from any of these sources. In the inaugural address, however, after saying that "we should make available to peaceloving peoples the benefits of our store of technical knowledge," the president went on to say, "and in co-operation with other nations we should foster capital investment in areas needing development." There is nothing explicit here to indicate that the plan was intended to be primarily a technical assistance program or even that it emphasized technical assistance over the export of capital, although the words implied, without saying so explicitly, that the capital export to be encouraged was private capital. Nevertheless, the financial aspect of the aid was generally ignored, so that the Point Four Program came to be regarded as one of technical assistance only.

In December 1948, in a conversation with David Lloyd at a small social gathering, I had said that I thought we ought to be giving aid to less developed countries on a continuing basis and that such aid should be elevated to a major role in our foreign policy. Besides promoting the development of those countries, which was desirable for a variety of reasons, I said that aid to these countries for capital development could be of substantial help to Western Europe. Lloyd appeared greatly interested, and we arranged to discuss it further at the office. (We were both housed in the Executive Office Building.) In elaborating the idea to him at our second discussion, I explained that we needed to think ahead about the situation of Western Europe in a few years. The countries there would probably not yet be in a position to finance needed imports when direct aid through the Marshall Plan ended, and we would not want to continue direct aid. However, the export of capital from the United States to less developed countries would permit them to finance increased imports. Western Europe would be in a position to compete in these expanded markets if, as appeared likely, its capacity to produce such goods had revived sufficiently by then. Obviously, this approach emphasized the capital aspect of aid.

Lloyd said that he was interested in this idea for possible use in "a major speech by a top official" and that it had the same general thrust and was consistent with, although not the same as, an idea that had come to the White House through another channel. He mentioned that this other memorandum concerned only technical assistance. I believe I expressed the opinion that such assistance would not have much impact if it was not accompanied by an increased flow of capital, and it would certainly contribute nothing to Western Europe's "dollar problem," as it was then called. He asked me to get a memorandum to him by the end of that day. Later, he told me that he had presented the idea to Clark Clifford—in what form I do not know—and that some combination of these ideas was being favorably considered.

One reason I never knew—and still do not know—whether I also belong on the list of "originators" of the Point Four Program is that I never knew—and still do not know—what the White House had in mind as the role of capital in this program. Was there a difference of opinion about this question in the White House? Did it even come up as an explicit issue? Was government money excluded because it was desirable for political reasons to introduce a program that would have, among its virtues, only modest budgetary requirements? Did the White House intend to confine the program to technical assistance, or did it envisage, as I did, giving expansion of the flow of capital an equal role? In the process of putting the program into legislative form was that aspect squeezed out by the State Department which was entirely unprepared for the policy statement contained in the inaugural address?

There are several points that I find of general interest in this whole episode. First, it is not easy to find out how an idea becomes government policy. As I have already said, different accounts have attributed the idea to different sources. Historians, each relying on only one account, would get entirely different impressions. Yet not one of these accounts appears to be positively incorrect; they are all merely incomplete, reflecting what the particular source happened to know. For ideas that come to the top of the government's structure, the sources at the top are not reliable: Top-level officials rarely can know with whom an idea originated. On the origin of the Point Four Program, Truman's memoirs appear to me of dubious reliability.[4]

This is probably true of all presidential memoirs, even those that are not rationalizing or justifying policies and actions. It is not a question of faulty memory; a president is not likely ever to have known the origin

---

[4] On the specific issue of the role of capital in relation to technical assistance, the *Memoirs* abound in inconsistency. In *Years of Trial and Hope* (volume 2), Truman refers to the Marshall Plan, one of financial aid, as having "hinted a new concept" (p. 230). He then calls the Point Four Program one of technical assistance (p. 230); says by way of background, "I knew from my study of American history that this country was developed by the investment of foreign capital"; and refers to his hope that stabilized governments would encourage "the investment of capital from the United States" (p. 231). And then he says, "We had both the capital and the technical 'know-how'. I did not see how we could follow any other course but to put *these two* great assets to work in the underdeveloped areas" (p. 232, my emphasis).

of an idea passed on to him by his immediate staff. To get a true view, the historian must consult many sources each of whom have seen events from a different vantage point.

My second general observation is that it is quite difficult for the White House, eager for fresh policy ideas, to get them from the bureaucratic machinery. There is nothing new about this, perhaps, but it should be noted that in the case of the technical assistance proposal the difficulty did not reflect any lack of creative ideas. According to the account in *War on Hunger*, the first State Department rejection of Hardy's idea was based on the objection that the department's budget had already been submitted. In short, an important policy initiative, which the White House apparently was eagerly seeking, was first blocked in official channels by a relatively trivial administrative consideration. The second time, the proposal got further in the department but was rejected on the grounds that it was not timely. The first rejection shows that something was wrong about the communication of policy ideas within the department; the second suggests that something was wrong with the communication of the administration's desires to the department or with the department's receptivity.

The third general observation—not covered by this illustration—is the problem of how the White House can ensure that a program is carried out according to the president's intentions rather than being altered by the department that develops and administers it.

THEODORE TANNENWALD, JR.

It has occurred to me it might be helpful if I recited an episode which occurred while I was on the White House staff and which indicates how Mr. Truman viewed his responsibilities as president.

This involved the troops-for-Europe resolution and occurred, I believe, in February 1951. The resolution was an attempt by the Congress to limit the president's right to send more than six divisions to Europe. Charlie Murphy, Sen. Brian McMahon, and I went to see the president one evening in Blair House. The president said that he himself did not really care whether the resolution passed or not because he had no intention of sending more than six divisions; but he was going to fight the resolution's passage to the maximum degree because he was not going to be responsible for the establishment of a precedent which might embarrass a successor, fifty or one hundred years hence. President Truman understood very clearly what it meant to be president of the United States.

Now let me turn to three areas of White House, or Executive Office, operations in which I was involved.

Preparation of Presidential Speeches

The system for preparing presidential speeches usually involved a stable of four or five people who, in pairs or triplets or even four at a time, would prepare drafts. Charlie Murphy was in charge. Other members of the group were David Lloyd, Dick Neustadt, Dave Bell, Ken Hechler, and myself from the White House; occasionally Marx Leva and/or Frank Nash from the Defense Department; and Marshall Shulman, who was Acheson's speechwriter. The initial drafters would meet together in Murphy's office and discuss the framework of the speech. Then, usually one person would undertake to prepare a rough draft; after that the initial drafting group would assemble in Murphy's office the next day, or perhaps even the same day if the draft was ready, and go through it page by page and line by line. Murphy had the final say. After one or two drafts had been prepared, if Murphy thought that the speech was in reasonably good shape, he would take it to the president to get his preliminary reactions. Usually Murphy went alone. He would come back and give us the benefit of his discussion with the president, and then the drafting group would go back to work on the speech—doing one, two, three or more drafts. After the framework had been pretty clearly developed, a draft would be circulated to the departments involved and their comments would be requested. When these comments came back, they would be incorporated, if they were acceptable, into the final (or next-to-the-last) draft. When the speech had been put in final form as far as the drafting group was concerned, it would be submitted to the president at a meeting usually held in the Cabinet Room. The meeting would be attended by the heads of the departments (or their representatives) who were interested in the speech, plus, of course, the president, the White House press secretary, and the White House staff members who had worked on the speech. The president would go through the speech line by line and word by word, and some changes might be made. Additionally, there was a thorough discussion of the substantive problems involved in the speech. Upon completion of this process, the president would put his final stamp of approval on the speech.

The Office of the Director of Mutual Security

The organization of the Office of the Director of Mutual Security, which integrated all the foreign assistance programs, and its relationship to the other departments and agencies—particularly the Department of State and the European Recovery Administration—presented some very delicate questions.

Part of the problem arose out of the constant tension between efforts by the Department of State to retain jurisdiction over all foreign assistance programs and the pressures from other elements to keep the mutual security program outside of the State Department. The Office of the Director for Mutual Security was created at the last minute—in two hours during the course of a conference between House and Senate conferees on the Mutual Security Act of 1951 on a Saturday morning in October. The legislative sections creating this office, which were written by the conference committee without the benefit of participation by any representatives of the executive branch, gave the director for mutual security a dual role: first, to head the foreign assistance program, run through the Economic Cooperation Administration [ECA]; and second, to coordinate all the military, economic, and technical assistance programs. Harriman, with the president's approval, immediately delegated the responsibility for running the economic assistance program to a deputy (W. John Kenney); Harriman felt that no one person could both run the economic assistance program and coordinate all three programs effectively. Technically, there was no deputy on the coordinating side because no such position had been provided for in the legislation. However, to create a framework in which somebody could function on Harriman's behalf in connection with the coordination effort, one of the assistant directors for mutual security was assigned that job and given the additional title of chief of staff. This was my job.

Although Harriman had two deputies to act on his behalf, he believed that there had to be one official in charge of tying everything together. He also believed that that person should be outside the State Department, although he recognized the overriding need for a close working relationship between the head of the foreign assistance program and the secretary of state. The inherent problem of organization involved not only a theoretical concept but a practical one as well: it was often argued that if the right person was secretary of state and the right person was head of the foreign assistance program, it did not make any difference where the latter was located. By the same token, it was argued that if you did not have the right people in those two slots, any resolution of the question of where to locate the mutual security program would not solve the organizational problem.

The staff of the Office of the Director of Mutual Security always tried to operate as a coordinator. Our operations reflected Harriman's horror of interagency committees and his insistence that any committees which were set up were to be advisory only, with decisions to be made by one individual—usually the representative of the director of mutual security and chairman of the committee.

The legislative authority given the president to allocate funds between assistance programs was effectively delegated to the director for mutual security so that he would have the maximum power—after all, "he who controls the money controls the program."

Although the Office of the Director for Mutual Security had an independent status and function, we always operated under the principle that one of the regular departments, usually State, should take the lead and that our office would simply provide encouragement. In fact, however, we often had to play the leadership role directly.

The coordination of cabinet departments by the director for mutual security involved a delicate balance because he was really a layer between the cabinet officers and the president. Needless to say, there were many occasions, particularly in the field of military assistance, when the secretary of defense would try an end run by going directly to the president—if not to overrule our office, at least to embarrass us.

At the time the Office of the Director for Mutual Security was established, an overall Executive Order was required from the president. The wording of this order was extremely tricky because it had to synthesize two things. The first problem was to avoid infringing on the role of the State Department; obviously foreign assistance activities had to be conducted within the framework of U.S. foreign policy as determined by the secretary of state. To this end, the phrase "general direction" (as I recall) was left out of the Executive Order as it was finally issued. The second problem was to make sure that the director of mutual security in his coordinating capacity had channels of communication to, and influence over, the other government agencies involved in matters which affected the day-to-day administration of the foreign assistance program. For this reason, as I recall, there was language in the Executive Order dealing specifically with the relationship between the director of mutual security and the Defense Production Administration, the defense materials procurement administrator, and the secretaries of commerce and agriculture. Unfortunately, I do not have in my possession a copy of the Executive Order, so I cannot be more specific.

Transition between Administrations

I was also involved in the transition effort in 1952 and 1953. Upon instructions from Harriman, all of us on his staff gave the incoming administration the fullest possible cooperation. Several of us personally briefed Henry Cabot Lodge; and after Harold Stassen was selected to succeed Harriman, he was in continuous contact with us until the changeover. There was never any holdback; the key factor was the welfare and success of the foreign aid program.

JAMES F. LAY, JR.

The National Security Council was established thirty years ago by the National Security Act of 1947. The deficiencies exposed by the pre–Pearl Harbor period of diplomatic and military maneuvers, the handling of wartime problems involving relations between foreign, military, and domestic policies, and the development of policies for the postwar period demonstrated to many individuals, both in and out of government, the need for better machinery for coordinating our foreign and our military policies.

The National Security Act of 1947, passed by a Republican Congress and approved by President Truman, was best known as the legislation that provided for "unification" of the armed services. However, it also established the National Security Council to "advise the President with respect to the integration of domestic, foreign and military policies relating to the national security so as to enable the military services and other departments and agencies of the government to cooperate more effectively in matters involving the national security." The Central Intelligence Agency, created by the same act, was placed under the council. The act also provided for the establishment of a career staff headed by a civilian executive secretary appointed by the president.

Those who participated in the initial organization and work of the council were motivated by certain key principles. The central one was a recognition of and emphasis on the council's role as a policy advisory body to the president.

At the time the council was organized, there were some people within the executive branch who favored a somewhat different emphasis. They did not deny that the council was fundamentally an advisory body to the president. But they believed that when, in the absence of the president, there was consensus within the council on a particular matter, when the departments or agencies represented on the council were able to carry out the decision reached, and when that decision was within the scope of previously approved presidential policies, it would not be necessary to seek the president's approval.

It was decided, however, that the council's role should be limited strictly to advising the president. The advisory character of the council was the principal theme of the "Concept" of the council approved by the president in July 1948. The only qualification placed upon this proposition was the recognition that under the statute, the council members had certain corporate responsibilities for issuing general directives concerning the organization and coordination of the various departmental and agency foreign intelligence activities that related to the national security. Even this was not truly an exception, for the president retained the ultimate power of decision within the executive branch.

The advisory character of the council was reinforced by a general acceptance of the principle that divergent views on national security matters should not be suppressed but should be clearly reflected at each stage in the development of a policy.

Within this broad and basic concept the NSC officials responsible for organizing the council's work faced certain immediate practical decisions as to what kinds of problems should be tackled first. The council's functions, as stated in the statute, were very broad indeed. It was believed, however, that the council could most quickly establish itself as an organization of recognized usefulness to the president and to the departments and agencies if initially, instead of tackling some of the broader, long-range national security problems, it were to concentrate on developing policies to deal with problems that were of immediate, current concern to the agencies and that required a presidential decision. Finally, everyone recognized that under existing circumstances the NSC was likely to be concerned in a very considerable measure with problems involving foreign affairs and, accordingly, that the State Department would play a major role within the organization.

The act was approved by the president on July 26, 1947. Mr. Sidney W. Souers, the executive secretary–designate, began assembling a small, permanent council staff in August. The council held its first meeting on the effective date of the act—Friday, September 26, 1947. Mr. Souers was sworn in as executive secretary just prior to the meeting, together with the heads of two other new agencies established by the act, the director of the Central Intelligence Agency and the chairman of the National Security Resources Board.

Although President Truman presided at the first council meeting and at occasional meetings thereafter, he did not attend regularly until the beginning of the Korean War. The president's decision not to attend the NSC meetings was based, first, upon his concern that discussions might be terminated prematurely by any expression of his own views and, second, upon his conviction that by not attending he could best preserve his full freedom of action with respect to NSC policy recommendations.

Following its meetings, the council's recommendations were ordinarily brought to the president for his consideration by the executive secretary who served, in effect, as an administrative assistant to the president for national security matters. The president was kept regularly informed of the status of council business through regular briefings by the executive secretary. The executive secretary saw the president daily to brief him on the latest foreign intelligence as well as on council matters. From the beginning, even though the president did not regularly attend, council meetings were held in the Cabinet Room of the White House.

The council established standing committees or subcommittees from time to time. Such standing committees occasionally included members from noncouncil agencies.

The initial organization of the staff of the NSC, drawn from the agencies that participated in its work, performed two basic functions. Individual staff members were responsible for bringing the resources of their respective departments and agencies to bear on the council's work; and these individuals, as a group, prepared the papers considered by the council. The permanent career staff of the council provided certain central services as well as independent analyses of the subjects before the NSC and its interdepartmental staff.

As initially organized, the council staff had three principal components: first, the Office of the Executive Secretary; second, a secretariat which performed such usual duties as circulating papers, preparing agenda, and recording council actions; and third, a unit called "the staff" which developed studies and policy recommendations for council consideration. The Office of the Executive Secretary and the secretariat were composed entirely of permanent council employees; the staff initially consisted wholly of officials detailed on a full-time basis by the departments and agencies represented on the council. Because it was anticipated that the majority of problems falling to the council would relate primarily to foreign affairs, the State Department was asked to provide an official to head this interdepartmental group.

First and most important of the four principal categories of policy papers considered by the NSC were the basic overall policy papers that covered a wide range of national security problems and contained related political, economic, and military strategies. Second were the papers covering individual foreign countries or larger geographical regions. A third category might have been called "functional" policies. These covered such matters as mobilization, atomic energy, free world–Sino-Soviet bloc trade, and the regulation and control of armaments. Organizational policies constituted the final category. These included policies relating to the council's own organization, policies on internal security organization, and general policy directives relating to the organization and coordination of foreign intelligence activities, issued pursuant to the National Security Act.

At its first meeting, on the recommendation of the executive secretary, the council made the assessment of U.S. objectives, commitments, and risks in relation to actual and potential U.S. power a continuing, long-range study assignment of the NSC staff. It was decided very early that this assignment should initially be tackled through studies of certain critical areas of the world. And it was agreed that these studies should subsequently be incorporated in an overall appraisal of U.S. objectives, commitments, and risks.

The great majority of the policies considered by the council dealt with particular foreign countries or large geographical regions that presented critical problems at the time. Papers of this kind were focused on single (though major) problems and in some cases provided quite detailed policy guidance. Papers dealing with a single foreign country did not attempt to cover all aspects of U.S. relations, focusing only on certain key aspects. As the months and years passed, the council and its staff progressively tackled broader, longer-range problems and widened the scope and coverage of country and regional policy papers.

During this initial phase, relatively few policies of the "functional" variety were acted upon by the council. However, because the NSC was establishing many of its own basic organizational arrangements during this period and was also making recommendations for organizational changes in areas of governmental activity related to the council's work, organizational policies constituted an important part of the council's business. The council began in December 1947 to discharge its responsibilities under the National Security Act for issuing general policy directives concerning the organization and coordination of departmental and agency foreign intelligence activities that related to national security. In January 1948 the council initiated a general survey of foreign intelligence activities.

On May 4, 1949, the executive secretary met with State Department officials to discuss the work of the interdepartmental staff and the type of reports they had been preparing. On May 26 the executive secretary issued instructions to the coordinator of the staff requesting the staff (a) to conduct a periodic review of all current national security policies to determine what revisions were necessary; and (b) to undertake a program of studies on major policy problems, appraising their national security aspects and analyzing alternative courses of action open to the United States without making policy recommendations.

Members of the staff, although assigned to the council on a full-time basis and physically located together in the NSC offices, also maintained offices in and regular contact with their respective agencies. The first step in the preparation of any paper was a staff meeting to discuss the problem and to define the scope of the particular report. Then each staff member obtained staff-level views from his respective department or agency.

The usual policy paper prepared by the staff during this period consisted of three basic elements: first, a very brief and quite general statement of the problem being addressed; second, an analysis of the problem; and third, the conclusions. The conclusions were the only section of the paper normally acted upon by the council.

After several meetings, the staff draft was sent to the departmental representatives for their views on whether the paper was suitable for council consideration. Following such clearance, the paper, including any continuing divergent views, was submitted to the council for consideration. The views of the Joint Chiefs of Staff were obtained by the secretary of defense on any papers having military implications and were circulated to the council prior to its consideration of the paper.

The policy proposals acted upon by the council were prepared by the staff. Where a council member submitted a policy proposal directly to the council, it was usually referred (sometimes after preliminary discussion) to the staff for preparation of a report and recommendations. The council also acted directly upon a report submitted by one of its members (generally, the secretary of state).

During the latter part of the period under review, there was increasing use by the NSC of ad hoc committees to prepare reports. Such committees were generally composed of higher-level agency representatives than was the staff.

From the start the council agenda included a variety of different types of report. Some were submitted for consideration as the basis for policy recommendations to the president; others were submitted for council information.

In a typical council meeting, the executive secretary introduced each subject on the agenda, but generally did not attempt to summarize the contents of the reports on the assumption that each participant had done his homework in advance. A general discussion of the policy paper followed.

At the beginning of the council's existence a decision was made not

The Executive Office Agencies

to prepare written minutes reflecting the council's discussion; the reasoning was that to do so would have inhibited the discussion. The only permanent, official record made during this period was a record of the council's actions on the various subjects it considered. This record was prepared by the executive secretary, but it was not routinely circulated to council members for clearance before being submitted to the president. Council members could, of course, raise questions about the executive secretary's interpretation of what had occurred in the meeting, following circulation of the approved record.

Occasionally, when it did not appear necessary to have a formal discussion of a report, the council acted by a memorandum of approval.

After each council meeting, the executive secretary submitted to the president the record of the council's actions and the policy papers as amended and adopted by the council, including any remaining differences of views. He also submitted any Joint Chiefs of Staff views on the paper. The president then acted on the council's recommendations, approving or rejecting only the conclusions of the policy paper. If approved, they became the national security policy on the subject.

Following the president's decision, the record of the council's actions and the approved policy papers were circulated to all council participants. When the president approved policy recommendations submitted to him by the NSC, he directed that they be implemented "by all appropriate executive departments and agencies of the U.S. government under

ACME Newspictures—UPI
National Security Council meeting, January 25, 1951. *Left to right:* James S. Lay, Jr. (NSC executive secretary), W. Stuart Symington (chairman, National Security Resources Board), W. Averell Harriman (presidential adviser on foreign affairs), Gen. Walter Bedell Smith (director, CIA), Gen. Omar N. Bradley (chairman, Joint Chiefs of Staff), George C. Marshall (Defense), Dean G. Acheson (State), President Truman, John W. Snyder (Treasury). Vice-president Alben W. Barkley was not present at this session.

the coordination" of the department or agency head who had primary responsibility for implementing the policy involved. The head of a department or agency that had been assigned responsibility by the president for implementing a council action or for coordinating the implementation of a policy paper was informed of his responsibility by an individual memorandum from the NSC executive secretary. It was the responsibility of the coordinating agency to notify all other departments and agencies of the actions for which each was responsible in implementing the paper and to ensure that such actions were taken in a coordinated manner. The coordinating agency was also responsible for ensuring appropriate dissemination of the policy, or extracts from it, to government agencies which were not members of the NSC.

DISCUSSION

E. H. Hobbs (chair): I would like to open with a short statement concerning the Executive Office of the President. I am sure that all of us know that in 1937 the Brownlow Report—the report of the President's Committee on Administrative Management—proposed, among other things, that there be added to the White House staff additional administrative assistants, that the number of agencies reporting directly to the president be reduced, and that an Executive Office of the President be created. We also know that, after a brief gestation period, the Executive Office was formed in 1939. In itself, the formalizing of the Executive Office of the President did not give the president any new powers, duties, or additional responsibilities, yet it was a very significant action in the history of the presidency.

But when, on September 9, 1939, Executive Order 8248 was issued implementing the new structure, it was given very little attention in the press. In part, no doubt, this was because on that same day President Roosevelt proclaimed a limited national emergency. Needless to say, over the years—and particularly during the Truman administration—the Executive Office has grown in importance. Two major units which have endured the test of time were formed during the 1940s and added to the office by congressional enactment: the Council of Economic Advisers in 1946 and the National Security Council in 1947.

I want to start with a key question: Were there problems in coordinating the work of the various units of the Executive Office, and were there any pressures on Mr. Truman to set up a coordinator of their work?

Elmer B. Staats: You have to remember that when President Truman took office, the Executive Office was made up primarily of the Bureau of the Budget. There had been established under President Roosevelt a variety of agencies for the civilian wartime programs, virtually all of them under the president's authority. But the Office of War

Discussion

Mobilization, which James F. Byrnes (and later Fred M. Vinson) headed up, was really about the only unit that served the president directly; the rest were creatures of the president's legal authority but did not, in practice, report to him directly.

At the time the Executive Office was established, there was a National Resources Planning Board, chaired by Frederick Delano; it was abolished by Congress in about 1942. There was an Office of Facts and Figures under Archibald MacLeish and an Office of Government Reports that Lowell Mellet headed up; both were later merged into the Office of War Information. There was a Central Statistical Board; it was merged into the Bureau of the Budget.

So, in the early days of Mr. Truman's tenure, the only problem of coordination was between the Bureau of the Budget and the Office of Defense Mobilization.

There were some strains between Harold Smith (director of the Bureau of the Budget) and Justice Byrnes as to who had primacy; but generally the arrangement worked very well, and there was no particular need for the White House staff to intervene. Later on, as you have indicated, the Council of Economic Advisers, the National Security Council, and also the National Security Resources Board were established, adding to the number of units. By the time President Truman left office there were some seven units within the Executive Office, if you include the White House itself. In contrast, by the way, there were some fifteen units at the time President Ford left the White House.

As to your specific question on whether there was pressure to provide for coordination among the various units: During the Truman administration there was very little of this. (To be sure, there were differences of opinion in terms of the advice given the president from time to time.) The fact that we were all physically located in the same building helped a great deal: People often had lunch together, and it was no problem to pick up one's papers, walk down the hall, and discuss a problem with a counterpart in the Executive Office.

When we had a problem involving a mutual interest of two units of the Executive Office, we went together to see the president, or we went together with a member of the White House staff to see the president.

Hobbs: May I ask a follow-up question: Did the White House staff meetings include, with any regularity, the various directors of the other units within the Executive Office?

Staats: I do not recall that there was ever any participation by the Bureau of the Budget in those morning staff meetings. We frequently knew what was coming up because we would get calls from members of the White House staff on something that was going to be discussed or following those staff meetings, if there was some interest in following up or in the Bureau of the Budget doing some staff work. I do not recall that we ever sat in on any of the staff meetings.

ROGER W. JONES: After Mr. Webb became director of the Bureau of the Budget, even though he was, on occasion, invited, he felt that his role was different from that of the remainder of the staff and that he ought to stand more or less aloof from the White House staff's own work.

LEON H. KEYSERLING: I think the history of the Council of Economic Advisers is a prime example of the ability of President Truman to provide for coordination. The Employment Act of 1946 was in itself an attempt at coordination because it was based on the idea that it was not enough for the president to get economic advice from segmented parts of the government, expert though they were, but that there ought to be a unified national economic policy with an agency devoted to that purpose. That was why the Council of Economic Advisers was established.

The main vehicle for this coordinated policy was the Economic Reports which the president sent to Congress. During my period on the council (although this was not the case later) the reports were sent to the Hill twice a year. The reports carried the printed notation "Prepared with the assistance of the Council of Economic Advisers." This reflected the aim of the 1946 law that the CEA was to be the primary instrument for the development of the president's coordinated economic policy.

How did President Truman implement this? The first Economic Report was prepared for issuance in January 1947. It was a single document, perhaps fifty printed pages, a thorough economic analysis, factual, analytical, accomanied by program recommendations.

Recognizing that it was a little incongruous for the president to sign a document of that length, about two years later, at my suggestion, we broke it down into a short Economic Report from the president and a long accompanying report transmitted to the Congress in the same package and called "The Annual Report of the Council of Economic Advisers." But in one sense there was no real distinction between the two. Obviously both reports contained policies; the council's report contained the analysis on which the president's report was based. Therefore, one might say that the president's report was a summary of the longer report, cast in presidential style. The council, of course, prepared both the president's report and the council's report.

At the very beginning of the budget preparation cycle we provided the Bureau of the Budget with certain economic assumptions to be used, though not mandatorily, in the preparation of the budget.

Discussion

We established a group of interdepartmental staff committees paralleling the working committees within the council; a council staff member chaired each interdepartmental committee. These continuous staff relationships served to reconcile differences so that as we approached the time when our reports had to be submitted to the White House proper, the groundwork had been laid. Presumably, the heads of the various departments had been kept informed by their staff representatives; but before the reports went to the White House, I directly contacted the various cabinet members. I remember a particular occasion when Secretary Snyder called me up about some point in the draft that he had concern about: we settled it in two minutes on the phone, and there was no problem. That was the way it worked.

Then the process moved to the White House. What we did was get together, with the council's draft as the basis. We sat around the table and made changes—just as any group working together makes changes in details. The policies were already known; the White House staff never attempted to override us on policy. We made changes in phraseology, and as the council became more mature, as our contacts increased, and as our respect for each other increased, those changes were usually quite minor.

Now, let me come to some of the other ways in which President Truman improved this relationship between the Council of Economic Advisers and other parts of his administration. At least beginning with the Korean War, President Truman treated me like a member of the cabinet. This was a recognition by President Truman that the old-line cabinet, composed of legislatively established departments, no longer reflected the major concerns of the government, especially in wartime. He recognized that the postmaster general was less important (to put it frankly) than the chairman of the Council of Economic Advisers or the director of the budget.

Secondly there were certain other groups established, of which I was a member. One of these was especially important and had a bearing upon the increasing familiarity and friendship between the White House and myself (first as vice-chairman and then as chairman of the Council of Economic Advisers). Immediately after the 1946 congressional elections, when the Eightieth Congress took over, President Truman set up an unpublicized group which met every Monday night for dinner and conversation. That group included Charlie Brannan, Clark Clifford, Charlie Murphy, myself, and a few other people; the group continued until President Truman announced his intention not to run again in 1952. This group really was set up for the purpose of reexamining the position of the Democratic administration and its policies, and it was quite influential with the president.

During the Korean War there arose the question of coordination between the Council of Economic Advisers and Mr. Wilson's office [the Office of Defense Mobilization]. President Truman took a great interest in that. It was a difficult problem, because to have subordinated the council to Mr. Wilson would not have worked: economic policy is—or should be—broader than war policy. On the other hand, it was politically impossible to subordinate Mr. Wilson to the council. President Truman solved the problem. He told me, "I don't want you in any way to be responsible to Mr. Wilson, but I want you to participate in the meetings Wilson holds every week with the chief operating people in the war program." That was done, and I attended as a representative of the president.

There was also a mobilization board—I do not remember the exact name—but it was a representative public board with [William] Green and [George] Meany from the AFL, [Philip] Murray and [Walter] Reuther from the CIO, business representatives, and public representatives, of whom I remember William H. Davis. I believe that the president was technically the head of that group, but as a practical matter Mr. Wilson was the chairman. Maybe Mr. Wilson was the technical chairman as well. In any event, the president insisted from the beginning that I attend all of their meetings and that every week I brief this group on the economics of the war program.

I think I have covered various ways in which Harry Truman personally took a deep interest in the effort to coordinate. You never do this by organizational charts, you do this by taking account of the people you are working with, who is good for what, and how you can put them together. I think President Truman did a superb job on that.

HOBBS: Are there any comments?

JOHN W. SNYDER: Mr. Truman certainly took a great interest in Mr. Keyserling's operation, and he did consult with him continuously. But Mr. Truman never considered him a member of the cabinet.

KEYSERLING: He may not have considered me a member, but he had me there.

CHARLES S. MURPHY: I would like to add a footnote to this discussion.

First of all, there is no statutory basis for the cabinet; it is whatever the president says it is at any given time.

But I want to talk about the participation of Mr. Keyserling and the

Discussion

Council of Economic Advisers in the Korean War effort and also in connection with the work of the National Security Council.

About Christmas of 1949, the president gave me a paper to read which, as I understood it, had been prepared by the Departments of State and Defense. It had to do with the overall view of our defense posture and the risk and dangers to which the nation might be subjected. This was not a field in which I had done very much work up until that time or in which I had a great deal of background, but I was enormously impressed by this paper. I thought that the situation really was very serious and that it was extremely important that something be done about it. This was, as I say, at the end of 1949, when the government had been operating on the theory that the defense budget could not be more than about $14 billion without bankrupting the country. Louis Johnson, who was secretary of defense, was generally credited with being responsible for that view. I have always been doubtful that he really was the one who originated that view; I am inclined to think he was more in the position of a man who was given instructions and then tried to carry them out. But that is the background against which this paper came.

The president asked for my recommendations with respect to this paper, and I recommended that it be referred to the National Security Council and that Mr. Keyserling be asked to work with the NSC, particularly because of the acute question of the economy's capacity to support an expanded defense effort.

The president did refer the document to the National Security Council where it became known as NSC-68. I asked for permission to work with the NSC on this.

One of the things that was discussed a great deal in the NSC senior staff group was the capacity of the economy to support a larger defense effort. From time to time we would turn to Leon and ask, "How much can the country afford to spend on defense?" And Leon would say, "I don't know exactly, but you have not reached the limit yet."

And this, it seemed to me, was enormously important.

HOBBS: I would like to move a step further and ask a question that is really a matter of public administration theory. It is this: A well-established principle of public administration is that the hostility of line agencies toward staff agencies is inevitable. Were there examples of this during the Truman administration? Did any of the department heads find the Bureau of the Budget, for example, and the controls that it exercised bothersome, frustrating, and what not? Were there clashes of any sorts with any of the agencies within the Executive Office of the

President? All of you indicated that you felt that you had free access to the president, but were there problems with his associated agencies and at lower levels?

JONES: From which side of the table do you want an answer on that one?

HOBBS: Either side.

SNYDER: You will find in my paper a discussion of the Treasury's relationship with the Bureau of the Budget. Mr. Truman's notion about the budget operation was a little different from Mr. Roosevelt's, but the Treasury and the Budget Bureau worked very handsomely together. Through four different budget directors during my administration as secretary of the treasury we got along splendidly, with Mr. Webb in particular.

STAATS: I would like to support everything that John Snyder has said but add to it also the importance that we both attached to developing common assumptions about the revenue side of the budget. Now this is very important. When the Council of Economic Advisers came into the picture, it was factored in, along with the Commerce Department and the Federal Reserve System. But the Treasury Department–Budget Bureau relationship was particularly important; all along, there was consultation between the two. In the briefings we had with President Truman, it was Secretary Snyder and Mr. Webb and myself, with some others, who sat around the table talking over the budgetary situation. At the time of the press briefings on the budget, the president sat in the middle with John Snyder on one side and the budget director on the other.

I would also like to address myself more directly to your question. Were there clashes over the budget recommendation that went to the president for a particular department? It would be almost a truism to say that there was a difference of opinion in every case. The question was, how did it get resolved? Charlie Brannan can tell you that every year we had discussions about what should be the proper budget level; to the extent that we could not work these things out directly, the department heads understood, as did the president, that the issue would come to him for resolution.

There were not too many cases where we had to do that, but everybody understood all along the line that the president's door was open. If it was a matter we knew the White House staff was interested in, certainly they became involved; all of us were interested in having complete staff work for the president.

Discussion

THEODORE TANNENWALD, JR.: Let me reinforce what Mr. Staats has just said. I mentioned an example earlier in which I was involved because Governor Harriman was in Europe on the "wise men" operation. In the finalization of the fiscal '53 budget, we ran into an irreconcilable dispute with the Bureau of the Budget. I have forgotten whether it was over the total level of funding for the aid program or only some major segment of it. But there was just no question that the way you got the answer was to go to the president. I went to the president with Mr. Lawton, and the president made the decision.

In terms of your question about hostility and tensions, the Office of the Director for Mutual Security—its history and how it worked—is probably a shining example. When Governor Harriman came back from Paris to do the coordinating job (or whatever you want to call it) plus his advisory job as the president's special assistant on foreign affairs, there were tensions between State and Defense. Governor Harriman found himself in the middle of these tensions. There were also some questions as to how this new office of special assistant to the president was going to operate. From the time the Economic Cooperation Administration was created, with Paul Hoffman as its head, until 1951 when

Treasury Secretary John W. Snyder and Budget Director James E. Webb review the mid-year budget with President Truman, August 20, 1947.

the first overall Mutual Security Act came into being, there was a constant argument about where the foreign aid program belonged. Did it belong in the State Department or should it be an independent agency? Indeed this struggle manifested itself in the fact that in the Mutual Security Act of 1951 the House bill provided for the agency to be independent and the Senate bill called for it to be part of the State Department (or maybe it was the other way around). Then, in two hours on a Saturday morning, in conference, without the benefit of any staff advice other than the very effective work of the then undersecretary of state and former director of the Bureau of the Budget, Mr. Webb, who was defending and protecting the interests of the State Department, there emerged a middle ground in which the Office of the Director for Mutual Security was created and given two tasks. One was to run what had been the old ECA; the other was to coordinate the military, economic, and technical assistance aspects of the foreign aid program. The technical cooperation program had been part of the State Department and remained there. The military assistance program was really an operation of the Defense Department and remained part of the Defense Department. When Governor Harriman was named by President Truman to be director for mutual security, the problem of State *vs* Defense immediately came to a head. It obviously portended tensions and reflected hostility.

Here for the first time was statutory layering: there was just no question that somebody was being put between the president and the departments involved—the statute required it. The question was how to handle it in a way that would produce the maximum result in a very important aspect of our foreign policy, with a minimum of difficulty and friction. Governor Harriman made the decision immediately; the problem of running the old ECA and doing the coordination job was too much for any one person to take on. He delegated authority to run the agency to John Kenney and retained for himself the coordinating function given him by the statute. But he wanted it understood, and he made it very clear to his staff, that we were to operate by encouraging the underlying agencies to take the lead and to resolve the problems, with our being only the catalyst.

The hostilities were reflected, for example, in the Executive Order that assigned certain responsibilities nominally given to the president under the act and spelled out the role of the Office of the Director for Mutual Security. I remember there was a great argument about whether the director should be given the authority, as I recall the language, of "general direction of the foreign aid program"; the phrase was finally taken out and some compromise language substituted. The power given

Discussion

to the president under the act to allocate funds between the various types of programs was delegated by the president to the director for mutual security. While it was a power that gave us, in many ways, ultimate control over a program, it was a power that remained in the background and was rarely used directly to accomplish the purpose that we had in mind. When that power was exercised, it was usually done only after a very strenuous effort had been made to produce a consensus between the State and Defense departments and our own office.

The special assistant's office and the Office of the Director for Mutual Security are shining examples of the fact that it often does not make any difference what is on paper, or indeed even what is in the statutes, because authority depends so much on the relationships between the warm bodies in the key positions. It is a tribute to Governor Harriman and to President Truman, who had such great rapport with Governor Harriman, that relations with Secretary Acheson, Secretary Marshall (and later Secretary Lovett), and, of course, with John Kenney (and before him Paul Hoffman) were such that the latent hostilities never became open conflicts. But the problems were there, make no mistake about it.

HOBBS: In your paper, Mr. Tannenwald, you refer to "end runs" by the secretary of defense as a means of embarrassing the Office of the Director of Mutual Security, if not to overrule the office. What were the results of these end runs—negative or positive—and did Truman try to minimize them, and if so how?

TANNENWALD: There were some examples, and as I recall, the end runs were often made more by way of the Joint Chiefs of Staff than they were by the Defense Department itself or by the secretary of defense. The shining example is the one that I mentioned earlier, when there was a real argument in September or October of 1951 as to where tanks were going to be sent—to the armored divisions in Texas or to the NATO forces. We thought we had it all settled that the tanks were going to go to the NATO forces, and then I found out that there had been an end run and that the president was of the mind to have them sent to Texas. That was the one episode where, as I recall, Secretary Lovett and I could not reach an agreement. We went to the president and it got resolved: the tanks went to Europe.

W. AVERELL HARRIMAN: Well, I think there were very few end runs. This one I recall.

HOBBS: Judge Tannenwald, do you think the president recognized these approaches by the secretary of defense as end runs, and if so, what did he do to discourage that kind of administrative procedure?

TANNENWALD: I would not put it in terms of President Truman recognizing these moves as end runs and then doing something about it. I would rather put it that the president would recognize a problem when it was brought to him as being one on which he would like to have the benefit of somebody else's point of view. He would, therefore, make sure that he knew what that other person's views were before he made a decision.

It is a little bit like what I said on the subject of a chief of staff of the White House: Charlie Murphy was not Chief of Staff, but it was a pretty good idea to talk to Charlie about a matter before it went to the president because if you did not talk to him before, you were likely to find yourself talking to him afterwards.

HARRIMAN: Of course, this was really a conflict of interest between two responsibilities of the Defense Department—to carry out the foreign mutual security shipments and to look after their own requirements. It either had to be settled by the secretary of defense, or if I disagreed, it had to be settled by the president. So it was not really an end run, but rather a conflict of interest, which we thought had been decided in the wrong way.

HOBBS: Let us move into an area I do not believe we have touched on so far, and that is the establishment of presidential study commissions. Was Mr. Truman effective in obtaining results from these commissions and, if so, what were the relations of these special commissions to the Executive Office agencies?

PHILLEO NASH: I would just point out that the whole country's attitude on civil rights and on majority-minority group relations was turned around by the President's Committee on Civil Rights. It was set up with the idea that there had to be a change in national sentiment. The president's powers of persuasion, of setting up a forum, and of calling on citizens to discuss important differences was made use of. It was a very carefully thought-out decision on Mr. Truman's part, and it was enormously effective. Some of the effects are still being felt today, and some of the processes that commission initiated can still be seen as ongoing processes today.

HOBBS: Mr. Nash, did that commission have a liaison arrangement with your office?

NASH: Yes. Mr. Niles and I provided the staff assistance and sup-

Discussion

port. Everything was discussed very fully with other members of the White House staff and with Mr. Truman, but basically we provided the liaison, helped select the committee members, looked up the authorities, etc. We also did a little help with the committee itself in ensuring as unanimous a report as possible with a minimum of dissent in a highly controversial area. Then there was also the question of whether there would be further support by legislation; here, of course, we went straight to the president and to his counsel.

STAATS: It seems to me that the answer to a question of that type has to be in relative terms. I can think of two commissions that I was involved in. One was the Fahey Commission which was set up to look at the whole problem of materials, supplies, and shortages. This was a commission set up at the recommendation of Stuart Symington and the Budget Bureau, and staff liaison between the bureau and the NSRB was very close. Out of that came some better guidance—on stockpiling policy, for example, and on incentives for minerals exploration—but certainly not a complete acceptance or recommendation.

The other commission I can think of was one on water resources policy, chaired by Morris Cooke. That again was a commission established by the president at the recommendation of the Bureau of the Budget, which was having great problems with the water resources development agencies on what the reimbursement policy should be. We had this out with the Soil Conservation Service and with the Corps of Engineers and with the Bureau of Reclamation. Again some recommendations were accepted, and some were not. I think that would be pretty much par for the course on any commission.

JONES: We need a footnote here that the Truman concept of the presidential commission was quite different from the wave of "taskforc-itis" that began to hit us a few years later. I find that in some of the literature the distinction between the two has not been maintained, that task forces of later administrations are being treated as similar to those Mr. Truman established, and that is not true—as Elmer just pointed out on both the Fahey and Cooke commissions.

THOMAS BLAISDELL (University of California, Berkeley): I would like to make just one comment with regard to the special commission the president appointed dealing with the armed services that Philleo Nash was talking about. When Charlie Fahey was asked to become chairman of that particular commission he went to the president and said, "Mr. President do you want a commission which will give you a report, or do you want something done?"

223

The president's answer was, "I want something done."

Fahey replied, "I'll take the job."

The difference between commissions that are appointed to bury problems and those that appointed to do something is very important and one that President Truman recognized.

KEN HECHLER: In 1951 President Truman asked the American Political Science Association to set up a commission on soldier voting. They made a very comprehensive report with recommendations that were subsequently sent to the Congress in a message by the president, and the Congress did enact legislation to ease the process of voting by members of the armed forces. I thought this was a very clean-cut example of a commission that did a thorough report, legislation resulted, and improvements were made.

NASH: Could I offer an aside to Tom Blaisdell's story? I think that Dave Niles was the one who first suggested Judge Fahey. Niles described Fahey to me as the reason why he would be an excellent choice for this committee: "He is little, he speaks in a little voice, and he is tough."

I said, "That certainly sounds like the right fellow to me." And he was. He spoke in a way that required you always to lean forward to listen to him. And as we came to admire the work he did, Dave and I referred to him as "Whisper" Fahey.

HARRIMAN: There is one agency which the president used to coordinate the activities and mediate the opinions of different departments or agencies; it has not been mentioned and I think should be mentioned. The president appointed the National Advisory Council which gave directions to our representatives on the International Monetary Fund and the World Bank. The secretary of the treasury was the chairman of it; State had a representative; I was represented as secretary of commerce —I can't remember all of the other agencies. There were definitely differences of opinion, particularly (as I remember it) between myself and the representative of State on different loans to be made. Here was an agency to resolve differences. I don't know how active it is today, but it performed a very important coordinating activity which functioned very effectively.

WALTER S. SALANT: For the record, that was a statutory body set up in the Bretton Woods Agreement Act.

HOBBS: Let us turn our attention now to another vital unit of the Executive Office and that is the Bureau of the Budget. One of the bureau's most formidable responsibilities is legislative clearance as well

Discussion

as several other important duties in this particular field. What I would like to know is how this institutional responsibility for legislative clearance meshed with the political orientation of the White House toward legislation?

JONES: Elmer Staats was the first real head of what was then called the Division of Legislative Reference in the Bureau of the Budget. I was his deputy and also the congressional liaison man. My job was to say in touch with the committees of Congress, particularly during the Eightieth Congress which was Republican controlled, to keep them advised of presidential programs, and in turn, to try to bring back certain institutional advice from the committee staffs. But this process could not have succeeded if we had not had the almost total backing of President Truman and certainly the total backing of the White House staff, particularly Mr. Murphy. Later on, Dick Neustadt and other people from the Budget Bureau moved over, people who were familiar with our working processes—Dave Bell, Harold Enarson, Russ Andrews, Dave Stowe. All of them in one way or another had been involved in the rudimentary processes of legislative clearance which had grown up—some since the early days of the Roosevelt administration. Dick Neustadt has traced the history of legislative clearance in his articles in the *American Political Science Review.*

Very early on the president approved the concept of trying to get together a total picture of what legislation might be recommended to the forthcoming session of the Congress. Accordingly, the Budget Bureau annually called for the legislative programs from all of the departments and agencies; subsequently the bureau's staff separated the proposals into several categories. First there were those items important enough to be considered by the president for inclusion in his legislative program. Then there were items which were of a minor nature, but about which the president certainly had to know since he would be asked to support them in his budget.

Another category consisted of items which had to do with expiring laws; this was an important category and one to which not enough attention had been given before Elmer and I started working on this operation. There had been a number of instances in which the White House of an earlier era had been caught short with a sudden realization that a law would expire on the thirtieth of June and that nothing had been done about setting the stage to get it continued.

And finally there were those items which seemed to us, on the first go-round, to be so far afield that they should not receive serious considerations by the White House. As the president's agents, after clearance with the White House staff (and if necessary, with the president), we would go back to the departments or agencies and tell them that this or that proposal was not timely or was something the president did not want or created the wrong kind of conflict with other agencies or programs.

As the fall months proceeded, this work of categorizing and refining was tied in closely with the budget process itself. The various proposals were worked into the process of evaluating the cost estimates sent in by the agencies. Elmer, as the first head of this operation, quite wisely made the decision that we would not attempt to second-guess the budget division and that we would not set up a large staff which would dupli-cate the budget preparation divisions. We kept our staff small and worked through the other divisions. This general concept and philosophy of operation continued not only through the Truman and Eisenhower administrations, but well into the administration of President Kennedy and to some extent the administrations of President Johnson and his successors.

The key to what I consider to be the outstanding success of the whole operation was the availability of the White House staff. Almost any issue could be taken there, some of them calling for the development of legislation. I remember one instance in which we worked very closely with Admiral Dennison who—I guess because he wore a blue suit—had been saddled with the job of trying to straighten out the whole problem of what the economics of our maritime policy should be: the amount of subsidy for ship construction in American yards, the amount for paying higher wage rates to crews in the American maritime unions, and some of the other issues involving the redoubtable Mr. [Harry] Bridges and his organization. Through Mr. Murphy's intervention, and with the pres-ident's full support, we were able to move anywhere in the White House staff in this developmental process.

Once Congress took action on legislation, whether it had originated at our end of the avenue or in the Congress, there was an improvement in the ensuing procedures which had been in force during the Roosevelt years. Facsimile copies of all enrolled enactments came to the Budget Bureau and were circulated by us to all agencies interested or affected. Fred Bailey, my predecessor, had tended to send copies of enacted bills only to the agency of chief concern. This was extended somewhat during the latter years of Harold Smith's directorship. But Webb, Pace, and Lawton wanted the bills sent to all interested agencies. They directed us to gather departmental views and then pull them together into a summary which was forwarded to the White House. To keep the insti-tutional character of this procedure, our memoranda were all addressed to Bill Hopkins. (In those cases, however, when we had a veto message

Discussion

or something of the sort to work on, the memoranda went to the president.)

We always tried to get everything to the White House so that there would be five full days for consideration there, but we frequently failed on this. I remember one occasion when we were unable to get an enrolled bill memorandum to the president until the very night that the bill was to expire. President Truman actually took action over in the White House about 11:30 P.M. This was repeated once more in the Eisenhower administration. I guess after that everybody got religion and decided we couldn't impose on the president to such an extent.

Then there came the question of the follow-up: What else was necessary? To the greatest extent possible, the budget director became a channel back to the agencies to develop the necessary structure for administering new legislation.

One final note. I referred earlier to an institutional relation with the committees of the Congress. This began largely in the Eightieth Congress when the Republicans were in control and there was a Democratic president. It seemed wise to have some kind of channel of communication to let the committees know through their own staffs what administration reactions were to all kinds of things. And we rather expanded the process of clearance of agency reports. We never really told an agency outright that it could not report to Congress whatever its views were—except, of course, on presidential items when the agencies were not free to depart from the president's position. Our effort was to let the committees know, in an informal, fairly stereotyped way, whether there was any strenuous objection from the administration to the nonpresidential items. All of this was covered by a Budget Bureau circular which, although it has been revised a couple of times, is still in effect. This circular (A-19) lays out the formal, almost ballet-like, rules for handling agency testimony on legislation.

STAATS: I think Roger has covered it extremely well. I will just add two very brief points. One of the reasons that we felt it important to have a legislative program was to preserve the integrity of the budget itself. Previously many legislative proposals had gone up after the budget was submitted and had not been provided for in the president's budget. So our intention was to see that every item of legislation involving $10 million or more became incorporated in the budget.

The other point I would make is that given the close adjunct relationship which this function had with the special counsel's office (first Mr. Clifford and then Mr. Murphy), we were never quite sure who we were working for, the budget director or the counsel, but that didn't really make too much difference. The only time that the budget director said we had to come and check with him was if a very large amount of money was involved; otherwise we went ahead and worked with Clark Clifford and Charlie Murphy.

JONES: One little footnote on this. In the next administration, when Rowland Hughes was director of the Budget Bureau, he decided that every enrolled bill that went to the White House should be personally reviewed by the director. I did not like this much and decided there was only one way to handle it. I think this was one of the few times that I have been engaged in subterfuge with my boss.

I waited until we had a total of nearly fifty minor pieces of legislation, put them all in one of those big archives-type baskets that you push around, took them into Rowland's office, and said, "Here is the legislative package that the president must take action on within the next three or four days." The freedom of Legislative Reference to operate with the White House staff was almost immediately restored.

RICHARD E. NEUSTADT: Let me add three comments. This operation, which my two colleagues have just described, was absolutely crucial. The tie to the special counsel and the special counsel's bundle of functions, as described by Charlie Murphy, has been dispersed around the White House in other administrations. As a result the ability of Legislative Reference to serve has been seriously crippled so that it now takes a bureaucracy in the White House itself to backstop this operation.

Secondly, during the period we are talking about, the Truman administration, there was no formal legislative liaison staff in the White House. That has several implications. Administration bills were not drafted by the administration, nor were they presented by the White House; they were presented by a department head, if there was one. The White House only got directly involved if it was a sphere of legislation in which there was no department. The bills might have been drafted in a working session that came out of the White House–Budget Bureau relationship, but that was in fact, not in form. In form, administration bills were sent by a department head and introduced by a member of Congress as a courtesy or were given to a member of Congress to introduce.

Mr. Truman had sensitive feelings on this subject. Thus, the practices during his tenure differed enormously from those of subsequent administrations. Among his aversions were an unwillingness to license formal lobbying from the White House and an unwillingness to have formal liaison across the board, as is now done. The liaison operation began under Eisenhower and has continued ever since. But it was distinctly *not* a feature of the Truman administration. But I defer to Charlie who, as I recall, when he first arrived in the White House as an administrative assistant, was instructed not to draft any bills.

MURPHY: I do not remember any instructions not to write any bills, Dick. But I am sure that when I first went there to work, there was no organized effort anywhere on the White House staff to keep up with the progress of the legislative program in Congress. The Bureau of the Budget did some of this, but the White House staff did none at all. Since I had come from working on the Hill and was interested in legislation, I began to keep a kind of crude record for myself of what was happening to the administration's program. That eventually grew into something that was somewhat more orderly and better organized. And from time to time there did develop some effort on the part of the White House to encourage Congress to act favorably on the administration's legislative program.

Now, this consisted mainly of the efforts of the president himself, in person. He met regularly with the leaders of Congress, he had a weekly meeting with them. This, I would say parenthetically, is an extremely important institutional arrangement. Along with the president's daily staff meeting, one of the most important recommendations I would make to any administration any time is to have a regular schedule for meeting with congressional leaders.

In the case of President Truman, a supplementary practice also developed. He would make phone calls to key people in Congress in support of a piece of legislation if I made a recommendation that he do so and if he thought the recommendation was right. A good deal of this went on; these phone calls were usually very short, but they were usually quite effective.

Later President Truman did appoint two liaison people to the staff. This was within not more than two years before the end of his administration. Charlie Maylon worked on the House side and Joe Feeney on the Senate side.

I have never known, for sure, why President Truman had the attitude he did about legislative liaison with the Congress and the responsibility of the president to make Congress perform its constitutional functions and not the president's, but I have always suspected that it was a part of the result of his Senate experience and the attitude in Congress toward President Roosevelt's efforts to get his legislation through, including the attempted purge of a number of members of the Senate in 1938. I suspect that President Truman went to the White House with the belief that it was the president's responsibility to make recommendations to the Congress for legislation and that it then was up to Congress to pass it, not up to the president to whip Congress into line.

JONES: I think all of us who worked with President Truman and who have been students of the presidency would recognize, without any doubt, that President Truman was the great constitutionalist among our twentieth-century presidents. He knew about the office; he had both an innate and an intellectual sense of the powers of the presidency and how they should be exercised; and this set a tone and an example for all of us. It made us feel that we were extensions of his own tremendous concept of what the office was.

SNYDER: I want to call attention to the fact that under the OWMR operation, which was set up under President Roosevelt and operated by Jimmy Byrnes and Fred Vinson, there was a responsibility placed on OWMR to follow through on *any* presidential recommendations to Congress. That probably grew out of the transition from peace to war, but it was President Roosevelt's notion that when he sent up recommendations for legislation, it was wise to follow-up and see how it was progressing in Congress. When I first went into OWMR, Fred Vinson had set up a rather effective group of contacts in Congress to follow-up on White House recommendations. Of course, when we dissolved the OWMR, that function disappeared. But for the record, you may find that there was some organized arrangement to follow-up on White House or presidential recommendations.

HARRIMAN: I have already mentioned one case in which the president did not want to become involved with Congress on matters which he thought were his responsibility. But when I was mutual security director, there was one case which confirms what has just been said.

Towards the end of the administration we were having trouble getting the amount of money that we thought we needed for mutual security, and the Congress suggested a watchdog committee. I went to the president and recommended that we accept the watchdog committee. I said I knew these men, and it was just as easy to let them in before an operation than to try to defend it to them afterwards. He said, "Averell, you don't understand. The greatest responsibility that I have as long as I am sitting in this chair is to preserve the authority of the president of the United States. This suggestion is an invasion of the administrative responsibilities of the president by the Congress. And if the Congress ever gets control of the president's authority, we will have chaos in this country."

Well, I readily understood that, because I had just come from Paris

Discussion

where the legislative branch had had complete domination of the executive branch and the average cabinet lasted only five or six months. I can give you four or five other cases where the president drew the line against congressional interference in his authority as president.

STAATS: The issue of the seventy-group air force was a good case in point. As I recall the president had recommended about forty-four or forty-five groups. Congress overrode that and appropriated funds for seventy, and he was going to impound the funds. The Bureau of the Budget and the attorney general both advised him that he did not have the legal authority.

He said, "I am commander in chief, am I not?" And he never let the money be spent.

HARRIMAN: There was another case. President Truman wanted to appoint Dean Acheson to run the Marshall Plan because Dean Acheson had been one of the originators of the idea. But Senator Vandenberg wanted a Republican, and the president was indignant that Vandenberg should interfere with his responsibilities of nominating an administrative officer. Of course, he never could have gotten the legislation through Congress without Vandenberg's approval, and Vandenberg was right that Congress needed a Republican to administer this program, a Republican businessman.

TANNENWALD: There is a counterpart to the watchdog committee story. I have forgotten whether it was in 1950 or 1951, but there was a provision which I believe the Senate put in the foreign aid bill directing the president to spend $25 million for aid to Spain. The president was adamant: Congress could authorize him to do it, they could give him the money (or not give him the money), but the one thing they could not do was give him the money and tell him how he had to use it. We succeeded in getting the provision knocked out in conference, but this was a very clear indication of the president's understanding of the role of his office.

HOBBS: Let me move the discussion now toward the budgeting process itself. Maybe we can start off by going back to a criticism which the Hoover Commission leveled against the Bureau of the Budget, charging that the bureau did too much of the budgeting for the departments and that the budgeting process should be more decentralized. Are there any reactions to that criticism?

JONES: Yes, I will react to it: They did not know what they were talking about. President Hoover himself admitted it a little bit later on.

231

comments about the coordination among the various agencies and the budget process—as a kind of general wrap-up observation.

SALANT: I would like to point out that as we came out of World War II, there was a big change in the role of the budget as an element of economic policy. The budget was much bigger, but more importantly, ideas about the role of fiscal policy in the effective functioning of the economy had changed a great deal since before the war. The budget process consisted not only of details, of adding up the requirements of particular operating agencies (which Elmer Staats has referred to), but also encompassed the overall question of economic policy. This was the main concern of the Council of Economic Advisers.

The Bureau of the Budget was still the expert on expenditures; the tradition had been that revenues were estimated in the Treasury. But there had not been any tradition, or indeed much practice, about who was responsible for estimating the budget's impact on the national economy. That, of course, became the responsibility of the Council of Economic Advisers.

The possibilities for conflict between the Bureau of the Budget and the Council of Economic Advisers was seen by many people when the council was established. I recall that there were some people who thought that there was a very dangerous risk of conflicts between these two agencies within the Executive Office.

As it turned out, however, there was very little conflict, for reasons that Elmer Staats covered earlier: There were very good personal relations, helped along by physical proximity. Furthermore, one of the staff members of the Council of Economic Advisers, the one charged with responsibility for fiscal policy, Gerhard Colm, had come from the Bureau of the Budget where he had been the chief economist on fiscal policy. But I think there was something more than personal relations and physical proximity involved in this lack of conflict: namely, the similarity of views about economic policy that prevailed among the people at the top of the Budget Bureau during that period and those on the council, the staff as well as the members.

HOBBS: There is one question that I cannot resist asking. The CIA was created during Mr. Truman's presidency. Did he ever express any concern about its intelligence-gathering activities or about political intervention by the CIA?

LAY: I would not think so because he was right there, giving instructions and deciding what he wanted done.

ROBERT L. DENNISON: The answer to that question is, no. I think

Discussion

that in the early years of the CIA, the agency was not involved in matters that would lead to that kind of uneasiness on the part of the president.

MURPHY: I would like to pursue that a little bit. It is my recollection that President Truman regarded the creation of the CIA as a means for him to get intelligence—and intelligence that was coordinated. He said he was getting intelligence from a number of different sources and somebody ought to pull it all together.

So far as I remember that is the only function he had in mind for the CIA, and I do not remember that he foresaw the CIA engaging in extensive covert operations or political intervention. I was not very deeply involved in the details of that, and I would like to know from Mr. Lay and Admiral Dennison if they share my same impression that President Truman would be startled, shocked, and very unhappy at some of the things that the CIA has done in recent years.

LAY: I agree completely.

DENNISON: I do, too.

LAY: He looked upon the CIA as an intelligence operation to give him the information he needed, and that is what he wanted.

SOME PRIMARY SOURCES
ON THE TRUMAN WHITE HOUSE

The following list is intended as a guide to the location and availability of papers and oral history interviews of members of the Truman administration. Most of the materials listed are housed at the Truman Library in Independence, Missouri; other archival depositories are shown in parentheses. The letter "c" has been used to indicate records that are still closed to researchers; "p" means that special permission must be obtained; and "s" indicates that the records are not yet available for use by researchers.

Name	Papers	Oral Histories
Dean Acheson	x	
Clinton P. Anderson	x	
Eben A. Ayers	x	x
David E. Bell	x	p
Thomas C. Blaisdell, Jr.	x	
Roy Blough	x	
Charles F. Brannan (Columbia University)	c	
Oscar L. Chapman	x	s
John D. Clark	x	
Tom C. Clark	s	x
Clark M. Clifford	x	s
Gerhard Colm	x	
Matthew J. Connelly	x	x
Jonathan Daniels	p	p
Donald S. Dawson		s
Robert L. Dennison	x	x
George M. Elsey	x	x
Harold C. Enarson	x	
Oscar R. Ewing		x

Some Primary Sources

Name	Papers	Oral Histories
James H. Foskett	x	
Martin L. Friedman	x	x
Clayton Fritchey		p
John T. Gibson	x	
Dallas C. Halverstadt	x	
William D. Hassett	x	x
Ken Hechler	x	
William J. Hopkins (John F. Kennedy Library; Truman Library has copy)		p
John C. Houston	x	
Charles W. Jackson	x	
J. Weldon Jones	x	
Roger W. Jones	x	
Richmond B. Keech		x
Leon H. Keyserling		x
Robert B. Landry	x	s
Frederick Lawton	x	x
David D. Lloyd	x	
Edwin A. Locke, Jr.	x	x
James I. Loeb	x	p
Edward I. McKim	x	x
Cornelius J. Mara	x	x
Charles J. Murphy	x	x
Philleo Nash	x	c
Richard E. Neustadt	x	
Edwin G. Nourse	x	x
Frank Pace, Jr.	x	x
Edwin W. Pauley		s
Irving Perlmeter		x
Spencer R. Quick	x	
J. Leonard Reinsch		x
William M. Rigdon	x	x
Samuel I. Rosenman	x	x
Charles G. Ross	x	
Walter S. Salant	x	x
George J. Schoeneman	x	
Beth Campbell Short		x
Joseph H. Short	x	
Harold I. Smith	x	
John W. Snyder	x	s
Stephen J. Spingarn	x	x

Some Primary Sources

Name	Papers	Oral Histories
Elmer B. Staats (Dwight D. Eisenhower and John F. Kennedy libraries)		x
John R. Steelman		c
David H. Stowe	x	s
James L. Sundquist		x
Stuart Symington	c	
Theodore Tannenwald, Jr.	x	c
Roger W. Tubby (Yale University)	x	x
Robert C. Turner	x	
Harry H. Vaughan	x	x
James E. Webb	x	

In addition, numerous office files at the Truman Library contain material relevant to the administration of the presidency. Just two examples are the file of the president's naval aide, and the Bureau of the Budget file of reports to the president on pending legislation.

INDEX

Index

Index

Employment Act of 1946, 214
Enarson, Harold L., 98, 115, 142, 225
Ewing, Oscar R., 37, 88, 191, 195
Ewing group, 191–92, 215–16
Executive clerk, 45, 113–14, 142
Executive Office of the President, 20, 126, 140, 151, 167, 169, 212
Executive Orders, 74, 99

Fahey, Charles, 223, 224
Fair Employment Practices Committee, 52–53
FBI (Federal Bureau of Investigation), 49
Federal Loan Administration, 18, 26
Federal Reserve System, 185, 218
Federal Security Agency, 71
Feeny, Joseph, 115, 229
Fellman, David, xxii
FEPC (Fair Employment Practices Committee), 52–53
Fisher, Adrian S., 11, 25
Fleming, Robert, 82
Ford, Gerald R., 213
Foreign and military policy, 101, 123–25, 154–56
Forrestal, James V., 24, 55, 88–89, 189, 153–54
Foster, William C., 11, 25
Fowler, Henry H., 190
Friedman, Martin L., 51, 111
Fulton, Hugh, 65

Gardner, O. Max, 27
Gavin, Tommy, 50
Gelfand, Lawrence, 85
Gordon, Lincoln, 155
Green, William, 216
Greenstein, Fred I., 33, 85

Hagerty, James, 146, 157
Halberstam, David, 39
Hannigan, Robert, 51
Hansen, Alvin, 190
Hansen, Donald, 100
Hardy, Benjamin F., Jr., 197–98, 200
Harriman, W. Averell, xiii, 3, 9–16; comments by, 23, 24, 35, 36, 38, 39, 40, 67, 68, 76, 81, 84, 154, 155, 160, 163,

221, 222, 230, 231, 233; mentioned, xxi, 88, 140, 145, 149, 151, 155, 158, 171, 182, 202–204, 219–21
Hassett, William, 77, 109, 144, 158
Hechler, Ken, xiv, 92, 128–35; comments by, 141, 148, 149, 157, 161, 165, 224; mentioned, 70, 100, 115, 142, 201
Hess, Stephen, x, xix, xx, 4, 36, 37, 48
Hobbs, Edward H., xvii, 40
Hoffman, Paul, 11, 82, 219, 221
Holmes, Oliver Wendell, Jr., 138
Hoover, Herbert, 161–63, 231–32
"Hoovercarts," 163
Hoover Commission, 21, 161, 162, 231
Hopkins, Harry, 23
Hopkins, William J., xiv, 41, 43–48; comments by, 63, 65, 66, 67, 75, 76, 78, 84, 85, 149, 160, 162, 165; mentioned, 113–14, 134, 140, 142, 158, 226
Housing and Home Finance Agency, 71, 98
Hughes, Charles Evans, 30
Hughes, Rowland, 228
Hull, Cordell, 23, 24
Humphrey, George, 160

Ickes, Harold, 19, 23
Independence, 145
Intelligence activities, 152–54, 206, 232, 234–35
Internal Revenue, Bureau of, 26–27
International Development Advisory Board, 127
Iran, 10, 147
Italy, 33

Jackson, Robert H., 30
James, Dorothy Buckton, xvii, 36
Johnson, Eric, 190
Johnson, Louis, 12, 14, 136, 154, 155, 217
Joint Chiefs of Staff, 123, 137, 153, 221
Jones, Roger W., xiv, 167, 173–78; comments by, 89, 157, 158, 162, 214, 218, 223, 225, 228, 230, 231; mentioned, 137
Judges, appointment of, 27, 29–31
Justice, Department of, 29, 75, 76

Index

Index

Nash, Frank, 201
Nash, Philleo, xv, 41, 52–56; comments
by, 33, 63, 75, 77, 82, 86, 88, 141,
148, 222; mentioned, 51, 111, 115,
140
National Advisory Council, 224
National Commission on Higher Educa-
tion, 127
National Resources Planning Board, 213
National Security Act, 205
National Security Council, 68, 112, 123,
124, 126, 139, 154, 167, 170, 171,
205–211, 212, 232
National Security Resources Board, 73,
124, 126, 170, 206, 212
Naval aide, 112–13, 136–39, 226
Neustadt, Richard E., xv, 91, 93–117,
135; comments by, 140, 141, 149, 151,
164, 228; mentioned, 70, 100, 115,
142, 149, 201, 225
New York Times, 135
Newland, Chester A., xviii
Niles, David K., 41, 51, 52–55, 63, 75,
77, 111, 222
Norstad, Lauris, 13, 14, 124
Nourse, Edwin C., 11, 72, 180–84, 188,
189, 190, 194, 195
NSC. *See* National Security Council
NSC-68, 124, 217, 233
NSRB. *See* National Security Resources
Board

O'Connell, Joseph, 61
ODM (Office of Defense Mobilization),
111, 126, 170, 216
ODMS (Office of Defense Mobilization
and Stabilization), 94
Oechsner, Frederick C., 128
OES (Office of Economic Stabilization),
50, 196
Office of Civil and Defense Mobilization,
170
Office of Defense Mobilization, 111, 126,
170, 216
Office of Defense Mobilization and Sta-
bilization, 94
Office of Economic Stabilization, 50, 196
Office of Facts and Figures, 213
Office of Government Reports, 213
Office of Price Control, 50

Office of Wage Control, 50
Office of War Information, 213
Office of War Mobilization, 213
Office of War Mobilization and Recon-
version (OWMR), 26, 66, 73, 95–99,
167, 196, 230

Pace, Frank, 16, 175, 194, 226
Patterson, Robert, 30, 153–54
Paperwork, 45, 79–80, 113–14
Pauley, Edwin W., 19
Pearson, Drew, 75
Perlmeter, Irving, 115, 129, 144, 145,
149
Personal secretary, 21, 45, 78
Personnel, 6–7, 25, 49–51, 80
Peterson, Howard, 154
Phillips, Joseph, 129, 134
Pogue, Welsh, 108
Point Four program, 197–200
Porter, Paul, 182
Present at the Creation, 38, 40
President's Airport Commission, 127
President's Commission on Health Needs
of the Nation, 127
President's Commission on Immigration
and Naturalization, 127
President's Committee on Administrative
Management, 167, 212
President's Committee on Civil Rights,
30, 34, 88, 127, 222
President's Communications Policy Board,
127
President's Materials Policy Commission,
127, 223
President's Scientific Research Board, 127
Press secretary, 44, 106–109, 114, 125,
140, 145–49, 157
Public opinion polls, 85–87

Race relations, 34, 52–56, 63, 76, 77–78,
82, 222
Ramspeck, Robert, 62
Rayburn, Sam, 15
Reconstruction Finance Corporation, 17,
98, 103, 170
Reuther, Walter, 216
RFC (Reconstruction Finance Corpora-
tion), 17, 98, 103, 170
Ridgway, Matthew B., 13, 14, 15

245

Index

Index

by, 6–7, 11, 25, 29–31, 49–50, 80, 82, 87; budget, knowledge of, xxii, 20–21, 36, 232; cabinet meetings of, 11, 18–19, 34–35, 67–70, 76–77, 97, 185; chief of staff of, 57, 67, 72; consultation with advisers of, 15, 32–33, 60, 126–27; decision-making by, 7, 16, 32–33, 38, 46–47, 60, 80, 138–39, 147–48, 196–97; delegation of responsibility by, 6–7; history, interest in, 46, 150, 157, 163, 173; human qualities of, 46, 48, 114, 120, 138, 141, 144; intelligence activities of, 152–53, 171, 233–35; loyalty to associates of, xxi, 39–40, 47, 233; as "a man of few words," 10, 12, 118–19; modesty of, 9; orderliness of, xxi, 84, 119–20, 122, 165, 173; as a politician, xxii, 27, 145; presidency, regard for, 12, 48, 120, 173, 177, 201; press conferences of, 146–47, 176; punctuality of, 46; reading habits of, xxii, 9, 45, 78, 148, 193; role perceptions of, 137–38, 156–57; Senate experience of, 6, 229; speeches, preparation of, 59–60, 99, 124, 128–35, 148, 150–52, 201–202; staff meetings of, xxi, 43, 63, 78–82, 85, 116, 145, 171; transition planning by, xx, 157–61, 204; work habits of, xxi, 47

Truman, Margaret, 18

Tubby, Roger W., xvi, 92; comments by, 35, 87, 144, 146, 148, 157, 164; mentioned, 106–109, 115, 128, 129, 149

Turner, Robert C., xvii, 42, 57–60; comments by, 62, 65, 67, 69; mentioned, 65, 73, 98, 190

Underhill, Robert, 89

United States v. *United Mine Workers*, 27–28

Valentine, Alan, 190

Vandenberg, Arthur H., 12, 231

Vandenberg, Arthur H., Jr., 159

VanDevender, Charles, 134

Van Fleet, James, 15

Vaughn, Harry H., 112

Veto, 48, 74, 177–78, 226–27

Vice-president, 19, 70

Vinson, Fred M., 15, 30, 33, 144, 169, 213, 230

Voice of America, 128–35

Wage Stabilization Board, 103

Walker, Frank C., 18

Walker, Walton H., 14, 15

Wallace, Henry A., 10, 23, 105

War Department, 55

War on Hunger, 197–200

War Reconversion and Stabilization Board, 111

Washington, George T., 75

Water Resource Policy Commission, 127, 223

Watson, Edwin M., 105

Webb, James E., 115–16, 137, 143, 175, 194, 214, 218, 220, 226

Welles, Sumner, 23

White, Harry Dexter, 10

White House Loyalty Review Board, 51

White House Office, 75, 93

White House Staff: careerist character of, 115–16; chief of staff of, 57–58, 67–68, 70, 72, 87, 137, 167, 170, 222; function of, 62–65, 126, 164–65; relationship to cabinet, 36, 48, 63–65

Wiggins, Lee, 27

Williamsburg, 128

Wilson, Charles E., 34, 170, 190, 216

WRSB (War Reconversion and Stabilization Board), 111